D0907223

The Rhetorical Presidency of George H. W. Bush

NUMBER FOURTEEN
Presidential Rhetoric Series
Martin J. Medhurst, General Editor

THE RHETORICAL PRESIDENCY OF GEORGE H. W. BUSH

Edited by

MARTIN J. MEDHURST

Texas A&M University Press

COLLEGE STATION

The paper used in this book meets the minimum requirements
of the American National Standard for Permanence
of Paper for Printed Library Materials, Z39.48–1984.
Binding materials have been chosen for durability.

Library of Congress Cataloging-in-Publication Data
The rhetorical presidency of George H. W. Bush / edited by Martin J. Medhurst — 1st ed.
    p.   cm. — (Presidential rhetoric series ; no. 14)
Includes index.
ISBN 1-58544-471-5 (cloth : alk. paper)
1. Bush, George, 1924—Oratory. 2. Bush, George, 1924—Language. 3. Rhetoric—Political
aspects—United States—History—20th century. 4. Communication in politics—United
States—History—20th century. 5. Political leadership—United States—History—20th century.
6. United States—Politics and government—1989–1993. I. Medhurst, Martin J. II. Series.
E882.2.R47 2005
973.928'092—dc22
2005021929

★

In memory of
Richard B. Gregg
(1936–2001)

Contents

PREFACE

The chapters in this book address different aspects of George Bush as a rhetorical president. That approach may strike some as strange inasmuch as George Herbert Walker Bush was not known for his eloquence, nor will he be remembered for his oratory. Even so, he was a rhetorical president in the sense that he, like all of his predecessors and successors, made choices about what to say, how to say it, where and to whom to say it. A president cannot escape rhetoric—as much as some would like to do so. For good or ill, all presidents are rhetorical presidents.

It has been my privilege to know George Bush personally. From 1993 to 2003, I served as the head of the Program in Presidential Rhetoric, a research unit within the Bush School of Government and Public Service at Texas A&M University. During that period, I met the forty-first president of the United States on multiple occasions. My observations over the years have led to only one firm conclusion: George Bush is indeed as gracious and kind as many others have claimed. In the little part of the academy that I occupied, the former president took time to give a guest lecture in my class, to deliver a major evening lecture sponsored by our program, to drop in numerous times to greet the academics at our annual conference, and to endorse the participation of many of his former White House associates in the various activities of the Program in Presidential Rhetoric. We were privileged to host such people as Marlin Fitzwater, David Demarest, C. Boyden Gray, Curt Smith, and others from the Bush administration. None of that would have happened without the president's tacit approval.

The essays in this volume are another kind of testimony to the forty-first president because each is based on research conducted at the Bush Presidential Library, located on the campus of Texas A&M University in College Station. Taken together, they touch on many of the central issues facing George Bush from 1989 to 1993, starting with the "vision thing" and ending with the economy and the 1992 presidential election. I am under no illusion that George Bush will necessarily like all of the conclusions reached in these chapters. But knowing the nature of the man, I am thoroughly convinced that he will appreciate the honest effort exerted and the fact that his presidential library, less than a decade old at this writing, is already yielding useful data to researchers.

—Martin J. Medhurst

ACKNOWLEDGMENTS

No book comes together without the assistance of many hands. We are particularly grateful to the archival staff at the George Bush Presidential Library, which was under the direction of Douglas Menarchik at the time this volume was prepared. Chief archivist Warren Finch and archivists Melissa Walker and Robert Holzweiss were particularly helpful.

We are also grateful to the members of the Bush White House who took the time to talk with the various contributors to this volume: Andy Card, Jim Cicconi, David Demarest, Marlin Fitzwater, C. Boyden Gray, Roman Popadiuk, Curt Smith, Judy Smith, John Sununu, Sean Walsh, and Doug Wead. Thanks are also due to two of Bush's pre-presidential speechwriters—Sandy Muir and Craig R. Smith—and one post-presidential writer, Jim McGrath. To all of these we express our gratitude. The judgments reached in this book are, of course, our own.

We are indebted to the scholars of the Bush presidency who preceded us, particularly Ryan Barilleaux, John Robert Greene, Bert Rockman, Mark Rozell, Mary Stuckey, and Stephen Skowronek. And we thank our friend and former colleague George C. Edwards III for his unflagging efforts on behalf of presidential studies in general and studies of the George H. W. Bush presidency in particular.

Finally, we want to recognize three people without whom this work would never have materialized: Paul Stob and Terri Easley, our research assistants, and Mary Lenn Dixon, editor-in-chief of Texas A&M University Press. Mary Lenn has been a friend and advocate of rhetorical studies of the presidency for more than a decade. And it is because of her faith and foresight that both the Presidential Rhetoric Series and the Library of Presidential Rhetoric have flourished at Texas A&M University Press.

The Rhetorical Presidency of George H. W. Bush

CHAPTER 1

Why Rhetoric Matters:
George H. W. Bush in the White House

MARTIN J. MEDHURST

Presidents can no longer choose whether to engage in public leadership, only what form that leadership will take.
Mary E. Stuckey

It may seem intuitively wrongheaded to use George Herbert Walker Bush as an example of why rhetoric matters. Many would find the opposite proposition more likely—that rhetoric did not matter to Bush at all. There would be substantial support for that opposing hypothesis. Indeed, one former White House aide went so far as to claim that "George Bush's presidency was an anti-rhetorical operation."[1] A journalistic observer concluded that in the environment of the Bush White House, "rhetoric was judged to be of little use."[2] And the man who through four years of the presidency interpreted Bush to the world, Marlin Fitzwater, described his principal as "a man normally so impatient with words that he seldom used verbs."[3]

All these characterizations contain a certain amount of truth. George Bush did not like the public dimensions of the presidency very much, including the need to communicate directly to the American people. Some rhetorical aspects of the presidency—speeches, debates, public relations, image-building, and image maintenance—were not a high priority of the Bush White House. And the president himself was a decidedly indifferent communicator, both philosophically and practically. He believed, according to one of his speechwriters, that many aspects of the public presidency were "phony baloney, inauthentic, unpresidential."[4] Because of that belief, Bush often did not devote the time or energy needed to master presidential discourse.

Yet that is only part of the story, because it is based on a fundamental misconception: that rhetoric is only about the end product, speaking and persuasion. It is the thesis of this volume that George Bush's problems in the realm of rhetoric went far beyond the linguistic idiosyncrasies mimicked so effectively by comic Dana Carvey. Bush's problems started from a fundamental misconception about the role and place of rhetoric in governance. Like many other public figures, Bush seemed to believe that rhetoric only came into play once a decision had been made, and even then only as a means of publicly announcing what had already been decided. Not only did he show no appreciation of the role of rhetoric in the actual formulation of policy, he did not appreciate the inventional and judgmental aspects of the art.

Historically, the art of rhetoric has encompassed two parallel dimensions: the discovery or invention of ideas, and the judgment and decision making that followed from those ideas. These two dimensions found their end in a third—prudential action. Rhetoric is involved at each stage along the way: the analysis of what is needed to address a problem, the search for what the policy shall be, the internal debates over specific aspects of that policy, the final decisions as to how the policy shall be framed, the selection of the specific language in which the policy will be encompassed. The final step is the articulation of the policy to various audiences, using various means, times, places, and emphases, as dictated by the characteristics of the audiences one is trying to reach. Too often, critics focus only on this final stage of the process and reduce the art of rhetoric to the public delivery of a speech or press release.[5]

As this collection will demonstrate, the Bush administration's problems in the rhetorical realm extended over the entire process, not just the final stage of public delivery. And the problem started at the very top—with George Bush himself and his misunderstanding of what rhetoric is, how it operates, and what it could do for him and to him. The president entered office in January 1989 with a certain set of beliefs, one of which was that he was no Ronald Reagan and could not hope to duplicate Reagan's role as a "Great Communicator."[6] This belief, along with Bush's relative distaste for public speaking, combined with a third factor to deprive the new president of an important tool of leadership. That was the belief that there was a fundamental difference between politics and government, between what one needed to do to win the presidency and what one should do once in office, in short, a difference between politics and principles. In combination, these three factors disabled the Bush White House from being able to effect prudential action in ways that were both recognized and appreciated by the public at large.

In this chapter, I will explore these three interlocking elements to show how George Bush, in a very real sense, disabled himself before he ever uttered a word. That personal disability was then passed along to his lieutenants, in various ways, to infect the whole White House operation with an antirhetorical virus.

THE SHADOW OF RONALD REAGAN

The problem started even before Bush assumed office in January 1989, with an edict that barred any appointee from the Reagan administration from holding the same position in the incoming Bush administration. The transition director and soon-to-be White House director of presidential personnel, Chase Untermeyer, had issued a clear operational directive: "new faces in old places and old faces in new places."[7] All previous appointees, the vast majority of whom were loyal Republicans, were instructed to have their resignations on the desk of their superiors by January 20. This despite the fact that the incoming Bush administration had no way to fill the hundreds of positions thus vacated in anything like a timely fashion. One result was the creation of tremendous ill will between one set of Republican officeholders and the new administration. What was supposed to be a friendly transition from one Republican administration to another instead turned out to be a fractious, and totally unnecessary, exercise in power politics. A second result was that scores of positions remained unfilled months after the Bush administration assumed power. A third result was that truly talented people, particularly in the communications side of the White House—speechwriting, press relations, public liaison, media relations, public affairs, scheduling—were turned away, some without even an interview.[8]

The specter of Reagan, and particularly of Reagan's skills at public communication, seemed to haunt Bush from beginning to end. As Marlin Fitzwater recalled:

> During his first full day in office, President Bush met with his speech writers to discuss his style, his words, his themes, and the events ahead. He told the story of riding with President Reagan in his limousine to a last minute speech at a Washington hotel. As the president and vice-president were getting into the car, someone handed President Reagan a text of the speech, saying he was sorry it was so late. "No problem," President Reagan said, and he proceeded to read through it, marking the paragraphs for pauses and punctuations. "Is this the first time you've seen this speech?" Vice-President Bush said to the President. "Yes," President Reagan said, "but it will be OK, don't worry about it." President Bush told

his speech writers he thought it would be a disaster, but the delivery was perfect, the speech was magnificent. "And the lesson," the new President Bush said, "is I can't do that."[9]

But Bush seems to have drawn the wrong conclusion from this experience. Rather than concluding that he would have to work harder at public communication in order to approach Reagan's level, Bush retreated to the other extreme, relegating public rhetoric to a position of secondary importance as something that could be more or less ignored merely because he was not Ronald Reagan.

One early manifestation of this attitude involved the staffing of the presidential speechwriting office. During the Reagan years, speechwriting had been at the center of the ideological struggle to "let Reagan be Reagan." Several of Reagan's writers—Peggy Noonan, Tony Dolan, Ben Elliott—became well known even outside the Washington Beltway. Not so the Bush speechwriting operation. Not only did the Bush team fail to retain any of the Reagan writers, they intentionally set about hiring writers of lesser stature. The task of hiring fell to David Demarest, the new White House director of communications. According to Demarest: "I felt that during the Reagan administration the speechwriters had gotten out of control. . . . that speechwriters were trying to make policy. And I felt that wasn't the role of a speechwriter. And my view was speechwriters should be heard and not seen. And the Reagan folks—including Peggy Noonan—were much more visible than I thought they needed to be. And that, to me, did not serve the president as well as he could be served."[10]

So Demarest turned to the bureaucracy for his White House speechwriters. Recalling the staffing process, Demarest noted that he "first recruited Chriss Winston," who had been his deputy at the Labor Department, as director of speechwriting. He then hired five more speechwriters. "The initial group was Mark Davis, Curt Smith, Dan McGroarty. Mark Davis was chief speechwriter for the Republican National Committee. Curt Smith was chief speechwriter for [Richard] Schwiecker over at HHS [Health and Human Services]. Dan was chief speechwriter for [Frank] Carlucci. I then recruited Mark Lang a little bit later. He was chief speechwriter at Labor. I did know him before. And Ed McNally came on a little later, too. He was over at Justice. He was one that was not out of the speechwriting. . . . He was a lawyer. He was a former prosecutor, but he was a really terrific writer, too."[11]

In addition to hiring writers who were virtual unknowns, Demarest turned back the clock on pay levels so that each of the writers started at an entry-level rank and salary. No one could make more than $40,000 per year. In so doing, he effected thousands of dollars in salary savings, but at a cost—and he got precisely what he paid for. There would be no memorable phrases or soaring oratory coming from these pens. As one-time Bush speechwriter John Podhoretz noted: "No president had ever spoken more frequently than Bush; no president had ever said less. By the end of his four years in office, Bush had given more speeches and made more public appearances than Ronald Reagan had in eight years' time. And yet if people were asked what memorable things Bush had ever said, they could think of only three: 'Read my lips: no new taxes,' 'a kinder, gentler nation' and 'a thousand points of light.' All three came from his acceptance speech at the 1988 Republican convention. Once he was president, he never uttered a phrase worth remembering."[12]

Later some members of the Bush administration blamed the speechwriting operation for having failed the president. Bush's White House counsel, C. Boyden Gray, for example, said that "the speechwriters, with all due respect, were not of the same caliber as their predecessors in Bush's office when he was vice-president, and their absence did affect his ability to communicate."[13] This is a debatable proposition, but even if true it still leads back to Bush himself, for it was Bush, his personnel chief, Chase Untermeyer, and his chief of staff, John Sununu, who made the decisions about who would be hired in which positions and at what salary levels. Because Bush personally devalued public communication, his lieutenants merely followed his lead in deciding how to staff and budget his White House communications operation. They did precisely what the president wanted them to do—then turned on their own creations.

BUSH'S OWN ATTITUDE

While the long shadow of Reagan was a psychological barrier to Bush, no less problematic was his own attitude about public communication generally, and campaign rhetoric in particular. As already noted, after four years in the presidency the most memorable phrases associated with George Bush were words he had uttered during the course of the 1988 campaign. Perhaps the most notorious of those phrases was "Read my lips: no new taxes"—notorious, of course, because he subsequently did raise taxes. This, in turn, led to the whole question of credibility, and for good reason. Most people still believe that there is (and ought to be) a direct relationship between what a person says and what that person subsequently does. The electorate took the "no new taxes" pledge as a promise based on what Bush really believed about tax rates. In other words, the American people made an assumption about his character, the type of person he was, and his personal belief system. When Bush broke his pledge, he sent a message not just about his tax policies, but about his own character as well.

That Bush simply does not understand the relationship between public rhetoric and personal credibility is amply demonstrated in his own book, *All the Best, George Bush: My Life in Letters and Other Writings.* In that book, Bush records a diary entry from March 30, 1989, following a meeting with his economic advisers: "I tell him [Richard Darman, head of the Office of Management and Budget] that I can't raise taxes this go around, and it will be very hard in the future, but I want to see the options, and I'm not going to be held up by campaign rhetoric."[14] To George Bush the pledge not to raise taxes was nothing more than "campaign rhetoric," something that, apparently, could be abandoned at will. Bush clearly did not see the relationship between public rhetoric and personal integrity. Indeed, he repeatedly separated the two, as though what one said had no impact on one's future actions or on how one might expect to be judged. Several of the president's communication professionals, including Marlin Fitzwater, tried to talk him out of breaking this pledge, intuitively understanding that breaking the major pledge of one's campaign for office was tantamount to political suicide. David Demarest, director of the White House Office of Communications, also saw the danger on the horizon. He recalled:

> I didn't know it was going to happen until it happened. As hard as that is to believe—that the communications director of the White House doesn't know that the president is considering—and is about to—dispose of the most resonating line from his 1988 campaign—it was incredible. And it isn't that I was opposed from a policy standpoint on it. I was appalled that no one thought about how to bring the public along, to position us in a way. . . . Ronald Reagan raised taxes a bunch of times—nobody thought he was the great tax raiser. Well, he positioned it properly. Dragged, kicking and screaming, you know. We did none of it. We posted it on the bulletin board. It was horrible. . . . Politically, it was a disaster. . . . It was the ticking time bomb of '92. It sat there. It was totally masked by Desert Storm—Desert Shield and Desert Storm. And it just sat there and kept ticking. And so when we were in the thick of it with Clinton, when we wanted to go after Clinton for being untrustworthy, and he's going to raise your taxes— look who's talking. He broke the promise that he made and that promise was about taxes.[15]

But George Bush didn't see it that way, because to him campaigning and governing were totally separate realms. Different rules applied to each. Unfortunately for President Bush, that was not the way that most members of the electorate reasoned. Nor would it be the way that anyone trained in rhetoric would have thought, because they would have known, as the famous rhetoric teacher Isocrates put it in the fourth century B.C., that "nothing is more important, save only to show reverence to the gods, than to have a good name."[16] The very worst thing a rhetorician—or politician—can do is to throw away or cause to fall into disrepute his or her own good name. And breaking major pledges tends to do just that. Fitzwater knew that. Demarest knew that. All of the speechwriters knew it, too. But because communications had been so totally separated from policy formation, those voices were not even heard, much less heeded. As Bush speechwriter Curt Smith put it, "The spoken word was devalued in our administration and we paid the price."[17]

Even apart from the political damage caused by the breaking of the "no new taxes" pledge, Bush seemed uncomfortable with matters rhetorical. Michael Duffy and Dan Goodgame reported that Bush "resisted what he called the 'show-biz' aspects of his job. When NBC News came to film a 'Day in the Life' of Bush in 1989, the president greeted Tom Brokaw in the Oval Office and, while the videotape rolled, launched into a conversation with the unnamed, unknown, and obviously unseen camera crew—a gesture to remind viewers that Ronald Reagan's successor regarded such half-staged charades as silly."[18] Even standard speeches were challenges to his aides because Bush hated to have words put in his mouth, or in his texts. According to Marlin Fitzwater, Bush "resisted using any word that someone else gave him, mostly out of a stubborn resistance to the idea that he was being programmed or 'handled.' Thus his general disregard for written speeches, texts, or any document that could be interpreted as putting words in his mouth."[19]

When Bush did accept a speech text, he often edited out the most memorable phrases. On one occasion, during a trip to Hungary after the fall of the Berlin Wall, Bush announced that he was "tearing up my prepared text," while well over half a million people stood in the rain, waiting to hear what the leader of the Free World had to say. Instead of reading from the carefully prepared text, he chose to speak off the top of his head. This led Fitzwater to ask later: "Now, the question is, what makes a president more proud of tearing up his speech than of giving it? President Bush had disdain for the rhetoric, but he greatly cherished the symbolic act of joining the Hungarian people in their emotional release."[20]

Clearly, George Bush wanted to connect with his audiences. Just as clearly, he had great difficulty doing so. A large part of that difficulty came from his own attitudes about rhetoric generally, and public speaking in particular. One former speechwriter for Gerald Ford, who subsequently wrote for Bush when he was vice president, offered this summary: "The main problem with Bush's presidential rhetoric was Bush himself. He disdained rehearsal. His love of substance often caused him to neglect style, particularly in speeches he delivered from the Oval Office to television audiences."[21]

POLITICS VS. GOVERNANCE

Part of Bush's rhetorical self-immolation revolved around his insistence on separating campaign rhetoric (or politics) from presidential discourse (or governance). To Bush, politics meant the narrow, self-interested activities that one had to engage in to get elected to office: campaigning, taking ideological positions, appealing to the base, using strong language to differentiate oneself from one's opponent, and generating the emotions necessary to move people to active participation in the electoral process. Governance, in contrast, meant broad, consensus-building activities undertaken for the common good. It meant statesmanship, diplomacy, compromise, and legislative achievement. It called for negotiation rather than proclamation, for quiet diplomacy rather than public declarations. As one member of Bush's White House staff wrote:

> One must understand that George Bush is essentially a man of many modes. His tendency was to compartmentalize not only his staff but himself.
> The two most significant Bush modes are his governing mode and his campaign mode. In Bush's mind, the nitty-gritty boorishness of campaigning for office was wholly distinct from the lofty business of actually governing the nation. What you had to *say* to get elected had no real bearing on or relationship to what you subsequently *did* once elected. That modal mentality explains how Bush could so cavalierly jettison his "read my lips" pledge not to raise taxes and then mock his own vow by telling the media to "read my hips" when he was out jogging one day. That was then, this is now.[22]

A strong case can be made that no president of the post–World War II generation has ever tried to separate politics as completely from governance as George Bush. Eisenhower is, perhaps, the strongest challenger for that title, but even Ike knew how to do more than a little manipulating behind the scenes, and he knew the importance of thinking rhetorically.[23] Bush truly believed that one could be a consensus president, and that politics could, and should, stop at the White House door. In that sense, Bush's preference for governing principles over party politics was laudatory. Yet, as virtually every observer has noted, "had policy and politics been more fused, the president would have been enormously better served."[24] Politics was an ever-present reality, despite what George Bush may have wished. And it was precisely that lack of realization, that failure to take account of all aspects of the situation, that led to many of Bush's rhetorical failures while in office.

So the main problem was not that George Bush was a poor public speaker. As Wynton Hall notes, "The view that Bush was simply an inept communicator is . . . misguided. Bush was, in many ways, an 'episodic' communicator."[25] He could be very effective at one moment and totally ineffective the next. That is why a single focus on his skills as a public speaker will always miss the heart of the problem, for the problem in the Bush White House was not that the president had trouble giving speeches but that he refused to adopt a rhetorical stance toward governance or to encourage others in his administration to do so. There was an absence of long-term planning of messages, a lack of coordination between messages and actions, and a failure to realize how the speaker's perceived character (ethos) was directly, and in Bush's case negatively, affected by his ideational content (logos) and language choices (lexis).

Sometimes a failure to coordinate messages and actions is the result of oversight or mistakes. But in the Bush White House it was an intentionally chosen path. The person whose job it normally would have been to coordinate message and action was the director of White House communications, David Demarest. But according to Demarest: "Fred McClure [White House director of legislative affairs] and I were both told not to do something in the first two weeks in the White House. Fred McClure was told you're not going to have a legislative strategy group and I was told you're not going to have a communications strategy group, because legislative strategy is in the chief of staff's office and communications strategy is in the chief of staff's office. . . . That was the conundrum. The strategy group really was Sununu and Darman. And that combination drove most of the agenda in the first two years—until Desert Shield, really."[26]

The failure to have long-term strategizing led eventually to a breakdown in the coordination between messages and actions. Charles Kolb, who served Bush as chief of domestic policy, recalled: "Inside the Bush White House virtually no effort was made to connect legislative priorities, policy development and communications outreach through Public Liaison, speechwriting, and presidential scheduling. There were people carrying out each function, but few of them actually worked together in any coordinated way."[27]

The result was that Bush appeared to lack an agenda. But as several of the following chapters demonstrate, in many instances Bush did have an agenda. The problem was not lack of ideas, but the inability to mobilize those ideas in a coherent and persuasive way. Again, Kolb's views seem accurate: "The contention that Bush lacked a domestic agenda was belied by the facts and the fact sheet. You would never know it, however, if you had to depend on the ability of the White House to articulate a central message and, more importantly, to sustain that message or to frame it in a context that mattered to people."[28]

Kolb articulates the central elements of a rhetorical vision: ideas, the articulation and framing of those ideas, and the effort to contextualize those ideas in relationship to a particular audience. That is the heart of rhetoric, and it is precisely what was missing from the Bush White House. Its absence affected the public perception of Bush's character. Because there was a perceived lack of connection between what Bush said and the actions that followed (or failed to follow), people questioned the president's sincerity. Kolb got it exactly right: "At issue was the President's credibility."[29]

How did Bush get himself into such a fix? His personal history offers one possible explanation. First, there is no evidence that Bush was ever exposed to the art of rhetoric in any of his formal education—not at Greenwich Country Day School, not at Andover, and not at Yale. His only exposure to the liberal arts was a few scattered courses in English and history, courses in which he was, at best, an average student.

Second, from an early age Bush seems to have equated leadership with the ability to make friends and influence people through *interpersonal* communication channels. His was a highly personal and individualistic conception of persuasion. It was predicated on attributes such as personal friendship, trust, loyalty, camaraderie, and small-group identification. One succeeded in leadership by making the right contacts, befriending the right people, forging the right associations. Such an approach to life emphasizes private "people skills" over public communication skills. One tends to think narrowly about the person at hand rather than broadly about the overall situation and that person's place in a larger scheme of contexts and objectives. It is not surprising, therefore, that at Andover Bush ranked high in areas such as "best all-around fellow" and "most respected," but did not appear at all on the list of those "most likely to succeed." He was not seen, even then, as a strategic thinker or one with a political agenda. His was a highly personal world where good humor, good looks, and better-than-average athletic ability counted for more than intellectual mastery, debate skills, or public speaking ability.[30]

Third, from very early on, Bush displayed a penchant for secrecy, for keeping information inside the group, whether family, business, or bureaucracy. Intuitively realizing that information is power, Bush held his thoughts closely, sharing publicly only such values as God, country, patriotism, and duty. Even those themes were difficult for him to articulate in public because he felt them so deeply that his emotions often dictated silence rather than speech. In many ways George Bush was a product of his own upbringing and experiences. He had reached forty years of age before entering elective politics, and by that time most of his communicative habits had been established. Although he was involved in four political campaigns between 1964 and 1970—two for the U.S. Senate (1964 and 1970) and two for the U.S. House of Representatives (1966 and 1968)—most of his adult life did not require nuanced rhetorical analysis. From 1970 to 1980, he served in appointed positions where persuasion of the public was seldom necessary. As Reagan's vice president from 1981 to 1989, Bush was in a perfect position to observe a master rhetorician at work. But the only lesson he seems to have taken away from those years is that he was not Ronald Reagan. Bush's own White House years revealed a man uncomfortable with the public presidency and seemingly incapable of translating its vast rhetorical resources into a comprehensive communication program.

The following chapters each speak to a single issue, area, or event associated with the Bush White House. In a sense, they highlight specific "moments" that in some special way served to characterize the Bush presidency. Each of these moments is placed under the scrutiny of a rhetorical examination, constituting what David Zarefsky has called an exercise in rhetorical history. According to Zarefsky, in such an examination the scholar "views history as a series of rhetorical problems, situations that call for public persuasion to advance a cause or overcome an impasse. The focus of the study would be on how, and how well, people invented and deployed messages in response to the situation."[31] That is precisely the question that each of these chapters asks: How well did President Bush and his administration respond to these events, issues, and situations, and how might a more perceptive embrace of the art of rhetoric have allowed them to respond more successfully?

The volume moves more or less chronologically, from Bush's early problems with the "vision thing" to his last-gasp efforts to deal with the economy during the 1992 campaign. In between, the chapters touch on the fall of the Berlin Wall, Bush's Gulf War rhetoric, the search for a New World Order, Bush as the education president, Bush as the environmental president, and Bush's stormy relationship with the Religious Right.

In chapter 2 Catherine Langford explores the charge that George Bush lacked a coherent vision for his administration, a problem that Bush himself seemed to downplay by referring to it as the "vision thing." What Langford finds is revealing: a president who over the course of four years in office used the term *vision* more than 275 times, yet in more than half of those uses was referring to someone else's vision, not his own. Langford argues that Bush failed to create a public narrative replete with an exigence or problem, enemies, and an impending sense of crisis. There was no story line to the Bush presidency, no sense of how the whole was to unfold to achieve some sense of completion or closure. Although there were many individual dramatic episodes, there was no coherent drama being enacted. Bush seemed to understand his part in the drama of governance as being the defender of the status quo, one whose job was to prevent bad things from happening rather than inspiring the creation of new and better things.

If failure to articulate a specific vision hurt Bush initially, the drama of the fall of the Berlin Wall and its aftermath clearly provided an opportune moment for Bush to shine. Yet the president was roundly criticized in some circles for his failure to embrace rhetorically the rapidly changing situation in Eastern Europe and the Soviet Union. In chapter 3 William Forrest Harlow examines the situation that Bush confronted and reaches a diametrically opposed conclusion: that Bush was right, from a rhetorical point of view, to take a low-profile approach to the Berlin events and that his rhetoric of silence was a strategically wise choice. Harlow, drawing on recently declassified documents from the Bush Library, illustrates how Bush identified the exigencies of the situation and fashioned a rhetoric to meet them. In the end, he finds that Bush's rhetoric of silence was both prudent and effective.

But Berlin was merely a warm-up for what some critics have called "Bush's war"—the 1991 conflict in the Persian Gulf. In chapter 4 Rachel Martin Harlow examines the president's major speeches and press conferences during the war and finds a rhetorically sophisticated strategy at work. Drawing from the theories of Kenneth Burke, Harlow identifies the dramatistic strategies used by the Bush administration, particularly the president's use of terms referring to God and the Devil, his use of polarization, and his employment of definitional arguments. Through such strategically selected language, Bush persuaded the American public to see him as "a consummate crisis and PR manager." Harlow's study of documents from the White House Office of Communications lends credence to her interpretations.

In chapter 5, Roy Joseph traces the use of the term *New World Order*. What he finds may surprise some on both the left and right. Far from being a meaningless phrase with no substance or a harbinger of trilateral domination,

Bush's New World Order ends up being a close relative of the United Nations' founding document. For Bush, *New World Order* was a shorthand term for a new kind of moral leadership addressed to the world at large. It was an idealistic conception, borrowing from the ethos that followed hard on the heels of World War II: the hope that a new era of peace and harmony was about to dawn. But Bush failed in the rhetorical task of defining precisely what he meant by the phrase, and in the absence of such definition others stepped forward to provide their own interpretations.

In chapter 6 Holly G. McIntush examines Bush's claim to the mantle of "education president." While it is certainly true that Bush failed to become known as the education president, McIntush finds convincing evidence that he did make several serious efforts toward that end. The main problem, as she sees it, was a basic incompatibility between Bush's vision of the proper relationship between the federal government and educational policies, and the vision held by the majority of Americans. According to McIntush, Bush believed that the government's role was merely that of a catalyst for change, while the polls revealed that the public wanted both more involvement from the federal level and more federal dollars sent to states and municipalities. Once again, Bush found himself caught between his principles and the politics of the situation. And once again, he failed to find a way to bridge the chasm rhetorically.

Likewise, Bush failed to be perceived as an "environmental president," even though one recent book holds that he was more active in this area than any other twentieth-century president save Theodore Roosevelt.[32] Perhaps the most visible public event concerning the environment during Bush's presidency was the 1992 Earth Summit, held in Rio de Janeiro. In chapter 7, Martin Carcasson examines that event, which many critics have labeled an utter disaster from a public diplomacy point of view.[33] Yet Carcasson finds that Bush's rhetoric at Rio was perfectly consistent with his previously announced policies. While the focus at Rio was on international accords, Bush was speaking for and to a national audience. Bush might well have scored some rhetorical and diplomatic points by signing the final protocols, but he could not do so and still be consistent with his announced policy stances. Bush's rhetoric was thus consistent with his governing principles, though hugely unpopular in the developing world and among environmental activists in the United States.

By 1992 Bush was also under attack from members of his own party, particularly those aligned with the Religious Right. In chapter 8 Amy Tilton Jones tells the story of how Bush went from enjoying the near-total support from the Religious Right to having his credentials sorely questioned by them in the 1992 election. According to Jones, Bush was isolated from many of the events in his own administration. Public liaison with evangelicals and fundamentalists failed to satisfy their demands. One result, according to Jones, was that Bush came close to losing this part of his base, only to overcorrect at the 1992 Republican National Convention, a convention remembered primarily for the speeches of Marilyn Quayle, Pat Robertson, and Patrick Buchanan. Even though Bush seemed unwilling to take strong stands on many issues of concern to the Religious Right, he nonetheless held their support in the 1992 election.

In the final chapter, Wynton C. Hall looks at how George Bush tried to handle the issue of the economy in the 1992 election. As with most aspects of that campaign, Bush started too late and seemed out of touch with the reality of most people's lives. This resulted, Hall claims, from a poorly developed sense of ethos on economic issues. Bush appeared to be disconnected, disengaged, and uncaring. He allowed the media to frame him in this unfavorable light. The framing and priming functions of the media helped to create and sustain this image of an uncaring, out-of-touch chief executive. In a world where perception is reality, a rhetoric that ignores perception is, according to Hall, doomed to fail.

In a brief afterword, I pull together the lessons learned from these chapters. The main point is already clear: George Bush as president preferred principles to politics. He identified rhetoric as part of politics rather than as part of governance and thus rejected it, too. That was a costly misidentification, both to Bush personally and to the country.

NOTES

1. Charles Kolb, *White House Daze: The Unmaking of Domestic Policy in the Bush Years* (New York: Free Press, 1994), 3. See also Mark J. Rozell, "In Reagan's Shadow: Bush's Antirhetorical Presidency," *Presidential Studies Quarterly* 28 (1998): 127–38. For the latest comprehensive treatment of the Bush White House, see Ryan J. Barilleaux and Mark J. Rozell, *Power and Prudence: The Presidency of George H. W. Bush* (College Station: Texas A&M University Press, 2004).

2. Michael Duffy and Dan Goodgame, *Marching in Place: The Status Quo Presidency of George Bush* (New York: Simon and Schuster, 1992), 47.

3. Marlin Fitzwater, *Call the Briefing! Reagan and Bush, Sam and Helen: A Decade with Presidents and the Press* (New York: Times Books, 1995), 259.

4. Curt Smith, interview by author, tape recording, College Station, Texas, January 27, 2000.

5. For works that treat political and presidential deliberation from a rhetorical point of view, see Martin J. Medhurst, ed., *Beyond the Rhetorical Presidency* (College Station: Texas

A&M University Press, 1996); Leroy G. Dorsey, ed., *The Presidency and Rhetorical Leadership* (College Station: Texas A&M University Press, 2002); Wayne Fields, *Union of Words: A History of Presidential Eloquence* (New York: Free Press, 1996).

6. On Reagan's skills as a communicator see Kurt Ritter and David Henry, *Ronald Reagan: The Great Communicator* (Westport, Conn.: Greenwood Press, 1992); William Ker Muir Jr., *The Bully Pulpit: The Presidential Leadership of Ronald Reagan* (San Francisco: ICS Press, 1992); Martin Anderson, *Revolution* (New York: Harcourt Brace Jovanovich, 1988); Dick Wirthlin with Wynton C. Hall, *The Greatest Communicator: What Ronald Reagan Taught Me about Politics, Leadership, and Life* (New York: John Wiley and Son, 2004).

7. John R. Bolton, "The Making of Foreign Policy in the Bush Administration," in *The Bush Presidency: Ten Intimate Perspectives of George Bush,* ed. Kenneth W. Thompson (Lanham, Md.: University Press of America, 1997), 109.

8. One of the ironies of the Bush transition is that despite the edict from Untermeyer and the creation of much ill will, "the Bush presidency retained a greater percentage (12.5 percent) of the appointees of the preceding administration than did all other administrations since Kennedy" (Janet M. Martin, "George Bush and the Executive Branch," in *Leadership and the Bush Presidency: Prudence or Drift in an Era of Change?* ed. Ryan J. Barilleaux and Mary E. Stuckey [Westport, Conn.: Praeger, 1992], 43).

9. Marlin Fitzwater, *Real Time Communications and Diplomacy* (College Station, Tex.: Program in Presidential Rhetoric, 1994), 6–7.

10. David Demarest, interview by author, tape recording, College Station, Texas, March 29, 2001.

11. Ibid.

12. John Podhoretz, *Hell of a Ride: Backstage at the White House Follies, 1989–1993* (New York: Simon and Schuster, 1993), 197.

13. C. Boyden Gray, "The President as Leader," in Thompson, ed., *The Bush Presidency: Ten Intimate Perspectives,* 11.

14. George H. W. Bush, *All the Best, George Bush: My Life in Letters and Other Writings* (New York: Scribner, 1999), 420–21.

15. David Demarest, interview by author, tape recording, College Station, Texas, March 29, 2001.

16. Isocrates, "On the Peace," in *Isocrates,* vol. 2, trans. George Norlin, Loeb Classical Library (1929; reprint, Cambridge: Harvard University Press, 1992), 93.

17. Curt Smith, interview by author, tape recording, College Station, Texas, January 27, 2000.

18. Duffy and Goodgame, *Marching in Place,* 41.

19. Fitzwater, *Call the Briefing!* 112.

20. Fitzwater, *Real Time Communications and Diplomacy,* 8–9.

21. Craig R. Smith, "George Herbert Walker Bush," in *U.S. Presidents as Orators: A Bio-Critical Sourcebook* (Westport, Conn.: Greenwood Press, 1995), 349.

22. Kolb, *White House Daze,* 311–12.

23. On Ike's behind-the-scenes manipulations, see Fred I. Greenstein, *The Hidden-Hand Presidency: Eisenhower as Leader* (New York: Basic Books, 1982). On Ike as a skilled rhetorician, see Martin J. Medhurst, *Dwight D. Eisenhower: Strategic Communicator* (Westport, Conn.: Greenwood Press, 1993); Meena Bose and Fred I. Greenstein, "The Hidden Hand vs. the Bully Pulpit: The Layered Political Rhetoric of President Eisenhower," in Dorsey, ed., *Presidency and Rhetorical Leadership,* 184–99.

24. Curt Smith, interview by author, tape recording, College Station, Texas, January 27, 2000.

25. Wynton C. Hall, "'Reflections of Yesterday': George H. W. Bush's Instrumental Uses of Public Opinion Research in Presidential Discourse," *Presidential Studies Quarterly* 32 (2002): 540.

26. David Demarest, interview by author, tape recording, College Station, Texas, March 29, 2001.

27. Kolb, *White House Daze,* 241.

28. Ibid., 241–42.

29. Ibid., 210.

30. See Herbert S. Parmet, *George Bush: The Life of a Lone Star Yankee* (New York: Scribner, 1997), 38–41.

31. David Zarefsky, "Four Senses of Rhetorical History," in *Doing Rhetorical History: Concepts and Cases,* ed. Kathleen J. Turner (Tuscaloosa: University of Alabama Press, 1998), 30.

32. John Robert Greene, *The Presidency of George Bush* (Lawrence: University Press of Kansas, 2000), 75.

33. For a scholarly critique of Bush at the Earth Summit, written from a rhetorical point of view, see Tarla Rai Peterson, *Sharing the Earth: The Rhetoric of Sustainable Development* (Columbia: University of South Carolina Press, 1997), chap. 4.

Chapter 2

George Bush's Struggle with the "Vision Thing"

Catherine L. Langford

A vision without a task is but a dream; a task without a vision is drudgery; but a vision with a task is the hope of the world.
George H. W. Bush

From his 1988 campaign until he left the White House, George Bush was heavily criticized for lacking a "vision." Tom Collins of *Newsday* declared in August 1988, "the campaign lacks a soul, an ideal, or what George Bush unpoetically calls 'the vision thing.'"[1] When evaluating Bush's leadership style in December 1989, David Broder proclaimed that Bush lacked four out of six leadership qualities, the first of which was long-range planning. "This is the vision thing Bush has so often derided, and its lack threatens to limit his presidency," Broder predicted.[2] Similarly, in January 1991 an editorial in the *New York Times* stated that "the Bush Presidency continues to confound anyone seeking tidy definitions, let alone a convincing agenda."[3] And on Bush's re-election defeat, Robert Hawkins of the *San Francisco Chronicle* remarked, "In the end, the 'vision thing' was Bush's Achilles heel. Rather than be a visionary, the president chose to be a steward—a major difference. A visionary stakes the future on a plan for action. A steward takes a more passive and reactive approach to leadership."[4] These examples are only a small representation of the commentary on Bush's problem with "the vision thing"; the president experienced frequent public criticism.[5]

"The 'vision thing,' as he called it, bothered President Bush a lot," according to Bush press secretary Marlin Fitzwater.[6] "The press had labeled him as too practical or pragmatic a politician to have vision," Fitzwater noted. "A big part of that analysis was due to the fact that he was always compared to Ronald Reagan, whose vision was more visible, rooted in romanticism and dreams of 'morning in America.'"[7] Unfortunately for Bush, his presidency followed that of one of the most skilled public orators in modern times. Paul

Burka maintains, "It was Bush's bad timing that his shortcomings—a lack of ideological vision, the inability to articulate his ideas, the difficulty of getting across to the public who he really was—were the flip side of Reagan's strengths."[8] While Reagan emerged warm and comforting, Bush appeared cold and unfeeling. "The irony," Gail Sheehy argues, "is that Bush really lives the eternal values so dear to conservatives' hearts, while Reagan mouths them and winks."[9] Put simply, it was Reagan's ability to conceptualize and articulate a rhetorical vision that enabled him to be successful as chief executive, a skill Bush did not have.

Bush's difficulty in developing, articulating, and promoting a rhetorical vision meant the public did not know who George Bush was or for what he stood. His rhetorical ineptitude and trouble with the "vision thing" caused him to fall short of the demands of the modern rhetorical presidency whose "expectations do not suit very favorably a president who is cautious and believes, like Bush, that a good president is a strong steward abroad who does no harm at home."[10] And as Bush biographer Herbert S. Parmet accurately recognizes, "Those remembered for eloquence did not gain fame by asking for the status quo—they sent up flares for change, in each case, perceived by the newly empowered as sorely needed and eagerly awaited by much of the public."[11] Bush's belief that change should be slow and incremental prevented him from recognizing the need to create a coherent rhetorical vision until late in his presidency. But by that time he was already classified as a visionless status-quo leader and pejoratively dubbed a wimp.

That Bush mentioned the term *vision* 277 times in his presidential addresses over the span of four years complicates the notion that he himself had no vision.[12] Examination of all Bush's addresses in which he used the term *vision* shows that in 1989 he referred to vision 56 times; in 1990, 80 times; in 1991, 66 times; and in 1992, 75 times. In other words, Bush used the term the least during his first year, but then substantially increased its use over his last three years in office. This leaves us with the quandary of how someone who mentioned the term so often could be accused of not possessing a vision, especially if, as Murray Edelman notes, "political language *is* political reality."[13]

Yet if we judge Bush's political reality by his allusions to vision, we must conclude that the vision Bush had was not his own; of the 277 times in which Bush utilized the term, 143 references pertained to others. In other words, more than half the times when Bush mentioned a "vision," he was referring to some other person, organization, business, or movement: George Washington, Mikhail Gorbachev, the Republican Party, the Cuban government, business entrepreneurs, the American space program, small-town educators, athletes.

Laying aside Bush's dependence upon others' visions, his second most discussed "vision" resided unsurprisingly in a global arena. For example, he asserted on February 2, 1989, "The scope of America's vision is global, and we
will continue to shoulder the obligations that belong to a global power."[14] He
discussed vision within the context of foreign policy 78 times, almost one-
third of the total, covering such subjects as the United Nations and the flow-
ering of democracy in the East. Bush also stressed a "New World Order" in
which the United Nations would play an integral role in promoting freedom
and democracy around the globe.[15] Yet global rhetorical visions began to lack
resonance with the American people almost as soon as Bush took office. In the
post–Cold War era Americans wanted attention focused inward on domestic
problems, yet the president had an international vision. This left Bush to
mention vision under the auspices of domestic policy less than one-fifth of the
time, focusing mainly on economics, education, drugs, and crime.[16] Over-
whelmingly, the public called home while Bush dialed foreign dignitaries.

Why did Bush's vision discourse, attenuated though it was, fail to capture
public awareness? In two addresses, one on August 6, 1991, and the other on
June 23, 1992, Bush poetically stated, "A vision without a task is but a dream; a
task without a vision is drudgery; but a vision with a task is the hope of the
world."[17] While this statement might lead one to believe George Bush understood the importance of and actually possessed a vision, I argue that he missed
the "vision thing" because he did not create a public narrative that was simple,
repetitive, familiar, and artistic.

Effective rhetorical visions serve as public messages that increase community cohesion, encourage public action, and provide a common, shared
narrative. According to Ernest Bormann, "the fantasy dramas of a successful
persuasive campaign chain out in public audiences to form a rhetorical
vision."[18] Rhetorical visions include heroes, villains, validating forces, settings,
meanings, and calls to action, all transmitted in a stylish fashion. Using a
dramatistic form, rhetors perpetuate visions by constructing messages that are
simple, repetitive, familiar, and artistic. While all public servants are expected
to offer a "vision" to their constituents in the era of the "rhetorical presidency,"
the chief executive's espousal of a "vision" appears to be an unofficial require-
ment of the office. To help gain an understanding of George Bush's inability
to construct a vision—at least as perceived by the American public—I briefly
offer Reagan's rhetoric as an exemplar of an effective rhetorical vision.

In his examination of Reagan's use of the narrative form, William F. Lewis
concludes that "his story gave a clear, powerful, reassuring, and self-justifying
meaning to America's public life."[19] Reagan managed this by crafting a com-

plete drama in which the American people could engage. Lewis explains: "Reagan portrays American history as a continuing struggle for progress against great obstacles imposed by economic adversity, barbaric enemies, or Big Government. It is a story with great heroes—Washington, Jefferson, Lincoln, Roosevelt—with great villains—the monarchs of pre-Revolutionary Europe, the Depression, the communists, the Democrats—and with a great theme—the rise of freedom and economic progress. It is a story that is sanctified by God and validated by the American experience."[20]

Lewis tells us that Reagan's messages consistently reinforced the same themes. The American people were the hero of his tale, as "Reagan repeatedly tells his audiences that if they choose to participate in the story, they will become a part of America's greatness."[21] The villains of the tale, consequently, are whatever forces hinder the nation from achieving this "greatness," be it other countries, economic forces, or the government itself. Reagan played upon the American perception that the nation has been divinely blessed. He also capitalized upon the Puritan work ethic, claiming that through each person's effort America's continued prominence would be achieved. "To accept Reagan's story," Lewis maintains, "is . . . to know that the direction and outcome of the story depend on you. Proper action makes the audience member a hero; inaction or improper action makes the listener responsible for America's decline."[22] The Great Communicator's vision was simply a tale of good versus evil, a message he maintained throughout his tenure in office. It capitalized upon themes already present within the American culture and was effectively presented, maximizing the potential for its effect through his narrative style.

Bush failed to develop a simple, easily repeated narrative. Because Bush had trouble developing a master narrative, he ended up talking about a wide variety of "visions," which resulted in his "vision" seeming to be convoluted and continually changing. His topics ranged from the war on drugs to economic policy to the New World Order. "Bush would try to do the right thing, case by case," Michael Duffy and Dan Goodgame assert.[23] Consequently, Bush did not develop a singular, clear philosophy through which he could share his perception of America's story. Since he had no overarching vision, he did not have a central theme to recount when appropriate occasions presented themselves. This was a serious flaw, for as Mary Matalin observes, "The absolute rule of message dissemination and message penetration is consistency and repetition."[24] Bush's messages were neither.

As president, Bush never projected a message that resonated with the American public. His visions typically advocated rational policy choices involving such things as the environment, the space program, or capital gains, without grounding them in any national narrative. Whereas Kennedy had the New Frontier, Johnson the Great Society, and Reagan the American Dream, George Bush had his prudence, a pragmatic notion of government that renounced the very ideals of an inspiring vision. "I am hopeful," Bush remarked early in his presidency, "that 1989 will be remembered as the year when American labor, business and, yes, government first began to work together in a real partnership for the freedom and dignity of workers everywhere, *not out of some utopian vision* but because we simply believe in the same basic values."[25]

More often than not, the president lacked any consistent rhetorical strategy. He repeatedly joked about his lack of vision, criticized the concept, and then proceeded to contradict his own position. When questioned during a meeting with the White House Press Corps on November 29, 1989, Bush quipped, "In terms of the 'vision thing,' the aspirations, I spelled it out in little-noted speeches last spring and summer, which I would like everyone to go back and re-read. And I'll have a quiz on it."[26] Bush thus missed an opportunity to emphasize a vision. Yet the president created a contradictory pattern when he claimed, only five days later, "Real peace, like prosperity, doesn't occur by accident. It requires patience, vision, a meaningful dialogue."[27] Yet no definition or description of such a vision was forthcoming. Early in his presidency Bush mocked the notion of vision, thus providing a shaky foundation for any later rhetorical leadership. The lack of foundation undermined his later effort to persuade the public he held a vision for America, a vision of public service.

By examining six specific speeches, I will illustrate how Bush failed to articulate a coherent vision for the American public. These six speeches are his Republican National Convention acceptance address (1988), his inaugural address (1989), his remarks at the University of Michigan commencement ceremony (May 4, 1990), his remarks at the presentation ceremony for the All-American Cities Award (August 6, 1991), his remarks on the administration's domestic policy (June 12, 1991), and his remarks at a celebration of the Points of Light (January 14, 1993). I chose to analyze these particular speeches for one of two reasons. The first two speeches stand as landmark moments of the Bush presidency, speeches that should have served as vehicles for dissemination of his rhetorical vision to the American public. The last four speeches were chosen because in them Bush specifically talks about the role of "vision."

1988 REPUBLICAN NATIONAL CONVENTION ADDRESS

With the words, "For we are a nation of communities . . . a brilliant diversity spread like stars, like a thousand points of light in a broad and peaceful sky,"

George Bush happened upon a sound bite by which to be identified by the public. Bush speechwriter Peggy Noonan remarks, "No one knew what an impact 'a thousand points of light' would have."[28] Bush was trailing Democrat Michael Dukakis in national polls by a significant margin as he headed into the Republican National Convention. At this point Bush was more interested in creating public awareness of himself as a candidate than in asserting any ideological vision.

The vice president's 1988 Republican National Convention speech satisfied two rhetorical functions: first, to help the public know and identify with George Bush; and second, to attach Bush's philosophy to that of Reagan.[29] He did this not by developing a "vision," but by expounding upon his "mission." "I am a man who sees life in terms of missions—missions defined and missions completed," Bush told the faithful. Although some might consider the two terms interchangeable, Bush does not adequately articulate any of the dramatistic requirements of a vision.

Ironically, even though Bush seeks to cloak himself in Reagan's image, he does not construct his predecessor as a hero. He classifies Reagan as a "friend" and declares the president has his "loyalty," yet he does not present Reagan as a white knight who took back the country from the dark ages of Democratic control. He does, nevertheless, laud the accomplishments of the past eight years and asks, "When you have to change horses in midstream, doesn't it make sense to switch to one who's going the same way?" His message is that he is the continuation of Reaganism. Nor does Bush truly appropriate Reagan's traditional hero—the American people. Toward the end of this speech Bush declares that "the individual" is the "bright center" of his political philosophy, yet he does not boast about the accomplishments, tenacity, courage, or valor of the individual. He merely emphasizes that individuals should hold the reins of governmental control and lists a variety of groups, announcing that "this is America: the Knights of Columbus, the Grange, Hadassah, the Disabled American Veterans, the Order of Ahepa, the Business and Professional Women of America, the union hall, the Bible study group, LULAC, Holy Name." Bush does not boast about the role of the people but merely identifies who the people are. Nevertheless, for Bush the individuals in these groups are "a brilliant diversity spread like stars, like a thousand points of light in a broad and peaceful sky."

Just as Bush does not characterize a clear hero in this speech, he has no villain to serve as a foil for his absentee hero. If one looks back to Bush's description of the "points of light," one notices that the stars reside in a "peaceful sky." No turbulence, storm, or cosmic threat exists. Actually, the closest

Bush comes to crafting a villain in this speech is when he mentions "the liberal Democrats," "drug dealers," and "the people who dump these infected needles into our oceans." Communism and Big Government, Reagan's two arch-villains, are implied rather than demonized, and Bush's speech is optimistic, not accusatory, focusing on what he hopes to accomplish in office. "I intend to stand for freedom," Bush proclaims, omitting any political tyranny against which to stand. No enemy is identified, for no enemy truly exists.

Since there is no enemy, Bush does not craft any exigence to which to respond. Even though he argues that he "will keep America moving forward, always forward—for a better America, for an endless, enduring dream and a thousand points of light," America has no pressing need for George Bush in particular. *He* has a mission, but no national narrative in which *the people* can participate. "This is my mission, and I will complete it." The process relies solely on the capabilities of the president and does not demand public support or anyone's vote.

Furthermore, America is a blessed nation. "America is not in decline. America is a rising nation," Bush proclaims. As such, there is no crisis that necessitates a particular saving power. In addition to the lack of hero, villain, and specific call to action, Bush does not have a validating force that endorses his candidacy, nor does he frame his speech in any particular setting. "America is good, we should stay the course" encapsulates the overall idea of Bush's acceptance address.

Starting with the acceptance address, the call to action that begins to run throughout Bush's speeches is volunteerism, which he refers to as being a "point of light." Bush's "point of light" (POL) discourse spanned the period from his 1988 presidential campaign throughout his presidency and continues to be utilized in his post-presidential rhetoric.[30] First mentioned during his 1988 RNC acceptance address, this phrase arose out of Bush's need to promote a domestic agenda. It then evolved from a simple maxim in a political campaign to become a philanthropic movement. In other words, volunteerism as a "call to action" was not a concerted effort, used by Bush to lead the people in his national vision, but a "rhetorical flourish" that was well received and therefore utilized again and again.

JANUARY 20, 1989, INAUGURAL ADDRESS

While his 1988 RNC acceptance address sought to construct Bush politically in the image of Reagan, his inaugural address endeavored to separate him from his predecessor.[31] At the beginning of his address, Bush briefly identifies two American heroes: Ronald Reagan (ironic in light of one of this speech's goals), "who has earned a lasting place in our hearts and in our history," and George Washington, "the Father of our Country."[32] These two men are acknowledged, then dismissed as Bush moves on to set the scene, only to jump into beseeching his Heavenly Father's favor. His deity is not a validating force that empowers his presidency, but One from whom we seek help in order to accomplish His will, whatever that might be.

To say that "we meet on democracy's front porch" satisfies Bush's notion of a frame of reference from which to speak would be too simplistic. Yet Bush does not set a scene that elicits any need for action. America is "at a moment rich with promise," and "for the first time in this century, for the first time in perhaps all history, man does not have to invent a system by which to live." Why, therefore, would there be a need "to make kinder the face of the Nation"? And the only explicit villain that exists is the "scourge" of drugs; materialism is merely alluded to. Communism is not a threat; the nation is at peace.

The conclusion of his inaugural address sums up Bush's lack of interest in a strategic national narrative. "Some see leadership as high drama and the sound of trumpets calling," he declares, "and sometimes it is that." And sometimes it is not, his audience correctly intuits. He continues, "But I see history as a book with many pages, and each day we fill a page with acts of hopefulness and meaning. The new breeze blows, a page turns, the story unfolds." This is not a narrative, therefore, that the leader of the free world provides as a beacon for his people, it is a tale told in response to an ethereal wind passing through the life of a people. Bush, moreover, is not even certain of his own ability to accomplish visionary ideals. "But *if* the man you have chosen to lead this government can help make a difference; *if* he can celebrate the quieter, deeper successes that are made not of gold and silk but of better hearts and finer souls; *if* he can do these things, then he must" (emphasis added).

Aware of Reagan's era being marked by materialism and excess, Bush vowed that his presidency would foster community service. The new president emphasized that during times of national struggles "we will turn to the only resource we have that in times of need always grows—the goodness and courage of the American people." Thus, Bush's employment of the POL shifted slightly, but substantially; instead of simply using it as an identification mark, he sets it up in a problem-solution fashion. Volunteerism can solve national problems, while federal funding cannot. Or, as Bush stated in his June 22, 1991, radio address to the nation on the subject of his administration's domestic agenda, "dollars don't make visions; deeds do."[33] And just as dollars do not make deeds, this president offered no rhetorical vision at the outset of his presidential term to lead the American populace to philanthropic action.

MAY 4, 1991, REMARKS AT THE
UNIVERSITY OF MICHIGAN COMMENCEMENT CEREMONY

In his commencement address on May 4, 1991, at the University of Michigan, Bush exhorted the graduating class: "My vision for America depends heavily on you. You must protect the freedoms of enterprise, speech, and spirit. You must strengthen the family. You must build a peaceful and prosperous future. . . . Muster the courage to be what I call a Point of Light."[34] While this may seem to be the typical collegiate graduation address, a sort of "go forth and do good," this speech contains a key dramatistic element that earlier speeches neglected: the American hero.

The overall setting of this speech is placed on a cusp of history: the fall of communism. "Your commencement, your journey into the 'real world,'" Bush tells the graduates, "coincides with this nation's commencement into a world freed from cold war conflict." It is significant that Bush does not use the end of the Cold War to demonstrate how good triumphed over evil (as Reagan would have); instead, he uses it only as a springboard for protecting the free market, free speech, and free "spirit." Again, Bush does not produce an enemy for Americans to band together against. He rejects outright such an idea: "Define your missions positively. Don't seek out villains. Don't fall prey to obsessions about 'freedom from' various ills. Focus on freedom's promise, on your promise." This illuminates how Bush misses an important element of visions: something to fight *against*. While Johnson fought poverty and Reagan battled the Evil Empire, George Bush struggled against developing a rhetorical vision.

The strongest aspect of this speech is Bush's adoption of the American hero as the champion of his tale. Although the philanthropic concept had been implied or even mentioned in early addresses, in this message Bush signifies a concerted effort on the president's part to construct Americans as the center of past and future glories. His use of inclusive pronouns emphasizes this. "We . . . help others in need." "Our government has sent aid . . ." "Our economic strength, our military power, and most of all, our national character brought us to this special moment," where freedom trumps tyranny. We are people of ingenuity, creating a system of government that fosters opportunity and a free market system that encourages success. We value the dignity of individuals and prize fundamental freedoms, including the market, speech, and spirit. "You can lead the way," Bush proclaims. In contrast to Bush's acceptance address almost three years earlier, success is not something Bush can achieve alone; this is not solely his "mission," but a goal achieved only through the action of each individual American. The people, therefore, have found a part in Bush's drama.

The overall message of this address is that although democracy has prevailed over communism, the battle is not over. Government cannot solve American ills, the people have to step up, and government should empower them to do so.

JUNE 12, 1991, REMARKS ON
THE ADMINISTRATION'S DOMESTIC POLICY

Throughout the first part his presidency, Bush did not proactively advocate a distinct rhetorical vision because he understood his role in the national drama in negative, rather than positive, terms. His job was to be "head of government," preventer of bad laws, and protector of the status quo, not "leader of the people."[35] Ironically, one of George Bush's strongest moments in office, the Gulf War, immediately preceded and in some ways precipitated his political downfall.[36] Although Bush experienced criticism for his problem in articulating a vision before the war, his confident leadership during the Persian Gulf conflict highlighted his lack of a coherent domestic policy.[37] This led to an effort by the Bush administration in May 1991 to develop an ideological vision. The result was Bush's June 12, 1991, remarks on the administration's domestic policy.

On May 22, 1991, David Demarest, assistant to the president for communications, sent a memo to the president regarding a June 12 South Lawn speech. Demarest stated, "This can be a powerful moment in your presidency. With the proper promotion, audience, and message, this event presents an excellent opportunity to frame your vision for the nation."[38] Demarest noted that the goal of Bush's June 12, 1991, South Lawn speech was to focus on the president's domestic vision per se, not on whether he actually had a vision or not. In the memo Demarest specifically outlined Bush's vision for "An America Transformed," an agenda advocated primarily by James Pinkerton, Bush's domestic policy adviser, and Edith Holiday, Bush's assistant.[39] This vision was three-pronged; only through "the synergy of a compassionate and competent government, a vibrant, creative private enterprise sector, *and* a national ethic of service" would America be transformed.[40]

Again the great American hero takes center stage in Bush's narrative, but in a less forceful fashion than in his May 4 speech. The hero is in the shadows, as Bush merely remarks, "You are extraordinary Americans. . . . You bring to life the genius of the American spirit." Moreover, Bush fails to craft a concrete scene; his stage vacillates between the national and local levels without giving his listeners a chance to place themselves within his narrative. Neither does Bush call upon a validating force. Surprisingly, the president in this speech does not even play upon the commonplace of American civil religion.[41]

Consistent with previous addresses and his desire to be a positive president, Bush does not fully develop a villain in this address. Tangentially, Congress and Big Government *appear* to be evils, yet one element of the three-pronged plan is government action. Congress is part of the solution, and while Big Government has been shown not to work, it is not evil in and of itself. The closest Bush actually comes to setting forth a concrete problem is informing Americans that they can solve America's "most pressing problems." But Bush does not outline what those problems are beyond "impoverished Americans . . . Americans gone astray . . . Americans uneasy." Bush's construction of America's problem as certain vague classes of Americans presents a logical dilemma. How can the people, in general, be both the hero and the villain? He goes on to encourage the country to "become America whole and good" by "working the magic of America," but what is the problem? How is America not whole, and how can "the greatest and freest [country] on the face of the Earth" not be good?

While Bush does develop a call to action, it is not very specific or wholly inclusive of the American people. Bush tells his listeners that to make a nation that lacks clearly defined problems "great," "it takes all three forces of our national life. First, it requires the power of the free market; second, a competent, compassionate government; and third, the ethic of serving others, including what I call the Points of Light. These three powerful forces create the conditions for communities to be whole and free, and it's time that we harnessed all three of them." The president's first two "forces" do not necessitate any action by the people. America's system of government is based upon the free market ideal, and government operates separately from its constituents. It is important, however, that in this address Bush also stresses the limitations of the first two parts of his three-part vision: the legislature's gridlock hampers it from passing domestically beneficial policies, and the free market is held in check without both positive legislation and national service. This should create a need for an actual summons to service, yet his "points of light" cannot be taken as a true call to action. Rather, Bush informs the audience that service is an "ethic" that needs to be "harnessed." The spirit of volunteerism already exists within the American people, yet the president does not expound upon *how* Americans should go about serving; he merely says that such action should be harnessed.

AUGUST 6, 1991, REMARKS AT THE PRESENTATION CEREMONY FOR THE ALL-AMERICAN CITIES AWARD

In his August 6, 1991, presentation of the All-American Cities Award, Bush continues his trumpeting of the American people as heroes. Yet the drama in which they take part is not Bush's, but each community's own narrative. "To fight crime, Austin, Texas, inaugurated Youth at Risk, and Winchester-Frederick County in Virginia set up a teen center to foster a drug-free environment." These efforts exemplify the grassroots vision of the people. George Bush has no role in this story; this is not his tale but the nation's. In his address Bush acknowledges the nation's story and even gives credit for this vision to another president: "These communities recognize the responsibilities of citizenship, as Teddy Roosevelt admonished Americans to be actors not merely critics. And the central theme of all these stories is the unlimited power and promise of voluntary service to others. These communities show us the strength of the American character—people helping one another without expecting financial compensation for themselves. And today we call them Points of Light. But they've been the heart of our Nation for over 200 years." Once again Bush lacks every other dramatistic element. This speech is devoid of a broad national scene; Bush allows his listeners to craft their own stage, set at the local community. Once again no villain exists—not even drugs or crime—as each community being celebrated has triumphed over its own affliction. Bush does not appeal to a validating force, nor is there any need for a call to action. The form of Bush's speech, devoid of all but one element of a rhetorical vision, leaves the president with only one course of action: to thank the people for *their* vision and for *their* action. Or, as Bush says, "thanks to all of you, and all out here for giving us hope, for showing us the way."

JANUARY 14, 1993, REMARKS AT A CELEBRATION OF THE POINTS OF LIGHT

Even toward the end of his presidency George Bush struggled with "the vision thing" and crafting a rhetorical vision. His June 12, 1991, address on domestic policy attempted to define a broad "Bush Vision," and his January 14, 1993,

Points of Light speech sought to reemphasize that vision and to encourage the continuance of Bush's national service agenda as he prepared to leave office. This address, given during his final days in office, comes closer to crafting a rhetorical vision than any other speech Bush offered.

The hero of Bush's tale is once again the American people. They have been the ones to take charge of their communities and seek to better local life. Yet this speech has several distinguishing aspects. First, Bush sets a broader scene than he had before. The setting of "points of light" is now in the American landscape, for while he mentions one specific community and a few key leaders of the "points of light" movement, he emphasizes that "we've got Points of Light here today from all 50 States, shining all the way from Anchorage to Harlem, Miami to Maine." This is not a localized movement; "America" is mentioned again and again throughout this brief speech.

Second, Bush has a clear call to action for the first time. His five-point plan includes "changing attitudes" about the definition of a successful life, "identifying" existing avenues of service, "encouraging" others to engage in philanthropic activities, "reducing volunteer liability" to decrease the litigious impulse of the American people, and actually aiding people in finding service opportunities. Unlike earlier speeches in which Bush espoused the belief that communities knew their own needs and acted on their own, here Bush informs the people of his role in directing the drama—specifically, how he has used his office to smooth the way for their actual involvement in his vision.

Third, this speech stands as one of the most eloquent examples of Bush's oratory. Throughout the address he plays upon the metaphor of light, using such words as *shining, illuminates, shadows, dark, constellation, stars,* and *rekindling.* His word choice gives flow and meaning to the body of the speech. The form of the text reinforces the purpose of the speech: to encourage public service, to motivate people to beome "points of light." He uses similar words to emphasize antithetical notions. His goal is to guide America back to its "moral compass," the "changeless values that can and must guide change." He employs alliteration to increase audience attention and to make his message more memorable. The short phrase "people, not programs, solve problems" encapsulates Bush's political ideology and his rhetorical vision.

Unfortunately, Bush once again fails to clarify a national villain. He mentions that "no social problem" will be solved without the participation of the populace, but does not expound upon what constitutes those social problems. He also does not fully develop a validating force. Philanthropic service is "the Lord's work," but Bush does not ask for help in the labor.

CONCLUSION

What George Bush sought to accomplish was to leave the country with a vision of a "Renewed America." Even though he managed to develop certain aspects of a national narrative, the president never crafted a complete rhetorical vision. Bush did have a hero (the philanthropic American, abstractly referred to as a "point of light") and he had a call to action (to participate in community service), but Bush's tale lacked every other dramatistic element. Bush's domestic rhetoric emphasized America's positives devoid of clear insufficiencies or evils; he never identified a serpent in America's garden. For Bush, "the America we know is right and decent and good"; thus, the nation is fine in its present state of existence.[42] Nor did the president lay claim to any empowering agency; neither "God" nor "The People" commissioned presidential action. The power for change lay in the American people because of who they are internally, not due to some external force. As he stated in his acceptance address at the Republican National Convention, "any definition of a successful life must include serving others." This philanthropic call, however, was nebulous and not grounded in the American story. Bush contextualized his "points of light" from a global or localized framework instead of a broad domestic one. He declared, "We've changed the world. And now let's use that same energy and that same enthusiasm and that same vision to change the United States of America, to make life better for every single citizen in this country." Unconcerned with international affairs or someone else's community, the people wanted the president to root his dream in their American soil. The president's incomplete tale, therefore, failed to achieve resonance with the people. Since Bush did not fully construct the parameters of his vision, he did not create a space in which to speak. Unlike Ronald Reagan, George Bush did not fashion a narrative that captured the nation's attention or moved its people to action. Rather than being seen as simply a different leadership style, Bush's problem with "the vision thing" was perceived as a defect in his presidency.

Consequently, Bush left office without the populace knowing who he was and what America meant to him. Passionate about service to his country, Bush never adequately translated that emotion into a national vision. Visions, according to Bormann, include villains, heroes, validating forces, settings, meanings, and calls to action in order to increase community cohesion and motivate citizen participation by including them in a common narrative. Bush, unlike Reagan, never fully developed his interpretation of America's story. He had heroes without villains or crises. He had calls to actions without any validating force or context. He had "points of light" without darkness or a celestial galaxy.

In order for Bush's Renewed America to be understood by the nation, Bush should have communicated his message in a vehicle intuitively understood by his audience: a story. In this narrative his hero would still be the American people and his call to action would still be national service, yet he would develop his Great American Tale by completing the drama. His villain would be corruption and materialism, the self-centered focus of the late twentieth century, and whatever forces hindered humanitarian efforts. His validating force would be the divine architect of the moral compass, set within the American heartland, each local community, from coast to coast. The altruism of Americans, moreover, could be applied both at home and internationally with the American people helping each other and the world.

Once he had established a simple, coherent narrative, the president would need to incorporate within his speeches specific initiatives; he could set explicit objectives for the people's public service. George Bush's "points of light" initiative could be labeled a glorified advertising campaign in disguise—an advertisement for a nonexistent product. The Bush administration spent on public marketing of the POL crusade ten times the amount it spent on actual POL programs. The first "Daily Points of Light" was awarded to a media group, and his administration announced press releases publicizing the "Daily Points of Light" recipient five days out of every week. Duffy and Goodgame report, "Some of his aides gradually realized that Bush saw the 'points of light' not so much as a complement to a domestic policy strategy, but as a substitute for one."[43] Rather than furnishing strategic rhetorical leadership marked by clear goals, Bush just articulated bits and pieces of a heroic narrative, never really completing the dramatic frame.

In the end, Bush's endeavor to create a vision floundered because he failed to develop a coherent narrative to frame his commitment to public service and because he lacked a clear program of action by which to measure his conception. He gave lip service to a national service program and commended individuals and organizations for jobs well done, but he never implemented a comprehensive policy to call forth action. "What Bush offered," Duffy and Goodgame argue, "was a trickle-down social policy to match his trickle-down economic policy. His message to the country on domestic policy, essentially, was: Do it yourself."[44] With communities in need, the people felt Washington was content with the status quo.

During a panel on leadership that former president Bush moderated in the spring of 2000, I had the opportunity to question him about the role of "vision" in leadership. His response:

> My problem, very frankly, was that I wasn't articulate. I didn't feel comfortable with some of the speechwriters' phrases, so I would cross them out. I didn't quote Shelley and Kant. I didn't remember exactly what Thucydides had meant to me when I was only twelve. And I felt there was something . . . not feeling those things, I would ex them out. Part of—and I think it was maybe a mistake— because part of being seen as a visionary is being able to have flowing rhetoric, and . . . you know, coming out of the clouds and being quoted all the time. My vision was for a kinder and gentler nation, my vision was for more freedom, more democracy around the world. My vision, as it turned out in the war—stand up against aggression and let some able people do the job. So I feel comfortable with what I felt was a vision. But I think it is very fair to say . . . [I] wasn't particularly good at articulating this—about . . . flowing rhetoric that can rally people along the way. And so maybe that's part of why I was hit on the vision thing. And, some of it, because when I talk about there could be no definition of a successful life that does not include service to others, being one of a thousand points of life, being one of what this guy is doing in the inner city of Baltimore, when he could be—I mean Wilmington—when he could be doing anything he wanted in life—that's a vision. And it's a good vision. But it didn't fit. Some would say, "Oh, he's just doing that to avoid his responsibilities as a government leader. He doesn't want to put money into the cities, so therefore he says other people ought to do it." So the vision . . . didn't fit with what some thought makers thought the vision ought to be. And I'm guilty of not having the soaring enough rhetoric to get above it. Even convince people the economy had recovered. Hell, I wasn't good enough to do that.[45]

Seven years after he left office Bush still did not get "the vision thing." He had a goal, but did not understand that his mission was not simply to provide an end objective but to craft a national narrative in which the people could take part. Rhetoric is not merely sophisticated artistry but a vehicle for presidential leadership.

NOTES

1. Thomas Collins, "The Muse Is a Stranger to Today's Campaigns," *Newsday,* August 28, 1988, 10.

2. David Broder, "Mixed Marks for Bush on Leadership Skills," *St. Louis Post-Dispatch,* December 7, 1989, 3C.

3. Editorial, "The Bully Pulpit, Half Empty," *New York Times,* January 2, 1991, 16.

4. Robert B. Hawkins, Jr., "Bush Last over the 'Vision Thing,'" November 7, 1992, A20.

5. In addition to the articles already cited, see, for example, Editorial, "Bush: The Real Test," *Los Angles Times,* November 9, 1988, 6; Bob Sipchen, "Cartoonists Draw a New Line for Bush," *Los Angles Times,* February 16, 1989, 1; "First Anniversary," *Newsday,* January 21, 1990, 3; Editorial, *New Republic* 204 (February 25, 1991), 7; Michael Krepon, "Bush States His Doctrine by Omission," *Los Angeles Times,* October 6, 1991, 2; Douglas Harbrecht and Howard Gleckman, "It's Not Too Late for Bush to Get 'the Vision Thing,'" *Business Week* 3280 (August 24, 1992), 26; Virginia I. Postrel, "Free Trade Is Bush's Economic Ace," *Los Angeles Times,* August 28, 1992, 7; and Bob Adams, "Leadership: Many See President as Pragmatic, Not Visionary," *St. Louis Post-Dispatch,* September 15, 1992, 1B.

6. Marlin Fitzwater, *Call the Briefing! Reagan and Bush, Sam and Helen: A Decade with Presidents and the Press* (New York: Random House, 1995), 245.

7. Ibid.

8. Paul Burka, "The Revision Thing," *Texas Monthly,* November 1997, 136–41.

9. Gail Sheehy, *Character: America's Search for Leadership* (New York: Morrow, 1988), 167.

10. Mark J. Rozell, *The Press and the Bush Presidency* (New York: Praeger, 1996), 4.

11. Herbert S. Parmet, *George Bush: The Life of a Lone Star Yankee* (New York: Scribner, 1997), 380.

12. In a query of Bush's Public Papers, the term *vision* appears 319 times, yet these mentions also include addresses by other persons speaking with Bush or speaking for Bush (foreign dignitaries, Marlin Fitzwater), public statements, and executive proclamations, which I have not included in my analysis.

13. Murray Edelman, *Constructing the Political Spectacle* (Chicago: University of Chicago Press, 1988), 104.

14. Bush, "Remarks Following Discussions with Prime Minister Noboru Takeshita of Japan," February 2, 1989. All my citations of Bush's speeches refer to his Public Papers in the Bush Library, unless otherwise stated.

15. See, for example, the following addresses by Bush for a sampling of his foreign policy vision as found in his Public Papers: "Interview with Members of the White House Press Corps," November 29, 1989; "Remarks to the National Academy of Sciences," April 23, 1990; "Remarks at a Luncheon Hosted by the Venezuelan-American Chambers of Commerce in Caracas, Venezuela," December 8, 1990; and "Remarks at the Signing Ceremony for the Computer Trade Agreement with Japan," January 22, 1992.

16. While all of this could be more narrowly coded, I was looking for broad, sweeping patterns in Bush's use of the term *vision.*

17. George Bush, "Remarks at the Presentation Ceremony for the All-American Cities Award," August 6, 1991; and Bush, "Remarks at the Presentation Ceremony for the National Medal of Science and the National Medal of Technology," June 23, 1992.

18. Ernest G. Bormann, "Fantasy and Rhetorical Vision: The Rhetorical Criticism of Social Reality," in *Readings in Rhetorical Criticism,* ed. Carl R. Burgchardt (State College, Pa.: Strata Publishing, 1995), 244.

19. William F. Lewis, "Telling America's Story: Narrative Form and the Reagan Presidency," in Burgchardt, ed., *Readings in Rhetorical Criticism,* 309.

20. Ibid., 297.

21. Ibid.

22. Ibid., 298.

23. Duffy and Goodgame, *Marching in Place: The Status Quo Presidency of George Bush* (New York: Simon & Schuster, 1992), 21.

24. Mary Matalin and James Carville, *All's Fair: Love, War, and Running for President* (New York: Random House, 1994), 80.

25. Bush, "Remarks at the Biannual Convention of the American Federation of Labor and Congress of Industrial Organizations," November 15, 1989 (emphasis added).

26. Bush, "Interview with Members of the White House Press Corps," November 29, 1989.

27. Bush, "Remarks at a Fundraising Luncheon for Senatorial Candidate Lynn Martin in Chicago, Illinois," November 20, 1989.

28. Peggy Noonan, *What I Saw at the Revolution: A Political Life in the Reagan Era* (New York: Random House, 1990), 312.

29. "Acceptance Speech," Republican National Convention, New Orleans, August 18, 1988; reprinted in *Vital Speeches of the Day* 55 (1988–89): 3–5.

30. For an excellent synopsis of the "points of light," see Duffy and Goodgame, *Marching in Place,* 209–13.

31. "Inaugural Address: A New Breeze Is Blowing," Washington, D.C., February 9, 1989, reprinted in *Vital Speeches of the Day* 55 (1988–89): 258–60.

32. See Rozell, *Press and the Bush Presidency,* 3.

33. Bush, "Radio Address to the Nation on the Administration's Domestic Agenda," June 22, 1991.

34. Bush, "Remarks at the University of Michigan Commencement Ceremony in Ann Arbor," May 4, 1991.

35. For a discussion of the two concepts, see James W. Ceaser, Glen E. Thurow, Jeffrey Tulis, and Joseph M. Bissette, "The Rise of the Rhetorical Presidency," *Presidential Studies Quarterly* 11 (1981): 158–71.

36. Clayton Yeutter, "Accomplishments and Setbacks," in *The Bush Presidency: Ten Intimate Perspectives of George Bush,* ed. Kenneth W. Thompson (Lanham, Md.: University Press of America, 1997), 49.

37. See Duffy and Goodgame, *Marching in Place,* 210; and Rozell, *Press and the Bush Presidency.*

38. Memorandum, David Demarest to George Bush, May 22, 1991, box 98, folder "Domestic Challenges Facing America," OA/ID 13571, Office of Speechwriting, Speech File Drafts, Bush Library.

39. Evan Thomas, "An Infusion of Vision," *Newsweek,* December 3, 1990, 24–25.

40. This is part of an attachment to the May 1991 "Memorandum for the President" from David Demarest to George Bush pertaining to the June 12 South Lawn speech. See Memorandum, David Demarest to George Bush, May 22, 1991, box 98, folder "Domestic Challenges Facing America," OA/ID 13571, Office of Speechwriting, Speech File Drafts, Bush Library.

41. For a discussion of civil religion see Robert N. Bellah, "Civil Religion in America," *Daedalus* 117 (1967): 1–21.

42. Bush, "Remarks at a Bush-Quayle Fundraising Luncheon in New York City," November 12, 1991.

43. Duffy and Goodgame, *Marching in Place,* 211.

44. Ibid., 213.

45. Bush, remarks at Bush Library, February 3, 2000, copy in possession of author.

CHAPTER 3

And the Wall Came Tumbling Down: Bush's Rhetoric of Silence during German Reunification

WILLIAM FORREST HARLOW

In early November 1989 events of historical import were taking place in Germany. The Berlin Wall was being torn down, and refugees from throughout much of the Eastern Bloc were streaming into what was still known as West Germany to seek a new life of freedom. Yet the president of the United States said nothing.

As the magnitude of the changes taking place in Germany and throughout Europe became clear, leaders in the American press and legislature called on George Bush to stand in Berlin to deliver a speech conveying the joy with which U.S. citizens viewed these events. Still, the president of the United States said nothing.

As it became clear that the Soviet Union was losing its grip on Eastern Europe and that American allies in NATO would have to deal with profound changes, there was an outcry that George Bush make known his views on the events at hand. U.S. allies and enemies alike demanded to know how America would react to these revolutionary changes. Publicly, the president of the United States still said nothing.

The November 9, 1989, announcement that travel restrictions across Checkpoint Charlie had been lifted set off a euphoric celebration in Berlin. President Bush did not speak publicly on the matter until November 22—the day before Thanksgiving and nearly two weeks later. Secretary of State James Baker later explained Bush's silence about the fall of the Berlin Wall this way: "In politics, words are the coin of the realm. Used judiciously, they can build political capital, coalesce a public consensus, or enrich a nation. But when frittered away or ineffectively employed, words in political life can bankrupt a candidate, sell out a policy, or even dissolve a government."[1]

The Bush administration's effort not to "fritter away" words on the occasion of the Wall's fall met with heavy criticism. For two months leading up to the fall, Senate Majority Leader George Mitchell had been accusing President Bush of "timidity" in his handling of European affairs.[2] Complaining of Bush's lack of response to the fall of the Wall, Mitchell urged him to speak in Berlin and then call for a meeting of Western allies concerning the future of Europe.[3] The press also complained that Bush was "lacking eloquence at a historic time."[4] The *New York Times* even published a fictional version of a speech that Bush might have given to address the situation.[5] Mary McGrory of the *Washington Post* said that the events in Berlin showed "Bush's emotional wall," and that perhaps he should prepare for the next similar event by "studying how to be giddy."[6]

Bush was also the target of broader criticism of his foreign policy as a result of his decision not to speak about the events in Germany. One writer stated: "The Bush administration does seem to have a strategy of sorts, buried under the half-measures and bad syntax. In a more jingoistic era, it would be called 'defeatism.'"[7] *U.S. News and World Report* noted: "George Bush has never been considered much of a trendsetter, but after 10 months in office, he is adopting a foreign policy . . . by triage, based on the belief that America's relative decline doesn't matter because the victorious U.S. can and must concentrate its dwindling resources on the handful of international problems Americans care most about, such as drug trafficking and trade."[8]

Perhaps the most direct criticism of Bush compared him to General George McClellan during the American Civil War:

> President Bush has been taking a pasting for his diffident, begrudging, initial reaction to the great events in Berlin and Eastern Europe. Similar criticisms have been leveled at him repeatedly throughout his first year in office.
> Collectively, they add up to the kind of complaint that a frustrated President Lincoln expressed about his unduly wary Union Army commander, Gen. George B. McClellan, the self-styled "Little Napoleon." After yet another instance of McClellan being late to commit his vastly superior forces to battle with the Confederates, Lincoln remarked angrily of the general: "He's got the slows."
> Something similar can be said about Bush.[9]

To what end did President Bush endure this intense criticism of what opponents viewed as his failure to grasp the rhetorical situation with regard to Berlin? As Secretary Baker noted, the administration did not wish to waste words. George Bush's own explanation, given some years later, was that he did not wish to exacerbate a tenuous political situation in Eastern Europe and the Soviet Union "by having the President of the United States posturing on the Berlin Wall."[10] Specifically, Bush claims that he was warned by British Prime Minister Margaret Thatcher that the consequences for the Soviet Union could be dire if the United States pushed it too far, too quickly on the changes in Eastern Europe. President Mikhail Gorbachev was battling conservatives in his own party over his *perestroika* and *glasnost* reform plans. According to Bush, Thatcher warned, "Destabilize him [Gorbachev] and we lose the possibility of democracy in the Soviet Union."[11]

Did President Bush make the correct decision in not provoking the Soviet Union by giving a celebratory speech or insisting on new legislative initiatives to take advantage of the evolving situation? Scholarly inquiry on presidential silence is limited. Richard L. Johannesen argues that silence is "pregnant with meaning."[12] Edwin Black examines Lincoln's Gettysburg Address using silence as a framework, and he praises Lincoln for knowing what not to say.[13] Martin Medhurst criticizes President Truman's failure to challenge the Soviet Union rhetorically in the aftermath of World War II as a flawed decision that ceded the ability of the United States to define the postwar environment.[14] Barry Brummett defines "political strategic silence" as "the refusal of a public figure to communicate verbally when that refusal (1) violates expectations, (2) draws public attributions of fairly predictable meanings, and (3) seems intentional and directed at an audience."[15]

It is my purpose in this chapter to understand presidential silence more fully and to examine George Bush's choice to confront this rhetorical situation created by the fall of the Berlin Wall with "political strategic silence." I use Brummett's term to define the president's actions because Bush clearly violated the expectations of many in Congress and the press, because a charge of "lack of vision" was consistently attached to his lack of speech, and because, as I will argue, he was intentionally directing his silence at several foreign audiences. Bush's silence was not absolute, but the few occasions on which he did speak were strictly epideictic and devoid of deliberative meaning—thus "silent" from a strictly policy-making perspective. As Brummett notes, "Silence is relative to what might be said."[16]

I will compare a deliberative speech President Bush gave in Mainz, Germany, on May 31, 1989, to the ceremonial address Bush gave after the fall of the Berlin Wall. I will also attempt to document the constraints operating upon George Bush as a rhetor during this period. My argument is straightforward: George Bush's legislative silence and ceremonial whisper were the best choices among the available means of persuasion in this last great rhetorical battle of the Cold War.

BEFORE THE FALL: MAINZ, GERMANY

In the first months of his presidency, Bush was embroiled in a battle over John Tower's nomination as secretary of defense, and he devoted significant time to a February 1989 trip to Asia. His first major address on Germany came in a May 1989 tour of Europe. In what James Baker described as one of his finest foreign policy speeches, George Bush spoke to the people of Mainz, Germany, on May 31, 1989.[17] Speaking at a time when the Cold War was not quite over, Bush called for a Europe "whole and free."[18] Confrontational in tone, the speech contained such lines as, "And on the other side of the rusting Iron Curtain, their vision failed."

President Bush used this speech as an opportunity to advance several policy proposals. Starting with broad goals, he called for "self-determination for all of Germany and all of Eastern Europe." However, Bush quickly focused on specifics in offering to grant the Soviets a temporary waiver of Jackson-Vanik trade restrictions if they agreed to liberalize their emigration rules. He also reminded the audience of a decision made earlier in the week, as a show of good faith in superpower relations, to lift technology export restrictions initially placed on the Soviet Union in response to its involvement in the Afghanistan conflict.

President Bush continued with a four-point plan to "heal Europe's tragic division," including proposals aimed at reducing conventional and chemical weaponry held by both NATO and the Warsaw Pact.[19] Specifically, he sought a reduction to 275,000 troops for NATO and an identical number for the Warsaw Pact nations. This would have been a reduction of 20 percent for NATO and more than 50 percent (325,000 troops) for the Soviet Union. Bush also called for a "worldwide ban on chemical weapons."

Bush's speech was designed as a deliberative statement engaging the Soviets on several discrete policy initiatives. Facing no immediate crisis, Bush was free to engage the USSR in the policy arena. In the atmosphere of the Cold War, the president of the United States was expected to give meaningful policy speeches that would engage the Soviet Union. In Mainz, George Bush did exactly that. However, before those proposals could be meaningfully advanced, the rhetorical situation changed dramatically. With the fall of the Berlin Wall on November 9, debate began on the question of whether the United States was still involved in the Cold War. This uncertainty appears to have constrained the Bush administration's response to the fall of the Wall.

AFTER THE FALL: LEGISLATIVE SILENCE

Almost two weeks passed between the November 9, 1989, announcement lifting travel restrictions between East and West Germany and George Bush's first speech on the matter on November 22. The president received intense criticism during this time. For example, he was criticized for having "a pained look on his face."[20] At the same time, he was criticized for continuing "to defer what he awkwardly calls 'the vision thing.'"[21] However, the rhetor-to-be spent that time in assessing the rhetorical situation. Specifically, he had to consider the constraints placed upon him by his multiple international audiences.[22]

Discovering the situational exigence, what Lloyd F. Bitzer calls the "imperfection marked by urgency," was, relatively speaking, not a difficult task for the Bush administration.[23] With many thousands of people leaving Eastern Europe for the West and the political situation in East Germany in a state of flux, the exigence facing a leading partner in NATO was how best to see the situation to a peaceful and stable resolution. However, the administration's ability to identify the exigence did not translate into ease in resolving it. The reason for this difficulty lay with the constraints placed upon Bush by his multiple audiences. When the president of the United States speaks, his audience consists of almost all of the world's important policymakers. The only audience that seemed to be demanding that he take forceful rhetorical action was his domestic one. Bush knew that his words would receive close scrutiny by many outside of his own country. For example, the Germans were particularly concerned that they be allowed to take the lead in determining their own future.[24] An overly forceful statement from the American president might be seen as intruding upon their right to self-determination. In a telephone conversation between President Bush and West German Chancellor Helmut Kohl on November 10, 1989, Bush asked Kohl if he could tell the U.S. press that he had been given a thorough briefing on the situation by the chancellor.[25] If Bush was so constrained that he wanted the approval of the German chancellor before publicly acknowledging their conversation, then a deliberative speech certainly might have pinched some sensitive diplomatic toes in Bonn.

In addition to the feelings of the West German government, Bush had to consider as part of his audience the thousands of East German citizens who were demanding change in their own government. In the same telephone conversation in which Bush asked Kohl if he could publicly acknowledge their conversation, Kohl gave an account of his trip to Berlin earlier that day. According to Kohl, 230,000 professionals had emigrated from East Germany in the previous year, and many thousands more were involved in various demonstrations. Egon Krenz, the East German leader, was making changes to his nation's political fabric in an attempt to stabilize the situation. Kohl, however, had his doubts: "This will work only if the GDR really reforms and I have my doubts. Krenz will carry out reforms but I think there are limits. One of those limits seems to be one party rule, and this simply will not work. . . . I could imagine that this will continue for a few weeks—that for a few weeks people will wait to see if the reforms come and if there is no light at the end of the tunnel they will run away from the GDR in great numbers."[26]

With these words, Chancellor Kohl presented Bush with two constraints. First, an agitated public in an unstable political situation could easily be provoked to take drastic action—emigration or otherwise—that risked destabilizing both Germanies and the whole of Europe. A wave of emigration would have crippled the East German economy as well as causing profound damage to the economies of the nations, particularly West Germany, that had to absorb a sudden and massive influx of refugees. George Bush had to avoid words that could provoke such a situation. Second, if the East German government was still committed to one-party communist rule, it would scarcely accept U.S. interference in its internal affairs. East German communists were not shifting to a liberal democracy, but were instead trying to maintain their own power. Provoking the East German government could easily have led to a crackdown in the name of maintaining one-party rule, and such a crackdown might have reversed whatever gains had been made. Thus, both East and West German audiences imposed significant constraints upon Bush.

The audience-based constraints upon the American president did not stop at the German border. Any speech that Bush gave would inevitably be closely watched in the capitals of all U.S. allies in Europe. Secretary Baker notes in his book *The Politics of Diplomacy* that London and Paris were nervous about the prospect of German unification because it raised the ugly specter of German aggression in two twentieth-century world wars. British Prime Minister Margaret Thatcher put it this way: "This reinforced me in my resolve to slow up the already heady pace of developments. Of course, I did not want East Germans—any more than I would have wanted anyone else—to have to live under communism. But it seemed to me that a truly democratic East Germany would soon emerge and that the question of reunification was a separate one, on which the wishes and interests of Germany's neighbours and other powers must be fully taken into account."[27]

Since any deliberative speech Bush might give would necessarily have to address the question of unification, the president was left in a difficult circumstance. If he was perceived as favoring unification, he risked losing the support of crucial allies in London and Paris. If he was perceived as opposing unification, the West German government, another critical ally, would be angry that the United States was involved in its internal affairs and its right to determine the direction of its own country. National Security Adviser Brent Scowcroft noted: "It was, of course, not possible to be rhetorically opposed to unification, but there seemed to me little reason at this point to put the issue on the active agenda."[28] A presidential speech would have done precisely that—place the issue front and center. Clearly, the audience that was composed of U.S. allies posed another significant constraint upon the president.

However, the most important audience—and thus the audience that placed the tightest constraint upon Bush—was neither domestic nor an American ally. Rather, it was inside the Soviet Politburo, whose members were watching every word to come out of Washington. President Gorbachev was facing internal political difficulties stemming from his liberalization programs and a bad economy.[29] He wished aloud that change would proceed in a calm and peaceful manner.[30] He had even gone so far as to say that the Soviet Union would not interfere in the process of change.[31] Still, there were forces in the Soviet Union that might compel Gorbachev to act if they perceived things to be moving too quickly. Prime Minister Thatcher confirms that in her visits with Gorbachev, he wanted to see the pace of things slow down and he stood opposed to German unification.[32] In a telephone conversation between President Bush and Chancellor Kohl on November 17, 1989, Kohl confirmed that he had received the same message from Gorbachev.[33] Bush's response at that time was consistent with his claims after he left the presidency about how he had handled the situation: "In spite of Congressional posturing, the U.S. will stay calm and support reforms in just the way you talk about. The euphoric excitement in the U.S. runs the risk of forcing unforeseen action in the USSR or the GDR that would be very bad. We will not be making exhortations about unification or setting timetables. We will not exacerbate the problem by having the President of the United States posturing on the Berlin Wall."[34]

Gorbachev's public statements began to convey the same message. He said that it was "useless to clamor about victory in the Cold War" and that "interests should be balanced."[35] Soviet Foreign Minister Eduard Shevardnadze also warned the West against trying to exploit perceived Soviet weaknesses.[36] In spite of the assurances it had offered, it was clear that the Soviet Union was not willing to be shown to be the loser in the grand contest of the Cold War.

Baker argues that ultimately American presidential rhetoric would have been crucial to the Soviet Union's determination of how to respond to the changes in Germany: "My sense was that what we said publicly was going to matter more to the Kremlin than any private message. We decided that the President would bring reporters in to the Oval Office, and that I would do all the networks that evening and the morning shows the next day.[37] We wanted to welcome the change diplomatically, almost clinically—and try as best we could not to be overly emotional, so that Gorbachev, Shevardnadze, and other Soviets who saw our reaction would not feel, as the President put it, 'that we were sticking our thumb in their eye.'"[38]

Press Secretary Marlin Fitzwater confirmed Secretary Baker's perceptions that the rhetoric of President Bush was going to be crucial to Gorbachev's response. Fitzwater and others in the White House public relations operation were pressuring Bush to make some kind of statement or speech. Deciding that it would not be the prudent thing to do, Bush forewent the positive domestic press likely to come with such a speech in order to avoid provoking the Soviet Union. Speaking of Gorbachev, Fitzwater writes: "His concern was that he was being portrayed as the loser, or the USSR was being portrayed as without values, when people spoke of the victory for Western values."[39]

How would Gorbachev have reacted if he had felt his nation to be the loser in a geopolitical values debate or if the president had stuck a rhetorical thumb in his eye? At least two important historical analogies suggest how the Soviets might have responded had they felt threatened by Bush's words concerning Germany. In 1956 the Soviet Union was faced with the potential loss of a satellite nation and of a great deal of international prestige when Hungarian Prime Minister Imre Nagy instituted a series of reforms that eliminated the privileged position of the communists in running the government. Nagy denounced the Warsaw Pact, and on November 1, 1956, announced Hungary's withdrawal from that alliance. Soviet tanks were quick to enter Hungary, and by November 4 had entered Budapest. Over the next few weeks Hungary was brutally pulled back under Nikita Khrushchev's umbrella of "protection." Accepting that same guise of protection and safe passage, Prime Minister Nagy left the hiding place he had assumed when Soviet tanks rolled into his country. However, he was abducted, taken to Romania, and executed in 1958.

Similar to Nagy's rhetorical sin of denouncing the Warsaw Pact, Czechoslovakian leader Alexander Dubcek in 1968 instituted a series of social liberalization programs under the rubric of "socialism with a human face." The Soviet Union must have also seen this face as objectionable, for Warsaw Pact troops quickly rolled into Czechoslovakia and violently suppressed protests against Soviet domination. Both Dubcek and Nagy offended Moscow with moves to challenge the Communist Party's exclusive hold on power, and they witnessed Soviet tanks rolling in to their respective countries when they were so bold as to criticize their "allies" publicly.

Could such a situation have repeated itself in 1989? The historical record certainly seems to indicate a low tolerance among Soviet leaders for dissent among their client states. William Safire argued in March 1989 that the wounded Soviet Union of that day would have been particularly likely to strike out violently if it felt it had been provoked:

> The puppet regimes of Poland, Hungary and the Baltic states, under pressure from patriots, are adopting the new thinking at face value, becoming more flexible and nationalist; but communists in power in Romania, Bulgaria, East Germany and Czechoslovakia have become more Stalinist than Moscow. Sooner or later, as movement accelerates in the flexible nations or as pressures build in the most repressive states, one of these countries will blow. At that moment, the contagion of freedom will threaten to spread even into the Ukraine. Depend on Gorbachev to crack down as Stalin would have, fraternally rolling in the tanks and shooting the dissenters. The present Kremlin leader was not chosen to preside over the dissolution of the Soviet empire. That revolt and reaction would teach a forgetful world the true nature of Soviet imperialism, but at a great cost in human life.[40]

Safire points to a tendency in even a weakened Soviet Union to respond violently to loss of international prestige. By the time the Berlin Wall began to crumble, Gorbachev had softened his position and was willing to allow change to take place slowly. However, he and the rest of the Soviet Politburo were uniformly unwilling to allow a rhetorical point to be made of their defeat in the Cold War, and the thought of Soviet troops taking action in East Germany or pouring through the Fulda Gap into West Germany must have been a chilling one for President Bush.

Identifying the most immediate exigence was relatively easy for the Bush White House. However, that exigence having been identified, the task of satisfying multiple audiences proved onerous given the various constraints upon Bush. Upon identifying each audience a new constraint was discovered. One particular constraint weighed heavily upon Bush. For some time, he had planned a summit meeting with Gorbachev near Malta for December 2–3, 1989. Bush looked at that meeting as an opportunity to "once and for all end the Cold War."[41] This was important to Bush for several reasons, not the least of which was the resulting help he would receive in a domestic budget crunch from no longer having to fight a Cold War enemy that had declared peace.[42] Additionally, an end to the Cold War would allow Bush rapid progress on the arms control agreements he had proposed in Mainz during his May 31 speech.

Bush's critics charged he should go about ending the Cold War by standing atop the Berlin Wall and making a passionate demonstration for freedom. However, as Bush had expressed, such an exhibition from him would have been inappropriate and would have risked the anger of multiple audiences. Instead of provoking any of his audiences, Bush was content to wait until the summit to see what gains he could make through personal diplomacy with Gorbachev. Private diplomacy was more important to Bush than public words. Nonetheless, despite his deliberative silence, the president would eventually have to make a statement on the matter. The question became exactly how to craft the epideictic rhetoric for that moment.

FROM SILENCE TO CEREMONY: BUSH SPEAKS

Bush was hesitant to say anything at all about the situation in Germany. When the speech eventually came, it was almost two weeks after travel restrictions had been lifted and even longer since refugees had been pouring in to West Germany. The president continued to endure intense criticism during this time as "a follower instead of a leader."[43] He was also criticized for having an "aloof approach to the drama now unfolding in Eastern Europe."[44] Instead of standing atop the Berlin Wall, Bush was sitting in the presidential retreat in Camp David, Maryland. Neither the timing nor the setting was what was desired by his domestic opposition. However, the time and place in which a speech was to be given were crucial to Cold War rhetoric.[45] As Baker argued, giving even a simple speech atop the Berlin Wall might well have been perceived negatively by the Soviets, and the same constraint would apply to a speech seen as being given too hurriedly. Thus came President Bush's two decisions: to wait two weeks before speaking at all, and to deliver the address from Camp David.

Not a great deal was said about the speech in advance. Deputy Chief of Staff James Cicconi circulated memos to the chief of staff, secretary of state, secretary of defense, and a few other White House staffers marked CLOSE HOLD, asking for comments on an early draft of the speech.[46] This prevented early drafts of the speech from being released and unintended messages being received and interpreted by Bush's publics before their full political implications had been considered by the White House.

After the two-week delay and the close hold on early speech drafts, Bush's speech of November 22, 1989, did not even begin with a discussion of the German question. Instead, he began with a brief homily about the Thanksgiving holiday and then touched upon his domestic legislative achievements from his first year in office. Only after this did Bush finally broach the subject of the fall of the Berlin Wall.

Bush's general emphasis in this speech was ceremonial; he tried to celebrate a broadly conceived notion of freedom without advancing new policy initiatives designed to take advantage of the situation. There were several references to times when Bush had sought Gorbachev's cooperation in some area, but Bush's public words in this speech stopped well short of calling for specific action from the Soviet Union. In this, his tone was substantially different from when he had spoken in Mainz seven months earlier. Indeed, Bush made it clear that he wanted Gorbachev to hear his words "not as an adversary seeking advantage, but as a people offering support."

There was only one instance in the speech where President Bush entered the policy arena. Bush referenced his multiple-point plan from the earlier spring that he said was necessary if "we are to take his [Gorbachev's] new thinking seriously." However, after recounting his plan, Bush went on to praise Gorbachev for meeting its objectives of democratic achievement, human rights, and arms reduction. This was certainly different from the Mainz speech in which Bush had decried the "rusting Iron Curtain." Furthermore, Bush made it publicly clear that he did not think the time to discuss any of these matters was on the immediate horizon:

> The Soviet Union has made progress in these five areas. That is undeniable.
> With that in mind and the momentous changes in Eastern Europe, I invited President Gorbachev to meet me ten days from now. This is a first meeting—a time for exploration. *It is not a time for detailed arms control negotiations best left for next year's summit.* (Emphasis added)

With these words, President Bush dismissed the notion that the immediate aftermath of the fall of the Berlin Wall was the time for policy announcements and proposals. Rather, he used the speech as a generic celebration of democratic values, and he incorporated the Soviet Union into that praise. The speech was much broader than a discussion of just the situation in Germany. Bush also discussed democratic advances in Hungary and Poland, as well as what he saw as "democracy transforming the Americas with stunning speed."

Perhaps the most notable part of Bush's speech was the omission of the words *unification* or *reunification*. The president went to great rhetorical lengths in this speech to avoid debating the German question.

If Bush's rhetoric had changed so dramatically from Mainz, what did he say? The first paragraph in the speech that mentioned Germany discussed the 1961 building of the Berlin Wall and raised the specter of Thanksgivings past that reflected a reality of watchtowers and guard dogs. After that, Bush expressed the thanks of Chancellor Kohl for decades of German-American friendship and celebrated the NATO alliance that both believed responsible for democratic gains in Eastern Europe. To celebrate the relationships among Germany, America, and NATO, Bush advanced a decade-by-decade chronology of challenges that U.S. presidents had faced and overcome to keep West Berlin free.

Bush also used the speech to outline his hope for a democratic future for Europe:

> Change is coming swiftly. And with this change, the dramatic vindication of free Europe's economic and political institutions; the new Europe that is coming to be built—must be built—on the foundation of democratic values. But the faster the pace, the smoother our path must be. After all, this is serious business.
>
> The peace we are building must be different than the hard, joyless peace between two armed camps we've known so long. The scars of a conflict that began a half century ago still divide a continent. So the historic task before us now, is to begin the healing of this old wound.[47]

Instead of using the cold warrior's words of conflict and conquest, Bush now spoke of healing old wounds. Instead of delineating several specific policy proposals designed to gain strategic advantage over the Soviets, Bush now saw fit to put those items on hold until at least the following year. Why was Bush trying to build these rhetorical bridges?

Medhurst provides a framework by which to understand Bush's rhetorical decision to refrain from engaging the Soviets after the fall of the Berlin Wall: "In Cold War discourse five constraining factors are always present: the history of superpower relations, domestic political concerns, the status of both the domestic and world economies, present diplomatic negotiations, and the ever present possibility of military engagement."[48]

Each of these factors played a role in Bush's decision to refrain from rhetorically engaging the Soviets in the aftermath of the fall of the Wall. For decades, East and West had stood ready to destroy one another if the Cold

War were made suddenly warm. On this Thanksgiving, however, the historical situation had changed. Gorbachev had promised not to engage the West militarily so long as he was not provoked. If Bush had used words that made Gorbachev seem the loser of the Cold War to conservatives inside Gorbachev's own party, the suddenly declared Cold Peace might have changed to something more sinister. The history of superpower relations was changing, and the primary rhetorical constraint on George Bush in November 1989 was to avoid altering the course of that change.

As to domestic political concerns, Gorbachev's needs were more immediate than Bush's own difficulties. While George Bush had to deal with a Senate majority leader of the opposition party who might continue to say unpleasant things about him, Mikhail Gorbachev had to avoid taking on a sudden illness that might allow conservatives within the Communist Party to wrestle power from him. For Bush, congressional elections were a year away and his own reelection bid was three years in the future. Gorbachev faced a much more dangerous and immediate crisis from within his own party at an upcoming Soviet Plenum. Stressing that the Soviet Union could be brought along on the German question if not pushed too quickly, Secretary Baker later noted:

> The intelligence community believed that, in the end, Moscow was likely to acquiesce in a unified Germany's membership in NATO, with certain restrictions. But "the German question is a visceral one among the Soviet population," the National Intelligence Officer for the Soviet Union, Bob Blackwell, wrote on March 1, "and criticism of Gorbachev's policy is beginning to emerge from people like Politburo member Ligachev and from some military officials."
>
> Such criticism is no major threat to Gorbachev now. But if it were to appear that Soviet troops were being forced to retreat from the GDR, he had "lost" Germany, and the security environment for the USSR was now more threatening, the domestic fallout—when combined with other complaints—could pose a threat to his position. *Gorbachev at least has to have one eye on this contingency.*[49]

Given the relative instability in the Soviet Union, Bush recognized Gorbachev's domestic concerns as paramount and intentionally tried not to provoke the conservatives among the Soviet leadership.

The third constraint Medhurst identifies, economics, was also a key factor in the president's rhetorical choice. Bush had expressed his desire to let the Cold War end so that he could ease a domestic budget crunch with the peace dividend. Gorbachev also desperately needed a chance to allow his economy to recover from a Cold War–inspired arms race.[50] With both leaders wanting to lower military spending to help their own economies, the constraint upon

Bush was to say nothing that might provoke the Soviets and prolong the Cold War. Avoiding deliberative speech on the German question allowed Bush to avoid such a scenario.

As for diplomatic negotiations, Bush had expressed in Mainz a desire to move forward on a series of arms control initiatives. During his November 22 speech, Bush said he wanted those efforts to go forward even if they might be delayed until the following year. However, Bush's public words were far more reserved than his private diplomatic initiatives. Before the meeting in Malta, Secretary Baker began to hint that Bush did indeed plan to advance the arms reduction initiatives he had previewed in Mainz. Additionally, President Gorbachev was coming to the meeting with weapons initiatives of his own.[51] Bush and German Chancellor Kohl discussed immediately after the summit how important a broad range of arms agreements was to stability and for Kohl's domestic political purposes.[52] If the leaders privately planned to commence diplomatic negotiations over such critical matters, then the rhetorical constraint upon Bush was to avoid publicly provoking Gorbachev or his Politburo opponents. The arms control negotiations could go forward as long as public pressures did not derail them.

As for the final constraint of a potential hot war, Bush's task was again to avoid saying something that would provoke the Soviets. They had pledged peace as long as they were not made to seem the loser, and Bush chose not to call their bluff over Berlin.

CONTINUING SILENCE

After the Malta summit, Bush traveled to Brussels to brief NATO allies on the status of his discussions with Gorbachev. Bush was still the subject of criticism at this time. Some in the press asked that Bush "forgive us if we feel like gloating."[53] Others criticized his approach as "poised between caution and timidity."[54] However, Bush continued to move forward with his private diplomacy. In a meeting at Brussels between Bush and Kohl, President Bush told Kohl that much of the summit time had been spent on the German question.[55] Gorbachev had told Bush that Kohl was in "too much of a hurry" to unify Germany. Kohl conceded that it was not in his interest to "invite things to get out of control." Their conversation continued with the theme that Gorbachev could be brought along on the German question as long as the delicate political balance was not disturbed:

The President: Gorbachev's chief problem is uncertainty. I don't want to say he went "ballistic" about it—he was just uneasy. We need a formulation which doesn't scare him, but which moves forward.

Chancellor Kohl: That is one reason I will do nothing to disturb the smooth running course. The CSCE [Helsinki Final Act] says the borders can be changed by peaceful means. I don't want Gorbachev to feel concerned. I need to meet with him. I don't want to create difficulties.

With that conversation, the last great rhetorical battle of the Cold War was destined never to occur. President Bush recognized that such a battle would push Gorbachev in uncomfortable directions, and his international allies agreed. With movement happening on arms control fronts and the German leader satisfied with the pace of progress in his own country toward a decision about reunification, there was no warrant on which Bush could launch this battle.

Bush maintained his legislative silence in the following months. The next time he publicly spoke at any length about the German question was in his January 31, 1990, state of the union address. From that time until Germany formally unified in October 1990, Bush made only a limited number of statements on the question, usually speaking at a press conference with Chancellor Kohl by his side when he did so. These press conferences occurred on February 25, May 17, and June 8, 1990. Bush became progressively more vocal about the policy implications the newly united Germany held for world politics as the Soviet Union increasingly grew to accept the loss of its former satellite state. Eventually, Bush did "learn how to be giddy" in a signing ceremony for the German unification treaty on September 25, 1990. Bush extended his rhetorical celebration of freedom for East Germany in a videotaped message on October 2, 1990, to mark the all-German elections.

Eventually, Bush openly supported German unification. However, this rhetorical evolution occurred only slowly and always followed Soviet acceptance—however grudging—of moving forward. Bush's speeches eventually came to support the changing events in Europe, but his words were never those of the cold warrior.

DISCUSSION AND CONCLUSION

Did President George Bush choose correctly when he decided to maintain deliberative silence and a ceremonial whisper upon the fall of the Berlin Wall?

The documents available at this time certainly seem to support the view that he was correct in his choice. Germany appreciated America's help but did not desire its interference, and Bush's public silence avoided that potential conflict. The pace of German unification proceeded much more quickly than experts in either country had predicted. In Brussels, Chancellor Kohl had scoffed at the idea that unification could occur within two years, yet Germany reunited much more quickly than that without significant oratorical support from Bush. U.S. allies in Europe who would have to participate in signing over post–World War II rights in Germany were kept within the tent in part because they did not see the American president pushing them out. Perhaps most significantly, the Soviet Union ultimately allowed the unification of Germany to go forward. Allowed to come to this decision on their own, the Soviets acquiesced, but their response in the face of rhetorical pressure from George Bush would have been unpredictable at best.

What of Bush's domestic audience that clamored for him to go to Berlin when the first piece of concrete was sundered from the wall? Regardless of their critical initial rhetorical response, one might argue that their long-term interests were served by a peacefully united Germany, a peacefully dissolved Soviet Union, and arms that no longer menaced them. How exactly Bush's domestic critics responded, however, is difficult to measure precisely because of other events that drew the interest of the press and the public. One month after the speech from Camp David, Bush was explaining the U.S. military action in Panama. Before Germany was unified, Saddam Hussein had invaded Kuwait, and the attention of the press and the Congress turned to the Arabian desert. Bush's party lost seats in Congress in the 1990 elections, but tracing this to Bush's rhetorical response to the collapse of the Berlin Wall would be difficult at best. This holds doubly true for an analysis of the impact this rhetorical event (or nonevent) had on Bush's reelection campaign three years after the fact. Public opinion polls taken early in 1990 gave Bush a great deal of credit for his handling of Germany and Panama.[56] However, these events rapidly gave way to economic concerns that propelled Bill Clinton to the presidency. While the response of his domestic audience may have been lukewarm at best, the response (or lack of response) of his various foreign audiences was sufficient to label President Bush's rhetorical strategy as effective.

Aristotle informs us that the definition of rhetoric is to discover the available means of persuasion in each given case. However, the first function of the rhetor is not to determine what words to use. The first office of rhetoric is to determine whether to use words at all as one attempts to advance one's interests. While his choice to speak only ceremonially on the German question raised objections from some, Bush's lack of policy-making speech ultimately helped to make sure that Germany was not pulled from the path of democracy. This deliberative silence helped coordinate the efforts of U.S. allies and foes alike, and ultimately proved the correct choice in Bush's rhetorical management of the fall of the Berlin Wall and eventual German reunification. The Cold War ended without its last battle having to be fought.

NOTES

1. James A. Baker III with Thomas M. DeFrank, *The Politics of Diplomacy: Revolution, War and Peace, 1989–1992* (New York: G. P. Putnam's Sons, 1995), 153. This statement from Baker came in his chapter specific to the fall of the Berlin Wall, hence my claim that this statement is about Bush not speaking in this particular circumstance.

2. Helen Dewar and Ann Devroy, "Mitchell Urges Bush to Visit West Berlin: Response to Changes in East Bloc Criticized," *Washington Post,* November 14, 1989, A40.

3. Michael Ross and David Lauter, "As Bush Salutes Visiting Walesa, Democrats Press for Decisive Action on East Bloc," *Los Angeles Times,* November 14, 1989, A32.

4. Dan Oberdorfer, "Upheaval in Eastern Europe: The Superpower Challenge: United States: Events Take Bush, Aides by Surprise," *Washington Post,* November 12, 1989, A23.

5. Anthony Lewis, "Abroad at Home: What Bush Could Say," *New York Times,* November 16, 1989, A31.

6. Mary McGrory, "Berlin and Bush's Emotional Wall," *Washington Post,* November 14, 1989, A2.

7. David Ignatius, "While Washington Slept . . . : An Empire Is Crumbling, and the Germans Are Getting All the Goodies," *Washington Post,* November 19, 1989, D2.

8. Louise Lief et al., "A Shrinking American Role in the World," *U.S. News and World Report,* November 12, 1989, 22.

9. Haynes Johnson, "No Time for the Slows," *Washington Post,* November 17, 1989, A2.

10. George Bush and Brent Scowcroft, *A World Transformed* (New York: Alfred A. Knopf, 1998), 190. Scowcroft served as Bush's national security adviser. The book is written with particular parts of the text attributed to either Bush or Scowcroft; hence my assertions here that words were those of a particular individual.

11. Ibid., 190.

12. Richard L. Johannesen, "The Functions of Silence: A Plea for Communication Research," *Western Speech* 38 (1974): 25–35.

13. Edwin Black, "Gettysburg and Silence," *Quarterly Journal of Speech* 80 (1994): 21–36.

14. Martin J. Medhurst, "Truman's Rhetorical Reticence, 1945–1947: An Interpretive Essay," *Quarterly Journal of Speech* 74 (1988): 52–70.

15. Barry Brummett, "Towards a Theory of Silence as a Political Strategy," *Quarterly Journal of Speech* 66 (1980): 289–303.

16. Ibid., 290.

17. Baker and DeFrank, *Politics of Diplomacy,* 159.

18. I am using the text of the Mainz speech available online from the George Bush Presidential Library. It may be obtained at <http://bushlibrary.tamu.edu/papers/1989/89053104.html>. This same copy is used for all references to the Mainz speech.

19. The four points of Bush's plan were (1) to "broaden the Helsinki process to promote free elections and political pluralism in Eastern Europe"; (2) to "bring glasnost to East Berlin"; (3) to promote East-West cooperation on environmental issues; and (4) to promote arms reductions in Europe.

20. Thomas Eagleton, "A United Germany: All in Favor Say 'Ja,'" *St. Louis Post-Dispatch,* November 14, 1989, B3.

21. Editorial, "The Vision Thing," *Boston Globe,* November 16, 1989, 18.

22. I draw my concepts of audience and constraint from Bitzer's foundational article on rhetorical situation. See Lloyd F. Bitzer, "The Rhetorical Situation," *Philosophy and Rhetoric* 1 (1968): 1–14.

23. This is Bitzer's definition of exigence.

24. Baker and DeFrank, *Politics of Diplomacy,* 197–98.

25. The George Bush Presidential Library, College Station, Texas (hereafter cited as GBPL). Box: FOIA 99–0393-F Box 1/1. File: Pres. Telcons 11/10/89. Document: Memorandum of telephone conversation between President Bush and Chancellor Kohl on November 10, 1989, at 3:29 P.M. Washington time.

26. Ibid.

27. Margaret Thatcher, *The Downing Street Years* (New York: Harper Collins, 1993), 792.

28. Bush and Scowcroft, *World Transformed,* 189.

29. Baker and DeFrank, *Politics of Diplomacy.*

30. Andrea Rosenthal, "Clamor in the East: Bush Echoes Gorbachev Plea for Peaceful Change," *New York Times,* November 18, 1989, sec. 1, p. 6.

31. Baker and DeFrank, *Politics of Diplomacy,* 163. See also William Drozdiak, "Soviets Offer Assurances on Germany: U.S. Is Told Troops Will Not Intervene," *Washington Post,* November 16, 1989, A41.

32. Thatcher, *Downing Street Years,* 792.

33. GBPL. Box: FOIA 99–0393-F Box 1/1. File: Pres. Telcons 11/17/89. Document: Memorandum of telephone conversation between President Bush and Chancellor Kohl on November 17, 1989, at 8:15 A.M. Washington time.

34. Ibid.

35. Michael Dobbs, "Don't Export Capitalism to East, Says Gorbachev: Blocs Should 'Meet Halfway,' Soviet Urges," *Washington Post,* November 15, 1989, A23.

36. Michael Parks, "West Warned by Gorbachev on East Europe," *Los Angeles Times,* November 15, 1989, A1.

37. Baker is commenting on the decision made on November 9, 1989, directly after learning of the East German announcement lifting travel restrictions.

38. Baker and DeFranks, *Politics of Diplomacy,* 164.

39. Marlin Fitzwater, *Call the Briefing! Bush and Reagan, Sam and Helen: A Decade with the Presidents and the Press* (New York: Random House, 1995), 264–65. Pages 261–70 detail much of the interplay between Bush and Gorbachev during the period immediately after the fall of the Berlin wall.

40. William Safire, "Soviets' Real Policy Is Still Imperialism," *St. Louis Post-Dispatch,* March 9, 1989, B3.

41. David Hoffman, "Prague Calls Presidium to Emergency Session: U.S. Won't Exploit Unrest, Bush Says," *Washington Post,* November 23, 1989, A1.

42. Thatcher, *Downing Street Years,* 794.

43. Thomas Oliphant, "Bush Takes to the Sidelines," *Boston Globe,* November 19, 1989, A27.

44. Bill Javetski and Rose Brady, "Europe's Grand Drama: Waiting for Bush to Make His Entrance," *Business Week,* November 27, 1989, 66.

45. Martin J. Medhurst, "Rhetoric and Cold War: A Strategic Approach," in Martin J. Medhurst, Robert L. Ivie, Philip Wander, and Robert L. Scott, *Cold War Rhetoric: Strategy, Metaphor, and Ideology* (East Lansing: Michigan State University Press, 1997), 23.

46. GBPL. Box: Subject Files, Speeches, Box 108. Folder: SP628, Thanksgiving Address to the Nation 11/22/89. Document: Memos on White House stationary dated November 18, 1989, for various administration officials.

47. The text of this address is available from the *Washington Post,* November 23, 1989, A24.

48. Medhurst et al., *Cold War Rhetoric,* 21.

49. Baker and DeFrank, *Politics of Diplomacy,* 234 (emphasis added).

50. Bill Keller, "Visions of Europe: The View from Moscow," *New York Times,* November 30, 1989, A1.

51. Andrew Rosenthal, "Clamor in the East; Bush Hoping to Use Malta Talks to Speed Strategic Arms Pact," *New York Times,* November 30, 1989, A1.

52. GBPL. Box: FOIA 99–0393-F Box 1/1. Folder: Presidential Memcons Jan–Dec 1989. Document: Memorandum of Conversation between Bush and Kohl on December 3, 1989, at Chateau Stuyvenberg.

53. Fred Bruning, "Forgive Us If We Feel Like Gloating," *Maclean's,* December 4, 1989, 13.

54. Burt Solomon, "Despite Malta Successes, Bush Still Lacks Vision of a New Era," *National Journal,* December 9, 1989, 3008.

55. Conversation between Bush and Kohl on December 3, 1989, at Chateau Stuyvenberg.

56. R. W. Apple Jr., "Good or Just Lucky?" *New York Times,* February 18, 1990, sec. 1, p. 14.

CHAPTER 4

Agency and Agent in George Bush's Gulf War Rhetoric

RACHEL MARTIN HARLOW

Saddam Hussein had been president of Iraq for ten years when, in 1989, his government began to build up a military force along its border with the small, wealthy nation of Kuwait. In February 1990, Hussein denounced Kuwait, "advanc[ing] several political, territorial, and financial claims against" its government.[1] Though the Kuwaitis rejected these claims, by July 24, 1990, Iraqi soldiers were deployed on Kuwait's border. The next day, Egyptian President Hosni Mubarak initiated diplomatic talks between the two nations; meanwhile, "the United States Ambassador to Iraq, April Glaspie, emphasize[d] the United States' desire to improve relations with Iraq" and urged the United States "to avoid tough talk with Saddam Hussein," who had by that time sent U.S. President George Bush "a message expressing his desire to resolve the crisis peacefully."[2] Even so, Hussein proceeded with the military buildup, and on August 2, at 4:00 A.M Kuwaiti time, the Iraqi army invaded.

The world community responded quickly. Later that day, when the U.N. Security Council convened at the request of both Kuwait and the United States, "each of the five permanent members of the Council voiced opposition to the invasion. . . . Each also stressed the need for negotiation."[3] Other world diplomatic organizations denounced the invasion as well, including the Gulf Cooperation Council, the League of Arab States, the Organization of the Islamic Conference, the European Community, and Member States of the United Nations.[4] Over the next two weeks the international diplomatic community worked furiously, as the United Nations and European, Asian, Middle Eastern, and North American governments implemented trade sanctions and embargoes against Iraq and deployed military support to Saudi Arabia. By November 1990 U.N. trade sanctions were deemed insufficient, and on November 29 the Security Council passed Resolution 678, which permitted the use of force after January 15, 1991.[5]

President Bush, his press secretary Marlin Fitzwater, and deputy press secretary Roman Popaduik met with the American news media daily during the first month of the Iraqi crisis, in statements, briefings, informal question-and-answer exchanges with reporters, and formal news conferences. During the next eight months these rhetorical opportunities became important fora for disseminating the president's perspective of the war, and for gaining both American and international support for war activities. In this chapter, I will show that the dramatic elements of George Bush's war rhetoric reveal how he, as a diplomatic leader in the conflict, used his rhetorical situation to authoritatively define, defend, and shape the conflict through its many stages and to publicly manage issues of international authority and sovereignty. To support my arguments, I will briefly consider the contributions of the news media to the Persian Gulf War, as well as the relationship between Bush's "procedural" philosophy of governance and his rhetorical choices.[6]

In 1990–91 George Bush conducted "his" war in both the mediated public sphere and the more private diplomatic sphere and was undeniably a moving force behind the coalition that opposed Hussein's Iraq. But scholars are sharply divided over the nature of the president's influence in the conflict, with some condemning Bush as a wimpy warmonger—note the oxymoron—who led the world *to* war, and others hailing him as a brilliant diplomat who led the world *through* war.[7] Such polarization is not entirely accurate; as David Demarest, Bush's director of communications, explains, "'Wimp' was a fiction created in 1988 . . . it was buried in the Dan Rather interview. And so we never really had to deal with the wimp issue after that. . . . My recollection is that we didn't have serious concern about the warmonger issue. I mean, we managed the prosecution of Desert Shield very methodically. President Bush was never using extreme rhetoric throughout that process. The only time you heard warmonger was really out of the fringe."[8]

Aside from inaccuracy, neither the "wimp" nor the "warmonger" characterization sufficiently explains *how* Bush the diplomat worked; thus, neither can provide much insight as to how and why the Gulf War evolved as it did. As the documents most useful to such an analysis will not be fully available for some time yet, the researcher must look to Bush's public discourse for clues that may answer these questions.

The Bush presidency has received less scholarly attention than one would think; perhaps his presidency pales against that of Reagan the Great Communicator or the charismatic Clinton. Much of the scholarship that does exist is the work of rhetoricians who have studied Bush's public addresses about the Gulf War.[9] Few scholars have examined the body of Bush's war rhetoric as a whole or seriously considered its place in the way the American public received war information; two significant exceptions to this generalization are Timothy Cole and Mary E. Stuckey, who consider the role Bush's rhetoric played in U.S. foreign policy and in the Gulf War, respectively.[10] In these rhetorical artifacts, the scholar may find a great many clues about Bush's attitude toward the war as a whole, about his philosophy of government and diplomacy, and about his relationship with the news media during the conflict. In the course of critically analyzing what Bush said, one may find patterns in his rhetoric that further demonstrate *why* and *how* he conducted his presidency as he did—and, therefore, why and how an American perspective of war in the Persian Gulf unfolded as it did.

WAR AS DRAMA

In *A Grammar of Motives*, Kenneth Burke remarks, "Unfortunately, in the modern state, with its great diversity of interests and opinions, due to the dispersion of technological and commercial enterprise, the act that comes closest to the totality of tribal festivals and the agape is the act of war. But modern war ('total war') itself is so complex that we could hardly use it as our representative anecdote until we had selected some moment within war to serve in turn as representative of war."[11]

For Burke, conflict is the representative anecdote of modern humanity, and it is played out in the countless dramas in which humans participate. However, the twentieth century was one in which the dramatic character of war changed, becoming "more of a *confusion* than a *form*."[12] To compensate for this change, and to make sense of human interaction as we know it, people focus their rhetorical attention on aspects of war, each of which maintains a dramatic character. Good-versus-evil plotlines, appeals to group autonomy and identity (characters), and contemplation of scenic restraints are all incarnations of the representative anecdote of war. Because such dramatic elements characterize nearly all aspects of war, dramatistic criticism is an appropriate methodological framework for studying war rhetoric.

George Bush's discourse in the Gulf War clearly exhibits dramatic elements. Specifically, Bush uses dialectical opposites, including god-terms and devil-terms, to characterize the players: America and its allies (good) fight Hussein's Iraq (evil). Furthermore, Bush focuses much of his rhetoric on agent and agency in his many statements about international and domestic sovereignty. Finally, Bush recognizes scenic restraints in his statements about the international coalition and the diplomatic effort, and in his many references to other twentieth-century wars. Thus, the methodological basis of this chapter is a dramatistic analysis of formal speeches, remarks, and news conferences in which President Bush was the sole or major participant.

RHETORIC AND HISTORY

David Zarefsky notes that "history and criticism . . . are overlapping circles. And rhetorical history is done in the area of overlap. . . . Any rhetorical act is an interaction between text and context, and one can imagine a continuum of scholarship that gives greater emphasis to one or the other."[13] The Persian Gulf War—both Operation Desert Shield and Operation Desert Storm—presented a series of problems that invited rhetorical response.[14] The history of this conflict is "a series of rhetorical problems, situations that call for public persuasion to advance a cause or overcome an impasse."[15] In the Gulf War, the most obvious example of such a situation was Iraq's invasion of Kuwait, which invited condemnation from the world community. Furthermore, the omnipresent American news media were caught between their responsibility to investigate and challenge actions of political leaders and their citizen's obligation to support their government in the war effort. To maintain support from both the international community and the news media, Bush had to respond carefully and strategically; a study of the dramatistic strategies Bush used in his Gulf War rhetoric can help explain the historical conditions of the war.

Presidential rhetoric is all the more significant when it shows us how the president persuades us to see as he *wants us to see.* It is important to note here that a president who succeeds in this rhetorical objective is not necessarily ill-intentioned; rather, he or she may need this unity of vision to accomplish anything at all. The Persian Gulf War is known for press coverage above all else: to the American public, it was marked by CNN's twenty-four-hour reporting, by images of reporter Arthur Kent (the "Scud stud") and others on television, narrating air battles as night-vision cameras transmitted images of tracers and explosions in the background. Media access to the war zone was debated as a First Amendment issue, and dozens of scholarly and popular works have discussed the role of communications in the crisis.[16] With such an audience, Marion Pinsdorf notes, "Bush had to win in both reality and image," and he worked hard rhetorically to ensure success in both the diplomatic and public spheres.[17] In the case of the Gulf War, George Bush's speeches, news conferences, and other public leadership strategies persuaded the public to see him as "a consummate crisis and public relations manager. With apparent skill, he built alliances, macromanaged the military, quelled criticism so adroitly that the press seemed jingoistic and the Congress compliant."[18] To successfully prosecute the war, Bush had to persuade the public that both he and the war were worthy of support; to persuade that public, continually bombarded by news media reports, Bush produced a fairly simple set of personalized messages and iterated his position to the American public, to Congress, and to the world community at every available opportunity.

Kerry Mullins and Aaron Wildavsky characterize Bush as a "procedural" president, one who valued both moderate individualism—that is, the independent agent—and "inclusive hierarchy," or agents acting by appropriate means for appropriate ends. They argue that "because inclusive hierarchies are so accommodating . . . theirs is not a hierarchy of command but of *persuasion,* in which authorities have the right to say what ought to be done, but citizens need not comply unless they are persuaded."[19] In terms of agent and agency, many of Bush's rhetorical choices as a procedural president make sense; for instance, he frequently communicated with the news media, as they constituted "the proper institutional conduit to the public."[20] The Bush administration's near-daily meetings with the news media satisfied the president's obligation to persuade the American people to support the Gulf War and give their president the authority to prosecute that war.

OPERATION DESERT SHIELD

Good vs. Evil: The Dialectical Opposition of Agent

Much of George Bush's war rhetoric centered on the agents of the war—the characters of the drama. To establish and define the characteristics of each agent, Bush often resorted to antinomy, or identifying what something *is* (its substance) by dissociating it from that which it *is not.* One variety of such definition Burke calls "dialectic substance." "A poem, by shifting the imagery of its metaphors, permits us to contemplate the subject from the standpoint of various objects. This effect is dialectical in the sense that we see something in terms of some other. In a more restricted sense, however, the dialectical considers things in terms not of *some* other, but of *the* other. The sharpest instance of this is in an *agon* wherein the protagonist is motivated by the nature of the antagonist, as with the situating of socialist motives in resistance to capitalism, or the unifying effect of the Allied Nations' joint opposition to Hitler."[21]

As Bush often invoked images and arguments from World War II in his

Gulf War rhetoric, the concept of dialectic substance appropriately illustrates Bush's attitude toward both the allied nations and the enemy.[22] Throughout the Gulf War, the president repeatedly characterized the coalition forces as the forces of good, of light, and above all, of unity. *Unity*, and similar terms clustered around it, became the primary god-terms of Bush's rhetoric, which he applied both to international and to domestic activities. Any sort of action begun with the support of others could be justified or even praised, from a unanimous U.N. Security Council vote to a series of "consultations" between the president and members of Congress. Throughout the eight months of the conflict situation, Bush associated unity with consideration, respect, morality, peace, diplomatic protocol, and the appropriate use of authority by an agent.

Disunity was the primary devil term in Bush's rhetoric; activity in which nations or parties acted without so much as a nod to others (particularly to the American executive) was denounced. In Bush's characterization, the "anti-agent," or villain, was the renegade Saddam Hussein; those who did not denounce the renegade's actions strongly enough (for instance, Yasir Arafat and the PLO, which did not ally with the coalition nations) were toying with evil. Disunity, in Bush's rhetoric, was analogous to desertion, defiance, treason, and illegitimate use of authority to arrogate others' rights and authority.

A second dialectical pair, related to the unity/disunity pair, is *legality* vs. *illegality*. Legality and terms related to it are reserved for the coalition members, and most often refer to nations acting in concert with international laws to which they have given their prior approval, while terms of illegality are exclusively applied to Saddam Hussein's Iraq and describe illegitimate use of power that defies international law. Besides promoting unity, legal acts are strongly linked to morality and are characteristic of the good; illegal acts promote disunity and immorality and are characteristic of evil. Cooperation in the form of multilateral decision making was particularly tricky in the Gulf War, and Bush had to carefully juggle American and international authority in the coalition, as well as denounce the misuse of power by Saddam Hussein. His solution was to cite international law in his public discourse. By following the U.N. condemnation of Iraq, Bush avoided appearing independently belligerent, which would have severely damaged his ethos both in America and in the international community. At the same time, the president could stand with other sovereign countries, large and small, and accuse another sovereign country (Iraq) of breaking a *higher* (international) law.

Significantly, Bush characterizes America as a sovereign nation that *chooses* to abide by the rule of national and international law, as his many references to the god-terms *legality* and *morality* illustrate. From the beginning of the

Desert Shield period, Bush declares that "we are acting within our legal rights. And I think the world wants to see these [U.N.] chapter 51 sanctions carried out, and that's the role that the United States is trying to do. . . . we're doing it the way our attorneys and others around the world recommend. And I think we're doing it properly, and I hope we're doing it to the degree that all ships will turn back if they are in contravention of the U.N. action."[23] Bush repeatedly justifies Desert Shield and U.N. sanctions as "provoked by this illegal action—outrageous action" that was "perpetrated by the Government of Iraq."[24] In contrast to the "egregious" behavior of Hussein's Iraq, including "coercion on foreign nationals in some other country [which] is a violation of international norms," the United States and its allies act according to "certain principles here—right and wrong—moral principles," and are therefore justified in using sanctions "to bring these people to do what's right," that is, to leave Kuwait.[25]

As president of the United States and a member of the anti-Hussein coalition, Bush often made the point in his public addresses and news conferences that Hussein had numerous opportunities to repent his lawbreaking, receive appropriate punishment, and return to the international community. Once Bush publicly determined that Hussein was essentially a lawbreaker (a claim he advanced through his numerous negative characterizations of the Iraqi leader), "the line [was] crossed, the rules [were] changed and friendly competition [became] serious adversity" that the American president would not soon forgive.[26] Thus, the president's war rhetoric makes great displays of friendship and cooperation with "law-abiding" nations, while constantly reinforcing the collective decision with harsh characterizations of the enemy and his provocations to war.

In his Gulf War rhetoric early in Desert Shield, Bush is careful to include his domestic audience as members of an international, law-abiding, yet sovereign government, noting that "what we've done is right, and I'm happy to say that most Members of Congress and the majority of Americans agree."[27] Bush was aware that he was dealing with a Democratic Congress still smoldering from the budget debates of 1990, and thus went out of his way to encourage and acknowledge its support of the conflict, however slow that support was in coming. To the press, Bush remarked, "I go to great ends to make sure that I give proper credit to the Democrats and the Republicans in Congress—make clear that this is not a partisan effort that we're involved in here. I've been very gratified for the enormous support from both Houses of Congress and from the American people."[28] To Congress, the president addressed a similar message: "So, if there ever was a time to put country before self and patriotism before party, the time is now. And let me thank all Americans, especially those here in this Chamber tonight, for your support for our armed forces and for their mission. That support will be even more important in the days to come."[29]

Congressional support was indeed important, for, according to John Robert Greene, the legislative branch of the American government "stood poised to claim authority given it under the War Powers Act and to debate Bush's authority to send troops into combat."[30] Bush concurred with Counsel C. Boyden Gray's position that "the War Powers Resolution is unconstitutional insofar as it purports to allow Congress to compel the withdrawal of U.S. forces through inaction," but in time of war, neither Bush nor any other president "wanted to jeopardize congressional support for his actions by defying the resolution."[31] Thus, to placate Congress, and to demonstrate U.S. internal unity to the international community (particularly Iraq), Bush periodically met with congressional leaders to discuss the conflict, and eventually requested that both House and Senate "adopt a resolution stating that Congress supports the use of all necessary means to implement U.N. Security Council Resolution 678."[32] Though the Bush administration never expected to lose, congressional support would have been of utmost importance had such a situation developed; C. Boyden Gray later explained, "If [the war] went sour, [Bush] wanted Democrats with him. . . . He wanted a unified government. . . . it's a military, constitutional, moral, and political thing."[33]

In the pursuit of national unity, the Bush administration did not limit its focus to gaining congressional support; according to White House Press Secretary Marlin Fitzwater, the messages he presented to the press were primarily directed toward the American people, whose support was crucial to winning over Congress.[34] Within the White House Office of Communications, "a group of people within the various offices of the White House, and [public relations representatives from] the appropriate agencies" regularly met to "coordinate our communications efforts concerning the Gulf."[35] The goal of this group, which was "designed after Souter/S&L working groups" organized to deal with the savings and loan crisis, followed that of the general communications plan for Operation Desert Shield: to "reassure the American people as to the objectives and purpose of our deployment and strengthen public support for Operation Desert Shield [and later, Desert Storm]. *Ultimately, our goal is broad, grass-roots support for the President's initiative*" (emphasis mine). To this end, the group "manage[d] a sustained effort, aimed at delivering a consistent message and developing appropriate events" in a large-scale public relations campaign.[36] According to White House communications director

David Demarest and deputy communications director Deb Amend, within the Persian Gulf Working Group's first two weeks, its members had "distributed talking points and briefing material to nearly 20,000 individuals, groups and opinion leaders across the country"; reproduced and distributed "excerpts of recent speeches and testimony daily to key constituencies"; developed an extensive program of surrogate speakers; arranged opinion pieces and editorials "for placement in key newspapers across the country"; and planned numerous "Presidential and non-Presidential briefings for concerned constituent groups," such as American veterans.[37]

Bush's promotion of national unity merges with his promotion of international unity, as much of the international coalition "depend[ed] on support from Congress and the American people."[38] Most of the comments he delivered characterized international unity as a "collective effort," and one that was pitted *against* an enemy.[39] Some of Bush's most often-repeated comments throughout the eight months of war were aimed at dispelling the notion that the conflict was between (renegade) Iraq and the (coalition leader) United States; for instance, the president declared, "As the deployment of the forces of the many nations show and as the votes in the United Nations show, this is not a matter between Iraq and the United States of America; it is between Iraq and the entire world community, Arab and non-Arab alike. All the nations of the world linked up to oppose aggression."[40] Other common statements stressed the number of nations included in the coalition, the buzz of diplomatic activity, and the degree to which individual nations were "do[ing] their part" and "bear[ing] their fair share" of the effort to censure Iraq.[41] Saddam Hussein himself was the enemy, the neighborhood bully who must face the wrath of a unified coalition, as Bush explained to a reporter:

> I would think that if this international lesson is taught well that Saddam Hussein would behave differently in the future. And that's what has been so very important about this concerted United Nations effort—unprecedented, you might say. . . . But a line has been drawn in the sand. The United States has taken a firm position. And I might say we're getting strong support from around the world for what we've done. . . . Large countries and small countries—the world reaction has been excellent. And I would hope that all of this would result in Saddam Hussein or some calmer heads in Iraq understanding that this kind of international behavior is simply unacceptable.[42]

Here Hussein is the agent of disunity; by contrast, even the United States and the Soviet Union work toward unity of purpose in the conflict. Though the Soviets hesitate to join the coalition, Bush describes diplomatic relations with the USSR as "on the right track" toward "mutual understanding" with respect to the coalition, and he holds joint news conferences with Gorbachev, in which the two men outdo one another in praising the "frankness without rancor" of their meetings.[43]

Bush's most pervasive rhetorical strategy of the Gulf War was his constant reference to the Iraqi leader by his first name—an unmistakable sign of contempt consistent with his characterization of Hussein as "anti-agent." In Bush's rhetoric, "Iraq" could be translated "Saddam Hussein" without substantial change in meaning, for the man himself was enemy to both the coalition and to his own people. Not only did Hussein destroy international unity, but also his "aggression" against the Kurds in Iraq destroyed unity in his own country. The president pointedly and frequently claimed to the world community and to Iraqi citizens that "the Iraqi regime stands in opposition to the entire world and to the interest of the Iraqi people. It is truly Iraq against the world. But I want to make this point clear: We have no argument with the people of Iraq."[44] On the contrary, the president freely held the Iraqi leader responsible for "outrageous radical statements" that "[give] me reason to say, hey, you're going to be responsible. . . . I blame Saddam Hussein for that. Everything to do with that affects our forces—that's where the blame will be and should be."[45] Hussein's behavior was denounced as "adventurism" and "aggression"; he was uncivilized, unpredictable, bellicose, manipulative, and divisive.[46] Bush accused Hussein of "trying to whip up support and make this Iraq versus the United States" because as the Iraqi government "become[s] isolated from their Arab brothers—and they are—and as they become isolated from traditional trading partners—and they are—there is a sense of irrational urgency there" that was indicative of evil.[47] Of course, personal distaste for a foreign leader is not sufficient to fight a war, and Bush was careful to remind his audience that Hussein was in essence a lawbreaker, and that with every word the Iraqi raised against the United States, and thus against the coalition, "he puts himself in direct contravention of international law."[48]

Most damaging to Hussein's credibility (which Bush derides frequently) are tales of the Iraqi's brutality, such as the one Bush tells reporters in early October, regarding "the brutality that has now been written on by Amnesty International confirming some of the tales told us by the Amir [of Kuwait] of brutality. It's just unbelievable, some of the things at least he reflected. I mean, people on a dialysis machine cut off, the machine sent to Baghdad; babies in incubators heaved out of the incubators and the incubators themselves sent to Baghdad. Now I don't know how many of these tales can be authenticated, but I do know that when the Amir was here he was speaking from the heart.

And after that came Amnesty International, who were debriefing many of the people at the border. And it's sickening."[49] Because brutality is indicative of evil, and because Bush had already established that the coalition was not evil, but good, the implied conclusion reflects the binary opposition between heroes and villains characteristic of American justifications for war.[50] Furthermore, in a war fought under the auspices of the United Nations, brutality was not only illegal, but also was an isolating activity in which the villain independently steals and misuses means to achieve power—that is, agency. Both Marlin Fitzwater and David Demarest explain that Hussein's behavior, to an American audience, fit the stereotypical villain image. Fitzwater pointed out that Hussein was a single "bad guy on whom Americans could focus their response" to the war.[51] Demarest noted that Saddam Hussein

> was conducting himself in ways that were hard to describe in any other kind of term except evil. . . . If you look at Saddam Hussein's rhetoric, [it was] laced with really vivid and almost crazy and insane sounding [language]. . . . That may be something that is more cultural, that is really less disquieting to people in his marketplace than in ours. . . . But what he didn't recognize was that he was on a global stage, not a local one, so his behavior [would appear to be that] of a madman. . . . When we talked about him internally, I remember thinking and I'm sure saying, that this guy is a classic villain . . . in terms of a narrative or a storyline where you have a guy in the white hat and a guy in the black hat.[52]

President Bush's most serious charges against Hussein as villain lie in references to World War II. They consist of carefully phrased comparisons of Hussein and Hitler in which Hussein appears as evil as, if not *more* evil than, the German demagogue: "I was told—and we've got to check this carefully— that Hitler did not stake people out against potential military targets and that he did, indeed, respect—not much else, but he did, indeed, respect the legitimacy of the Embassies [unlike Hussein]. So we've got some differences here. But . . . I see many similarities by the way the Iraqi forces behaved in Kuwait and the Death's Head regiments behaved in Poland. Go back and take a look at your history, and you'll see why I'm concerned as I am."[53]

Comparing Hussein and Hitler served two purposes. First, demonizing the dictator made it much easier for Bush to persuade Americans that fighting him was justified and necessary, and that applying sanctions would forestall another Munich disaster. Second, fixing a comparison in the public mind between the Gulf War and World War II would distract the public from strongly negative associations of agents and agencies in Vietnam.[54] As the military buildup in the Persian Gulf strengthened, Bush employed specific references to Vietnam, stating flatly that "there will be no more Vietnams" and assuring his audience that "the sooner [American military personnel] are out of there, as far as I'm concerned, the better. . . . we have no intention [of] keeping them a day longer than is required."[55] The president often addressed his military audience directly, praising them and thanking them for their work, in explicit contrast to the American reception of Vietnam veterans.[56] Bush even referred to the Gulf troops as "GIs," using the World War II–era term to further offset images of Vietnam: "Let me conclude with a word to the young American GI's deployed in the Gulf. We are proud of each and every one of you. I know you miss your loved ones and want to know when you'll be coming home. We won't leave you there any longer than necessary. I want every single soldier out of there as soon as possible. And we're all grateful for your continued sacrifice and your commitment."[57] These words of encouragement would also have been reassuring to members of the international community anxious about the possibility of a postwar American presence in the Persian Gulf.

Ironically, Bush himself bridged the primary set of dialectic opposites with another god-term, *leadership*. Bush initiated diplomatic relations with coalition governments and with Iraq; he addressed both the United Nations and the Iraqi people; he "consulted" with Congress, but made significant decisions about using U.S. forces himself. In all these actions, Bush seemed to act alone; at the very least, the president himself was, from the American perspective, the one visibly calling the shots and directing the war effort. In his Gulf War rhetoric, such actions were not renegadism, but initial steps toward unity. Furthermore, it is significant that one who so vocally valued unity and coalition would have recourse to such heavy use of dialectical opposition. Perhaps the strength of the coalition depended on the strength of the enemy, and binary characterization was the most rhetorically effective means of bolstering unity.[58]

Between August 2 and early November 1990, during which period the United Nations imposed trade embargoes on Iraq, Bush's rhetoric was aimed toward leadership in coalition building. The president iterates a finite number of objectives in much of his discourse; he praises shows of unity against the enemy Hussein; and he highlights issues of international law and authority.[59] While the substance of his objectives (also referred to as "goals" or "plans") changes little, their expression varies. In his first scheduled news conference after the invasion, Bush articulates two broad objectives.[60] By the end of August these are formally stated by the United Nations. He maintains that "our goals, enshrined in five Security Council resolutions, are clear: the immediate and unconditional withdrawal of Iraqi forces from Kuwait, the restoration of

Kuwait's legitimate government, the stability of Saudi Arabia and the Persian Gulf, and the protection of American citizens."[61] On a more apparently personal level, Bush indicates to the news media in August that the coalition, under his informal leadership, has "a plan, and the plan is to work diplomatically, and the plan is to put on the ground a significant military force."[62] Though the military is present from the beginning of the conflict, Bush insists that its purpose and the purpose of the diplomatic work and the U.N. sanctions is to safeguard and promote "common political goals," including peace, before war becomes inevitable.[63] At the end of August Bush characterizes America as a sovereign nation that takes the lead in coalition diplomacy (note the association of the god-term *leadership* with agency): "What we're talking about here, Charles [Bierbauer, Cable News Network], is a consulting and coordinating effort . . . but now we're moving up a little bit and trying to take the lead here—leadership in helping sort out who should help whom. Somebody has to do that. And we've made a significant commitment in various ways. And so, it seemed appropriate that we take the lead in working with our friends and allies."[64]

Once the U.N. deadline was set, and armed conflict became a distinct possibility, Bush invoked World War II imagery, saying that "there has never been a clearer demonstration of a world united against appeasement and aggression."[65] He reiterated his earlier claims that the Gulf War would not look like Vietnam.[66] The day after Resolution 678 passed, the president spoke about the issue with uncharacteristic eloquence, and did so three separate times in a single news conference:

> In our country, I know that there are fears about another Vietnam. Let me assure you, should military action be required, this will not be another Vietnam. This will not be a protracted, drawn-out war. The forces arrayed are different. The opposition is different. The resupply of Saddam's military would be very different. The countries united against him in the United Nations are different. The topography of Kuwait is different. And the motivation of our all-volunteer force is superb.
>
> I want peace. I want peace, not war. But if there must be war, we will not permit our troops to have their hands tied behind their backs. And I pledge to you: There will not be any murky ending. If one American soldier has to go into battle, that soldier will have enough force behind him to win and then get out as soon as possible, as soon as the U.N. objectives have been achieved. I will never—ever—agree to a halfway effort.[67]

But peace was not to be—in fact, was highly unlikely after Bush's vivid descriptions of a "dictator" capable of the "rape of his neighbor Kuwait."[68] So the January 15 deadline came and went; Hussein did not withdraw, and the Desert Storm phase of the Gulf War began the next morning. As the coalition moved from Operation Desert Shield to Desert Storm, Bush continued to speak as a leader, an organizer, a person with goals and a plan to reach those goals. Yet he repeatedly argued that as president and coalition *member,* he was acting within his legal powers and with the best of intentions.

National Sovereignty: Managing Agency and Agents

Bush used antinomy in the form of dialectic opposition to identify the agents of Operation Desert Shield—that is, to answer the question of "who did it." By the same token, agency is the answer to the question of "how he did it"; agency refers to the "means or instruments" the agent used to perform the act.[69] To accomplish the goals Bush established, and to project to the news media such accomplishment, the president had to address carefully issues of authority and sovereignty—that is, issues of agency—that determine who has the power to do what in the conflict, and he had to do so before actual fighting began. In other words, the president had to link agency and agents in such a way that each party (Congress, the coalition nations, Kuwait, and eventually even Iraq) was acting in concert with others and of its own accord. Toward this end, Bush often bounced between first-person and second-person pronouns, on the one hand asserting his authority to make decisions and do his job as he felt best, while on the other hand carefully acknowledging unity and cooperation between the executive and legislative branches of the U.S. government, or among the coalition partners. While Bush, as chief executive, had final say on U.S. foreign policy decisions, it was the consultative side of his leadership that worked particularly well in the realm of international diplomacy.

Domestically, Bush's agency problem was an issue of constitutional interpretation. In spite of the War Powers Act of 1973, which limited the president's constitutional power to introduce U.S. armed forces into a war situation, Bush felt that he had the authority to use the military as he did.[70] However, the president was aware that members of Congress did not necessarily agree with his interpretation, and that presenting such a show of disunity to the public would have damaged his credibility (his agency). So more than simply acknowledging Congress for its cooperation with the plans of the United Nations and the president, Bush worked to balance his rhetorical representation of authority within the U.S. government. Though he often spoke of his duty to make decisions, he spoke of cooperation between the executive and the legislature in which war powers reside: "Let me just say that I appreciate the support that Congress is giving to the administration during this situation. It's good, and it's strong. And for my part, I pledge to continue to consult fully, consult regularly with the Congress. The United States stands determined and united in its quest to see the Iraqi forces withdraw from Kuwait fully and unconditionally."[71]

After mid-November, when the U.N. Security Council approved the use of military force after January 15, 1991, Bush altered the way he addressed the internal unity of the United States, focusing on maintaining the authority (agency) of involved agents. Though the Security Council had approved military action, Congress had not, and the issue of war powers became increasingly significant.[72] Bush maintained that as commander in chief of U.S. armed forces, and by "legal and constitutional interpretation and historical precedent," he had the authority to prosecute the war.[73] His many consultations with Congress "combined with congressional ambivalence over assuming responsibility for military actions . . . to obviate any war powers challenge to Bush."[74] Furthermore, the president's many insistences that he did have such authority were intended to persuade those within and outside America who might have disagreed with the position. It was important for his administration to claim such authority without so much as hinting that war in the Gulf was imminent; if Congress was notified of such a situation, as White House counsel C. Boyden Gray explained in a memorandum to Sununu, "this would trigger the [War Powers] Resolution's 60-day clock. . . . Once the clock was triggered, the President would be required by the Resolution to terminate the deployment of United States forces to the region unless Congress passed legislation specifically authorizing the deployment within sixty days."[75] In short, by acknowledging the limitations of the War Powers Resolution too early in the conflict, Bush would have relinquished his authority to Congress just when holding it fast was most important.

In news conferences, the president found a public forum for his argument that the commander in chief had the authority to command military action; regarding the use-of-force resolution Bush had requested from Congress on January 8, a reporter asked, "Do you think you need such a resolution? And if you lose it, would you be bound by that?" The president responded with an answer that addressed his supporters and detractors alike, as well as the international community: "I don't think I need it. . . . There are different opinions on either side of this question, but Saddam Hussein should be under no question on this: I feel that I have the authority to fully implement the United Nations resolutions. . . . I still feel that I have the constitutional authority— many attorneys having so advised me."[76]

Bush's agency-centered rhetoric was even more significant in maintaining the international coalition than it had been in balancing American constitutional powers. Because the United Nations is an international body, it only has authority insofar as the sovereign member states so grant it. Thus, Bush's rhetoric during the Desert Shield stage included many appreciative statements directed at coalition partners exhibiting their unity of purpose in autonomous acts: "Well, you know, we feel we have all the authority we need; and the world leaders I've talked to, particularly François Mitterrand and Margaret Thatcher, agree that we have all the authority we need. We have been trying, and I think prudently so, to work with other countries around the world; and the more unanimity we get out the of the United Nations, for example, the better."[77]

Furthermore, the president was careful to avoid the appearance of bullying, as when he commented at length on Jordan's self-initiated involvement in the coalition: "I, of course, was very pleased that King Hussein, who previously had announced his support for sanctions, his willingness to go with sanctions, reiterated that to me, making clear that this was a decision that Jordan had taken some time ago."[78] As Bush's news conferences were broadcast worldwide on CNN, such statements deflected the appearance of American influence. However, the president had to balance his affirmation of other nations (and condemnation of Iraq) against an assertion of American authority: it would not do to have the United States appear less powerful than the United Nations, especially to an American audience. To affirm American authority, Bush employed negative-face statements, or statements indicating the desire for autonomy from other parties, numerous times throughout the Gulf War.[79] In late August, as Iraq attempted to strike deals with the United States, Bush used such negative-face statements as "The United States won't be threatened [by Iraq]" and "We cannot permit hostage-taking to shape the foreign policy of this country, and I won't permit it to do that."[80] Negative-face statements such as these offset accusations of timidity and powerlessness without sounding too hawkish abroad, but they were not enough to persuade the American audience that the United States retained control of the situation. For this purpose, Bush used positive-face statements to indicate that American actions won approval both internally and externally. When asked by a reporter, "Do you feel that you are free to take offensive action without any kind of U.N. resolution authorizing it?" the president responded, "Yes, we have authority. But we've been great believers in going to the United Nations. I think one of the major successes has been the ability to have world opinion totally on our side because of U.N. action. The peacekeeping function of the United Nations has indeed been rejuvenated by the actions of the Security Council."[81]

Between mid-November and mid-January, Bush repeatedly contrasted the legality of coalition activity to the illegality of Hussein's invasion and takeover of Kuwait. Bush continued to denounce Hussein, being careful to demonize only the dictator and his government, not the Iraqi people. At this point, however, it was Hussein's challenge to American *authority* that condemned him. At the news conference the day after Resolution 678 passed, Bush told reporters, "This treatment of our Embassy [that is, holding Americans hostage at the U.S. Embassy in Kuwait] violates every civilized principle of diplomacy. It demeans our people; it demeans our country."[82] In retaliating against the U.S. Embassy, Hussein challenged American face and American sovereignty—which, in combination with his other "aggressions," was sufficient provocation to fight.

As the January 15, 1991, withdrawal deadline loomed, publicly denouncing Iraq's challenge to the authority of the coalition and the United States became increasingly important. Between mid-November and the deadline, the president repeatedly expressed a desire for peace *and* a willingness to lead the coalition if fighting was necessary.[83] Thus, even in proclaiming the leadership role of the United States, Bush again aligned himself and the United States with the coalition in two ways: not only did he represent himself as sensitive to the human costs of war, but also he challenged those who would equate a desire for peace with a desire to negotiate. The abrupt change in the status of negotiation from a unifying (therefore good) action to borderline betrayal shifted war from something to be avoided to something necessary: "I'm concerned some might say that [Baker's trip to Baghdad] is an ultimatum in which—all it is, is an effort to be sure that he understands the commitment of the United States; that he understands that anything that is done must be done inside the confines of the United Nations resolutions that have been passed; that there will be no contingency, there can be no face-saving—that's not what this is about. This is to be sure that he understands how strongly the President of the United States feels about implementing to a tee, without concession, the United Nations position."[84] In this statement, the president becomes an agent of U.N. authority, thus unifying agent and agency for his audience.

With the U.N. deadline set, Saddam Hussein was given some autonomy of action. Bush told reporters in early December, "It isn't too late. But now, as before, the choice of peace or war is really Saddam Hussein's to make."[85] Considering the characterization Bush had so carefully built for Hussein (which included insanity, brutality, and thirst for power), one can suppose that Hussein would be unlikely to accept such a face-damaging challenge. Thus, as the January 15 withdrawal deadline approached, Bush's news conferences indicated that the range of peace opportunities was narrowing.[86]

AGENT AND AGENCY IN OPERATION DESERT STORM

On November 19 Iraq claimed it would send over 400,000 more troops to Kuwait; Saddam Hussein attempted to bargain with the United States, offering to release some foreign hostages, including U.S. citizens, from Iraq in exchange for American nonintervention. Meanwhile, U.N. member states began to implement measures that culminated in the November 29 UNSC Resolution 678. If Hussein failed to withdraw his forces from Kuwait by January 15, 1991, Resolution 678 authorized the coalition to drive out Iraq forcibly.[87] After the United States entered the war against Iraq on January 16, 1991, Bush's public appearances occurred less frequently, and focused more on caution and on unity, both in terms of the strength of the coalition and the internal unity of the American people and government.

Rhetorically speaking, the actual fighting phase of the war was anticlimactic; having convinced the U.S. government and the American people to support a war, and having helped build a coalition to fight one, the task at hand was to keep morale up and press on to victory. Thus, the president's rhetoric in the Desert Storm phase maintained a high degree of consistency with his earlier rhetorical efforts. After nearly two weeks of combat, Bush gave a major news conference that summarized the events of the war to date. At this point, the president revived his emphasis on objectives; from a position of success, he stated a new objective negatively, and used it for a second purpose. His statement not only articulated his intentions, but also served as "evidence" convicting Hussein of more brutality: "We do not seek Iraq's destruction, nor do we seek to punish the Iraqi people for the decisions and policies of their leaders. In addition, we are doing everything possible—and with great success—to minimize collateral damage, despite the fact that Saddam is now relocating some military functions such as command-and-control headquarters in civilian areas such as schools."[88]

Bush and the United Nations successfully began the war on their own unified authority, and the Bush administration still had an interest in maintaining the public perception of that authority. To this end, his Desert Storm rhetoric revisited the god-terms of law and morality, this time incarnated as credibility. Hussein, of course, had "zilch, zero, zed" credibility in Bush's eyes.[89] Further condemnatory statements reinforced his villain-role established in August: "But here's a man that used chemical weapons on his own people. Here's a man that gassed the Kurds. Here's a man who has no hesitancy to recklessly throw city-busting Scuds, population-killing Scuds, into Israel or into Saudi Arabia. Here's a man that brutally parades prisoners of war. Here's a man that has launched environmental terrorism. I can't figure out what he's thinking, and neither do the coalition partners with whom I am in touch; neither can they figure it out."[90] On the coalition's side, Bush claims that the successful war effort granted to the United States and the U.N. peacekeeping function "renewed credibility."[91] For the United States, part of this credibility came from Bush's repeated assertions of authority and control: "Saddam Hussein will not set the timing for what comes next. We will do that. And I will have to make that decision if we go to ground forces, and I will do it upon serious consideration of the recommendations of our military, including our secretary of Defense and the Chairman, of course, but also of our commanders in the field."[92]

The credibility of the United States came from its internal unity, a god-term Bush revisited during the Desert Storm phase of the Gulf War. Two days after coalition air strikes began, the president remarked at a news conference, "Let me close here by saying how much we appreciate what our fighting men and women are doing. This country is united. Yes, there's some protest, but this country is fundamentally united. And I want that message to go out to every kid that is over there serving this country."[93] In essence, the president claimed that the United States could be trusted to do what it promised because the American public—the driving force behind the U.S. government—supported the U.S. presence in the Gulf. Likewise, the coalition's credibility stemmed from the cooperative spirit of its members, including the Soviet Union, France, the Middle Eastern nations in general, and the Arab nations in particular.[94] Bush skirts over "differences" of opinion among coalition nations, for such signs of disunity would have damaged the unified front indicated by his rhetoric. Instead, Bush chose to praise the whole and express empathy for the troops who were serving in the Gulf, invoking images of his own experience in World War II and again broadly trying to drive away the ghosts of Vietnam and Korea.[95]

After April 6, 1991, when a permanent cease-fire was accepted by Iraq, Bush again revived the "good" half of the dialectical oppositions raised at the beginning of Desert Shield (unity and leadership), as well as a reframing of postwar agency. The president again iterated the objectives of the coalition, repeatedly announcing them "fulfilled."[96] He set a final objective for the coalition—securing the peace. With peace comes autonomy, according to Bush. He repeatedly commented to the press that the coalition should not establish occupation forces in Iraq; rather, self-government should be left to the Iraqi people (against whom Bush claimed never to have been at war). Problems in

Iraq—namely, the Kurds—were not within the power of the coalition to address after the cease-fire. As Bush explained to the news media,

> It was never a stated objective of the coalition to intervene in the internal affairs of Iraq. Indeed, I made it very clear that we did not intend to go into Iraq. I condemn Saddam Hussein's brutality against his own people. But I do not want to see United States forces, who have performed with such skill and dedication, sucked into a civil war in Iraq. We will not have normal relations with Iraq until Saddam Hussein is out of there. But I made very, very clear from day one that it was not an objective of the coalition to get Saddam Hussein out of there by force. And I don't think there's a single parent of a single man or woman that has fought in Desert Storm that wants to see United States forces pushed into this situation—brutal, tough, deplorable as it is.[97]

Once peace was formally declared, Bush's mention of the war in his news conferences dropped dramatically, as did reporters' questions about it. The "1,000-Hour War" faded into questions of aid for refugees, summits with foreign leaders, and routine press conferences about a variety of normal matters.

CONCLUSIONS AND IMPLICATIONS FOR FUTURE RESEARCH

In this chapter I have used a dramatistic method to show how George Bush, as president and as diplomatic leader in the Persian Gulf conflict, used rhetoric to shape and defend U.S. participation in the conflict. Bush managed issues of international authority and sovereignty (agency) by framing the agents of the war in dialectically opposing terms. Once established, the god-terms of unity/legality and devil-terms of disunity/illegality allowed Bush to polarize the conflict and to identify who belonged to each side. Furthermore, the god-term of leadership allowed Americans to take diplomatic and military initiative without appearing as controlling and belligerent as would otherwise have been the case.

John Robert Greene writes, "In his one-to-one dealings with people, Bush was a master of the persuasive art. . . . Yet in the area of the public presidency—that part of leadership that requires the president to connect with the citizenry at large—historians will find Bush wanting. George Bush was, to put it charitably, an uninspiring speaker."[98] Despite Bush's lack of enthusiasm for public communication, the Persian Gulf conflict was a time in which the Bush administration had to convince Congress, the American people, and the world community that war was both justified and necessary, and had to cultivate and maintain these audiences' trust and assent.[99] Connecting with the "citizenry at large" was not Bush's forte; however, he and his communication organization managed to unite these audiences long enough to prepare for, prosecute, and end the war—a feat that seems particularly impressive when one considers the vast differences in culture and political power separating them. President Bush's public communication both responded to and shaped the events unfolding in the Persian Gulf and the United States, and studying this communication reveals a great deal about how and why the Gulf War evolved as it did. Future researchers will be the ones to further substantiate these claims, as more documentary information about the period becomes available; in the meantime, studying the public words of the president is a good place to begin.

NOTES

1. Boutros Boutros-Ghali, "Introduction," in *The United Nations and the Iraq-Kuwait Conflict, 1990–1996,* United Nations Blue Books Series, vol. 9 (New York: Department of Public Information, United Nations, 1996), 1.

2. Clayton R. Newell, "Chronology," in *Historical Dictionary of the Persian Gulf War 1990–1991,* Historical Dictionaries of War, Revolution, and Civil Unrest, No. 9 (Lanham, Md.: Scarecrow Press, 1998), xxxiii.

3. Boutros-Ghali, "Introduction," 14.

4. Five Arab League members voted against condemnation of Iraq or abstained from voting. See Newell, "Chronology," xxxiv. For the United Nations, see Boutros-Ghali, "Introduction," 14.

5. Newell, "Chronology," xxxviii.

6. Kerry Mullins and Aaron Wildavsky, "The Procedural Presidency of George Bush," *Political Science Quarterly* 107 (1992): 31–62.

7. Newell, *Historical Dictionary,* 64. The phrase, "George Bush's war" is used most notably by Jean Edward Smith, *George Bush's War* (New York: Henry Holt, 1992).

8. David Demarest, telephone interview by author, tape recording, College Station, Texas, August 31, 2000.

9. For example, Kathleen M. German, "Invoking the Glorious War: Framing the Persian Gulf Conflict through Directive Language," *Southern Communication Journal* 60 (1994): 292–302; Kathryn M. Olson, "Constraining Open Deliberation in Times of War: Presidential War Justifications for Grenada and the Persian Gulf," *Argumentation and Advocacy* 28 (1991): 64–79.

10. Timothy Cole, "When Intentions Go Awry: The Bush Administration's Foreign Policy Rhetoric," *Political Communication* 13 (1996): 93–113; Mary E. Stuckey, "Remembering the Future: Rhetorical Echoes of World War II and Vietnam in George Bush's Public Speech on the Gulf War," *Communication Studies* 43 (1992): 246–56; and Stuckey, "Competing Foreign Policy Visions: Rhetorical Hybrids after the Cold War," *Western Journal of Communication* 59 (1995): 214–27.

11. Kenneth Burke, *A Grammar of Motives* (Berkeley: University of California Press, 1945), 328–29.

12. Ibid., 329.

13. David Zarefsky, "Four Senses of Rhetorical History," in *Doing Rhetorical History: Concepts and Cases,* ed. Kathleen J. Turner (Tuscaloosa: University of Alabama Press, 1998), 21.

14. See Lloyd F. Bitzer, "The Rhetorical Situation," *Philosophy and Rhetoric* 1 (1968): 1–14.

15. Zarefsky, "Four Senses of Rhetorical History," 30.

16. See Newell, *Historical Dictionary,* 250–51, for a bibliographic listing of some of these works.

17. Marion K. Pinsdorf, "Image Makers of Desert Storm: Bush, Powell, and Schwarzkopf," in *The 1,000 Hour War: Communication in the Gulf,* ed. Thomas A. McCain and Leonard Shyles (Westport, Conn.: Greenwood Press, 1994), 40–41.

18. Samuel Kernell, *Going Public: New Strategies of Presidential Leadership,* 2d ed. (Washington, D.C.: CQ Press, 1993), 79; Pinsdorf, "Image Makers of Desert Storm," 39.

19. Mullins and Wildavsky, "Procedural Presidency of George Bush," 32 (emphasis added).

20. Ibid., 52.

21. Burke, *Grammar of Motives,* 33.

22. Stuckey, "Remembering the Future"; Stuckey, "Rhetorical Hybrids"; Cole, "When Intentions Go Awry."

23. George H. W. Bush, "The President's News Conference," August 14, 1990, *Public Papers of the President of the United States.* Available online at <www.presidentialrhetoric.com>. All subsequent references to speeches and news conferences are from the same source, and are noted by date only.

24. August 22, 1990; November 1, 1990.

25. August 16, 1990; September 21, 1990; August 16, 1990.

26. Mullins and Wildavsky, "Procedural Presidency of George Bush," 36. The emphasis on law and legality was central to the Bush administration's handling of the war. Among the "Gulf Policy themes" that the Persian Gulf Working Group of the White House Office of Communications distributed during Desert Shield is listed, "Morally, we must act so that international law, not international outlaws, governs the post–Cold War world." Gulf Policy Themes, revised December 14, 1990, Bush Presidential Records, White House Office of Communications, Paul McNeill Files, Persian Gulf Working Group: Notebooks of David Demarest, Folder 6 [OA/ID 03195].

27. November 8, 1990.

28. November 1, 1990.

29. Address before a Joint Session of the Congress on the Persian Gulf Crisis and the Federal Budget Deficit, September 11, 1990.

30. John Robert Greene, *The Presidency of George Bush* (Lawrence: University Press of Kansas, 2000), 126.

31. Memorandum for Governor Sununu from C. Boyden Gray, December 6, 1990, Subject: War Powers Resolution, Bush Presidential Records, Chief of Staff John Sununu Files, Persian Gulf War 1991 Files, Folder 11 [OA/ID CF00472].

32. Ibid.; Letter to Congressional Leaders on the Persian Gulf Crisis, January 8, 1991.

33. Quoted in Greene, *Presidency of George* Bush, 126.

34. Marlin Fitzwater, telephone interview by author, tape recording, College Station, Texas, September 1, 2000.

35. Memorandum to the President of the United States from David Demarest and Deb Amend, December 10, 1990, Subject: Communications Working Group on the Gulf, Bush Presidential Records, Office of Communications Files, Paul McNeill Files, Persian Gulf Working Group: Notebooks of David Demarest, Folder 6. [OA/ID 03195].

36. Memorandum for Governor Sununu from David Demarest, November 28, 1990. Subject: Communications Plan–Operation Desert Shield, Bush Presidential Records, Chief of Staff Files, John Sununu Files, Persian Gulf War 1991 Files, Folder 11 [OA/ID CF00472].

37. The Persian Gulf Working Group included David Demarest, Deb Amend, Chriss Winston, Bobbie Kilberg, Sichan Siv, Leigh Ann Metzger, Barrie Tron, Dave Carney, Rob Portman, Roman Popaduik, Michael Jackson, Bill Sittmann, Richard Haass, and Spencer Abraham. The staff included Sara Maltby and Paul McNeill. Bush Presidential Records, Office of Communications, Paul McNeill files, PGWG: David Demarest Notebooks, Folder 2, [OA/ID 03195]. Representatives from various government agencies attended the meetings as well; one list, dated December 3, 1990, included individual public affairs staff people from the Department of State, the Joint Chiefs Office, the Department of Defense, the Department of the Treasury, the Department of Energy, and the Department of Veterans Affairs. Bush Presidential Records, Office of Communications, Paul McNeill Files, Persian Gulf Working Group: Attendees of Meetings Folder [OA/ID 03195].

Memorandum to the President from David Demarest and Deb Amend, December 10, 1990, Subject: Communications Working Group on the Gulf. Bush Presidential Records, Office of Communications, Paul McNeill Files, Persian Gulf Working Group: David Demarest Notebooks, Folder 6 [OA/ID 03195].

38. September 21, 1990.

39. August 30, 1990; Remarks and a Question-and-Answer Session with Reporters Following Discussions with Allies on the Persian Gulf Crisis, December 17, 1990.

40. August 22, 1990. See also the president's news conference of December 18, 1990.

41. August 14, 1990; August 22, 1990; August 30, 1990; December 28, 1990.

42. August 8, 1990.

43. September 9, 1990; November 1, 1990; November 8, 1990.

44. August 30, 1990; November 1, 1990; November 30, 1990; Address to the People of Iraq on the Persian Gulf Crisis, September 16, 1990.

45. September 21, 1990. Bush makes similar statements throughout and after the war.

46. Remarks Following Discussions with Amir Jabir al-Ahmad al-Jabir Al Sabah of Kuwait, September 28, 1990.

47. August 22, 1990; September 9, 1990.

48. September 21, 1990.

49. October 9, 1990; see also Open Letter to College Students on the Persian Gulf Crisis, January 9, 1991.

50. Robert Ivie, "Images of Savagery in American Justifications for War," *Communication Monographs* 47 (1980): 279–94.

51. Fitzwater, interview, September 1, 2000.

52. Demarest, interview, August 31, 2000.

53. November 1, 1990.

54. A letter to Bush from the National Vietnam Veterans Coalition in Washington, D.C., commends the president for the "very careful diplomatic balancing that you have done to avoid the use of military force," and chastises the press for "inappropriately compar[ing] your handling of the Persian Gulf crisis to what we Vietnam veterans encountered in Vietnam." Thus, for at least one audience, the Bush administration's strategy was indeed effective. Letter to George Bush, December 4, 1990, Bush Presidential Records, Office of Communications Files, Paul McNeill Files, Persian Gulf Working Group: Notebooks of David Demarest, Folder 6 [OA/ID 03195].

55. Radio Address to the Nation on the Persian Gulf Crisis, January 5, 1991; September 9, 1990.

56. Christmas Message to American Troops, December 24, 1990.

57. November 8, 1990.

58. See Roderick P. Hart, "Introduction: Community by Negation—An Agenda for Rhetorical Inquiry," in *Rhetoric and Community: Studies in Unity and Fragmentation,* ed. J. Michael Hogan (Columbia: University of South Carolina Press, 1998), xxxv–xxxviii.

59. Message to Allied Nations on the Persian Gulf Crisis, January 8, 1991.

60. August 8, 1990. Bush makes similar statements at news conferences throughout the crisis; see transcripts of news conferences held on August 22, 1990, November 30, 1990, January 18, 1991, and February 5, 1991.

61. August 30, 1990.

62. Ibid.

63. November 8, 1990; September 9, 1990; November 1, 1990.

64. August 30, 1990.

65. November 30, 1990.

66. December 18, 1990; January 9, 1991; January 12, 1991.

67. November 30, 1990.

68. Ibid.

69. Burke, *Grammar of Motives,* xv.

70. Public Law 93–148, 93d Congress, H.J. Res. 542, November 7, 1973.

71. September 21, 1990.

72. November 30, 1990. See also Robert J. Spitzer, "The Conflict between Congress and the President over War," in *The Presidency and the Persian Gulf War,* ed. Marcia Lynn Whicker, James P. Pfiffner, and Raymond A. Moore (Westport, Conn.: Praeger, 1993), 25–44.

73. Spitzer, "Conflict," 33.

74. Ibid., 37.

75. Memorandum for Governor Sununu from C. Boyden Gray, December 6, 1990.

76. January 9, 1991. Many scholars, including George C. Edwards III in *The Public Presidency: The Pursuit of Popular Support* (New York: St. Martin's Press, 1983), argue that the press conference is of little influence on the public. Marlin Fitzwater, however, argues that the news conference is the second most influential form of presidential discourse, following televised speeches shown in their entirety (such as the annual state of the union address) because the news media are an integral part of the event and can "buy into the idea[s]" being presented to them (Fitzwater, interview, September 1, 2000).

77. August 22, 1990.

78. August 16, 1990.

79. Sarah Trenholm and Arthur Jensen, *Interpersonal Communication,* 3d ed. (Belmont, Calif.: Wadsworth Publishing, 1996), 263.

80. August 22, 1990; August 30, 1990.

81. November 8, 1990.

82. November 30, 1990.

83. Ibid.; December 18, 1990; January 9, 1991.

84. November 30, 1990.

85. December 9, 1990. Bush also made similar comments in his news conference of January 12, 1991.

86. January 9, 1991; Bush details these narrowing options in the Address to the Nation Announcing Allied Military Action in the Persian Gulf, January 16, 1991.

87. Newell, *Historical Dictionary,* xxxviii.

88. February 5, 1991.

89. March 16, 1991

90. February 5, 1991. See also March 1, 1991.

91. March 16, 1991; April 6, 1991; April 7, 1991.

92. February 5, 1991.

93. January 18, 1991.

94. March 1, 1991; March 13, 1991; March 14, 1991; March 16, 1991; April 6, 1991.

95. February 5, 1991; March 1, 1991; April 16, 1991; March 14, 1991.

96. April 4, 1991; April 6, 1991; April 7, 1991; April 16, 1991.

97. April 4, 1991. Later in April the United States began to aid Kurdish refugees.

98. Greene, *Presidency of George Bush,* 145–46.

99. Demarest notes, "I think the way he looked at [rhetoric in the presidency] was that he felt that his actions should speak for themselves. That there is a level of spin when it comes to certain kinds of rhetoric, he really wasn't very comfortable with. He thought that you have to marry the rhetoric with the persona and that he would not come across as real if he tried to do some of the things that great orators typically try to do. . . . he wanted to be a little bit more plainspoken" (Demarest interview, August 31, 2000).

CHAPTER 5

The New World Order: President Bush and the Post–Cold War Era

ROY JOSEPH

Until now, the world we've known has been a world divided—a world of barbed wire and concrete block, conflict and cold war. Now, we can see a new world coming into view. A world in which there is the very real prospect of a new world order. In the words of Winston Churchill, a world order in which the "the principles of justice and fair play protect the weak against the strong . . ." A world where the United Nations—freed from cold war stalemate—is poised to fulfill the historic vision of its founders. A world in which freedom and respect for human rights find a home among all the nations. The Gulf War put this new world to its first test. And my fellow Americans we passed the test.
George Bush to Congress, March 6, 1991

For over four decades, the world quivered under the specter of nuclear annihilation. The era of nuclear brinkmanship between the two superpowers, however, lost political fuel as the Soviet Union started imploding under the pressure of its own toppling economy. A world that had been divided by "barbed wire and concrete block," symbolized by the Iron Curtain and the Berlin Wall, was receding into the dustbin of history as President Bush saw a "new world coming into view."[1] President Bush conceived the end of the Cold War as a rhetorical opportunity to build a Churchillian vision of a new world in which "the principles of justice and fair play protect the weak against the strong."[2] Against this backdrop, Bush amplified his vision of the New World Order in which the United States "remains an engaged power for positive change."[3] The "New World Order" is a grand locution that promises much but at the same time raises, for some, frightening ogres of one-world government.

This chapter explores this polysemic concept, the New World Order. The New World Order is a concept that is associated with an individual, George Bush, and with an era, the post–Cold War period. The key question is, what did George Bush actually mean by the phrase a "new world order," and why did this locution fail to gain rhetorical traction with the public? The first part of the question can be answered by comparing Bush's vision of the New World Order with the Charter of the United Nations, and by tracing historical parallels with other American presidents and their visions of world peace. The second part is more difficult to answer. It can best be approached by examining ideological critiques of President Bush from both the left and the right, and demonstrating the vulnerability inherent in a situation in which the leader fails to clearly articulate his ideas.

WHAT IS THE NEW WORLD ORDER?

Rhetoric permeates the realm of public communication. Any political artifact, such as a presidential speech, press conference, or expression of ideology, has rhetorical implications, be they profound or prosaic. The conception of any political reality is impossible without the symbolic evocation of a concomitant rhetoric—one that gives impetus to the vision that is being enacted. Political language becomes rhetorical the moment it is mediated through metaphor and metonymy such that these linguistic utterances begin to evoke "mythic cognitive structures in people's minds."[4] The particular use of a metaphor or any type of accented syntax evokes in the minds of listeners a whole structure of beliefs and counter-beliefs. The rhetorical dimensions of a political utterance are potent in that they engender a sense of identification or repulsion (through either passive indifference or active rebellion).

The line between political doctrine and rhetorical expression becomes wafer-thin, especially in the realm of pubic persuasion. A rhetorical transaction occurs when the leader enunciates the importance of a particular doctrine, with a keen eye on winning public support. In this case, Bush's enunciation of the New World Order is carried out in an atmosphere in which the president as a political being is transposed into a rhetorical being to persuade his audience about the legitimacy of his doctrine. Presidential discourse is chiefly rhetorical, since it constitutes a rhetorical enactment of the symbolic power of the presidency. The spoken word of the president carries with it a sanctity and evocative power that recursively seek a form of self-validation within the parameters of the office of the presidency. The president is a rhetorical being who "understands that few things in life are given or inalterably determined; one who understands that most things are amenable to choice and to selection among several competing choices; one who understands that the ability to use symbols carries with it the power both to build and destroy."[5] President Bush used the most eloquent symbols and metaphors invoking the ideas of "peace, justice, fair play, [and] democratic values" to articulate his vision of the New World Order.[6] Bush presented his vision through generalized abstractions and by spelling out the qualities that the new international post–Cold War system would possess. Although Bush did not define the exact parameters that would constitute the New World Order, a comparative study of his vision with that of the United Nations Charter might help us get closer to a better understanding of his intention.

The charter of the United Nations was meant to represent the collective aspirations of peace-loving nations that were determined to accelerate the process of healing in the wake of mass destruction:

> WE THE PEOPLE OF THE UNITED NATIONS DETERMINED to save succeeding generations from the scourge of war, which twice in our lifetime has brought untold sorrow to mankind, and to reaffirm faith in fundamental human rights, in the dignity and worth of the human person, in the equal rights of men and women and of nations large and small, and to establish conditions under which justice and respect for the obligations arising from treaties and other sources of international law can be maintained, and to promote social progress and better standards of life in larger freedom, AND FOR THESE ENDS to practice tolerance and live together in peace with one another as good neighbors, and to unite our strength to maintain international peace and security, and to ensure, by the acceptance of principles and the institution of methods, that armed force shall not be used, save in common interest, and to employ international machinery for the promotion of the economic and social advancement of all peoples, HAVE RESOLVED TO COMBINE OUR EFFORTS TO ACCOMPLISH THESE AIMS.[7]

The charter formulated a vision for global politics in which nations of the world would come together to maintain international peace and security. In the aftermath of a catastrophic world war, the United Nations emerged as a corrective against any form of national aggrandizement or divisive provincialism that could result in more bloodshed. Chapter I, Article 1.1, of the charter declares that one of the purposes of the United Nations is "to maintain international security, and to that end: to take effective collective measures for the prevention and removal of threats to the peace, and for the suppression of the acts of aggression or other breaches of the peace, and to bring about by peaceful means, and in conformity with the principles of justice and international law, adjustments or settlements of international disputes or situations which might lead to a breach of peace." The U.N. charter represented a rather holistic picture of how international relations across the globe should look.

However, for the next few decades, the United Nations seemed more like an impotent organization, watching helplessly as the Cold War polarized the world into Eastern and Western Blocs. The United States and the Soviet Union were hostile to each other, and employed the principles of balance-of-power politics and the doctrine of mutually assured destruction (MAD), keeping the world in a state of fragile peace. The United Nations remained a shadowy entity struggling to assert itself since the superpowers continually ignored it, especially at moments in which there was a clear conflict of interest.[8] Two of the problems that beset the U.N. were as follows: "The United Nations was established to override the balance-of-power war system, yet its peacekeeping role has never been developed with such capacities in mind and, in fact, has been seriously diminished over the years; and the United Nations was established to sustain a common allied front against aggression, yet bloc voting and ideological rivalry have frequently paralyzed or politicized the organization when warfare breaks out, as was the case during the Iran-Iraq War (1980–1988)."[9] The relationship of the United Nations with the superpowers and with the other nations on the Security Council remained unclear. There was indeed a sense of selective compliance to the United Nations: "In fact, none of the Big Five in the Security Council has been willing to submit its claims to use force to the normative discipline of international accountability, seeking to the extent possible to avoid even a debate as to its propriety under the UN Charter."[10] Interestingly enough, the Yalta and Potsdam accords reflected "the willingness of the great powers to take responsibility for maintaining the international order, a responsibility best expressed in the Charter of the United Nations."[11] Not until the Gulf War, however, did the United Nations get close to the vision that its founders had originally envisaged in 1945. "The great power directorate of the Security Council was created based on the principle that power must be commensurate with responsibility. As a consequence what emerged in the United Nations . . . was a system that could only work against smaller powers—hardly a significant guarantee for making international peace and stability."[12] Furthermore, veto power was given to the permanent members of the Security Council, and this "decision was made not in the idealistic belief that the great powers would continue to live in peace and that the veto would never be used, but with the expectation that there would be occasions on which it would be used to avoid great power confrontation."[13]

In some respects, during the Cold War the United Nations found itself in self-defeating, Catch-22 situations. Contrary to its professed goals, the way in which the Security Council was set up acted against fulfilling the mission statement of the organization. The Iran-Iraq conflict was just one in a series of missed opportunities that confronted the United Nations. All five permanent members of the Security Council sold arms to both sides, earning higher profits as the war extended over an unusually long period.[14] Another problem that confronted the United Nations was the partisan manner in which the General Assembly voted, manifested along ideological lines that supported either the United States or the Soviet Union, or, in some rare cases, abstained from taking a stand.

From a Western perspective, the deadlock in which the United Nations often found itself would gradually disappear as the winds of reform started sweeping over its Soviet adversary. President Reagan, who called the Soviet Union an "Evil Empire" in 1983, seemingly underwent a softening of heart as he foresaw the emergence of Western-style freedoms in the Eastern Bloc. In his address to the United Nations in 1988, Reagan suggested that a new age was dawning in which the East-West stalemate that had hitherto stultified the United Nations would give way to a period of peace:

> For the first time, the differences between East and West—fundamental differences over important moral questions dealing with the worth of the individual and whether governments shall control people or people control governments—for the first time these differences have shown signs of easing, easing to the point where there are not just troop withdrawals from places like Afghanistan but also talk in the East of reform and greater freedom of press, of assembly, and of religion. Yes, fundamental differences remain. But should talk of reform become more than that, should it become reality, there is the prospect of not only a new era in Soviet-American relations but a new age of world peace.[15]

Reagan's optimism for change was passed on to Bush, who eagerly set about conducting the requiem for Soviet communism. "We live in a peaceful, prosperous time, but we can make it better. For a new breeze is blowing, and a world refreshed by freedom seems reborn. For in man's heart, if not in fact, the day of the dictator is over. The totalitarian era is passing, its old ideals blown away like leaves from an ancient, lifeless tree. A new breeze is blowing, and a nation refreshed by freedom stands ready to push on."[16] The beginning of the fall of Soviet communism precipitated a series of events. The overthrow of Nicolae Ceausescu's regime in Romania, the fall of the Berlin Wall, the reunification of Germany, and finally the disintegration of the Soviet Union raised hopes that a new international system was waiting to be born.[17] Even hordes of diehard communists rapidly discarded their long-held beliefs in the Marxist-Leninist revolution. In its place, amorphous and mutated forms of free-market capitalism began to take shape. The shift from communism to postcommunism was commencing. As Zbigniew Brzezinski wrote: "A new phenomenon—post-communism—is now appearing. . . . a post-Communist system will be one in which the withering away of communism has advanced to the point that neither Marxist theory nor past-Communist practice dictate much—if any—of ongoing public policy. Post Communism, very simply, will be a system in which self-declared 'Communists' just do not treat communist doctrine seriously as the guide to social policy."[18] The emergence of a postcommunist Eastern Europe had global ramifications. First, the United States and its Western allies were left without a principal adversary. Second, there was either a possibility of witnessing a unipolar world under American leadership or a multipolar world with diminished Western influence.[19] The world of post–Cold War politics was thus fraught with uncertainties. President Bush recognized the need to define America's role in this post–Cold War world and to articulate a vision that would encompass the international community as a whole. "In the emerging post–Cold War world, international relations promise to be more complicated, more volatile and less predictable. Indeed, of all the mistakes that could be made about the security challenges of a new era, the most dangerous would be to believe that suddenly the future can be predicted with certainty."[20] The absence of a political adversary did not necessarily eliminate the possibility of conflict. The uncertainties of international politics could manifest themselves in terms of nationalism or regionalism. Religio-ethnic conflicts and other wars, albeit fought on a smaller scale, could reduce the importance of the United States and its allies in world politics. Furthermore, conventional solutions such as "balance-of-power" politics would seem hopelessly out-of-sync in dealing with local conflicts proliferating across the globe.

Bush pictured an America that had an important role to play in leading the world in the new age of post–Cold War politics. "This is a time for America to reach out and take the lead, not merely react. And this is a time for America to move forward and cautiously—not retreat. As the freest and the fairest and the most powerful democracy on the face of the Earth, we must continue to shine as a beacon of liberty, beacon of justice for all the people of the world."[21] The United States as the world's leading political power should not abdicate its role as a model for the rest of the international community. The end of the Cold War vindicated the ideals of freedom, the free market, and the spirit of democracy. "History is moving decisively in favor of freedom, thanks in large part to American ideals and perseverance—the touchstones of the modern world which the emerging democracies are now striving for: free markets, free speech, free elections."[22] It was important that Bush universalized his post–Cold War vision in a way that applied to the rest of the world. By projecting the ideals of freedom and democracy that America cherished, Bush attempted to strike a sympathetic chord with his international audience. He appealed to an ethos of moral leadership, and projected his vision of leadership as one shared by the world: "A world once divided into two armed camps now recognizes one sole and preeminent power, the United States of America. And they regard this with no dread. For the world trusts us with power, and the world is right. They trust us to be fair. They trust us to be on the side of decency. They trust us to do what's right."[23]

It is important to note that President Bush's rhetoric was inclusive, creating a discourse of identification. As Thomas Kane explains, "the language used to express the meaning of national and international events needed a coherent and inclusive vocabulary in order to promote a variety of social concerns, economic interests, self-images and personal ambitions."[24] The end of the Cold War was construed not just as a victory for the United States and its allies, but as a "victory for all humanity" accomplished through "American leadership" that was "instrumental in making it possible."[25] President Bush might have risked alienation if he had used exclusive language, rather than the inclusive phrase "for all humanity," yet he does not diminish the preeminent role that the United States played in winning the Cold War.

The rhetorical exigency that Bush had to address pertained to the role of the United States in international politics. Crafting a vision that engaged both the United States and the United Nations in diplomatic or military forums would enhance the credibility of the president with the international community. Leadership meant "followership, goal-directedness, and commitment to a cause that transcended the self."[26] Bush's years of experience as a diplomat overseas helped him to have a broader vision for America in the context of global politics. His primary task consisted of having a coherent agenda for America in the tumultuous coliseum of international politics. Bush's America derives its moral leadership by entering into a global partnership with other nations to promote the new international order. "We have a vision of a new partnership of nations that transcends the Cold War: a partnership based on consultation, cooperation, and collective action, especially through international and regional organizations; a partnership united by principle and the rule of the law."[27] By apparently fostering an atmosphere of multilateralism as opposed to unilateralism, Bush wanted to communicate a powerful message

to the international community that his political style was based on consultative leadership and not on hegemony.

A New World Order had to be established that would fulfill the historic
vision of the founders of the United Nations. The New World Order would
revitalize the United Nations.[28] It would operate on the principle that "a lot
of countries—disparate backgrounds, with differences—can come together,
standing for a common principle, and that principle is: you don't take over
another country by force."[29] Bush popularized the phrase *New World Order*
in the wake of Saddam Hussein's invasion of Kuwait. Saddam was subjected
to the combined moral outrage of the United Nations. In the rhetorical vision
of the New World Order, Saddam symbolized the forces of tyranny and lawlessness against the grand collectivity of the United Nations. Therefore, to
Bush, the Gulf War was a necessary corrective against those elements that were
disrupting the fledgling New World Order.[30]

Saddam Hussein had clearly violated Chapter I, Article 2:4, of the U.N.
Charter, which states: "All members shall refrain in their international relations from the threat or use of force against the territorial integrity or political independence of any state, or in any other manner inconsistent with the
Purposes of the United Nations."[31] Furthermore, perhaps for the first time
since World War II a small nation had raised the ire of both the United States
and the Soviet Union. The willingness of the Soviet Union to turn its back on
Iraq, its former ally, was definitely a shot in the arm for Bush.

> It was enhanced by a more viable United Nations, a United Nations where big
> powers didn't automatically go against each other. In the cold war days, we'd say
> this is black and the Soviets would say, hey, that's white. And you'd have a veto,
> and nothing would happen. And the peacekeeping dreams of the founders of the
> U.N. were dashed. . . . So, part of this new world order has been moved forward
> by a United Nations that functioned. . . . but it was enhanced—it is far better to
> have this collective action where the world—not just the Security Council but
> the whole General Assembly stood up and condemned it.[32]

The New World Order enhanced the peacekeeping vision of the United
States, and the United Nations reinforced the New World Order, since this
new international system that Bush envisioned required the active support of
the international body. The New World Order presupposed a shared commitment to "international law," including those specified by the U.N. Charter.[33] International law is grounded "primarily in the prior consent of the
members of the world community," and by the same token "the role of the
United States as enforcer of international law thus rests, ultimately, upon

the consent of states."[34] Iraq was also a signatory to the U.N. Charter, and thus its violation of the charter demanded punitive action. While building up troops in the Gulf, Bush observed the following about the need to make Iraq comply with the U.N. Charter: "These goals are not ours alone. They've been endorsed by the United Nations Security Council five times in as many weeks. . . . We can point to . . . United Nations Security Council resolutions that condemn Iraq's aggression."[35] The Iraqi dictator's actions stood in dialectical opposition to the values of the New World Order. They were an aberration in an era in which the "nations of the world, East and West, North and South can prosper and live in harmony."[36] They represented most importantly, a "grim nightmare of anarchy" trying to obstruct the emergence of a new world in which "the rule of the law supplants the rule of the jungle."[37]

The rhetoric of the New World Order coincides with the events leading up to the Gulf War, the duration of the war, and a brief period thereafter. The articulation of this concept is closely tied to the moral might of the United Nations in its mission of accomplishing peace, buttressed by the military support of the United States and its allies. With the Soviet Union now an ally, the Security Council of the United Nations could also pursue common goals. As outlined in the charter, one of the chief aims of the Security Council was to "determine the existence of any threat to the peace, breach of the peace, or act of aggression" and "make recommendations, or decide what measures be taken. . . . to maintain or restore international peace and security."[38] Article 41 states: "The Security Council may decide when its measures not involving the use of armed force are to be employed to give effect to its decisions, and may call upon the Members of the United Nations to apply such measures. These may include complete or partial interruption of economic relations and of rail, sea, air, postal, telegraphic, radio, and other means of communication, and the severance of diplomatic relations." Article 42 declares:

"Should the Security Council consider that measures provided for in Article 41 would be inadequate or have proved to be inadequate, it may take such action by air, sea, or land forces as may be necessary to maintain or restore international peace and security. Such actions include demonstrations, blockade, and other operations by air, sea, or land forces of Members of the United Nations."[39] When Saddam failed to comply with the U.N. resolutions, Bush invoked Article 42 to receive the blessing of the United Nations in the allied forces' military campaign against Iraq.[40] Bush was interviewed by a reporter about the double standard that the United States was adopting: on one hand, the United States was signing a treaty with Gorbachev for a reduction of conventional arms, but on the other hand, it was pursuing a military option

against Iraq without exhausting diplomatic possibilities. Bush responded as
follows:

> I don't see any irony in it whatsoever. What I see is the fact that we're able to en-
> ter into a CFE agreement with full cooperation and support of the Soviet Union
> who, heretofore, has been an enormous adversary of the West. And now this re-
> duces practically to nil the tensions that have existed. . . . So, what it does is show
> a solidification of forces that in recent history have been on opposite sides of
> some of these questions. So, if there is any message coming out of CFE for Sad-
> dam Hussein it ought to be: Look what you're up against here. Here are people
> that since World War II have tension and, at times, conflict; and now they are to-
> gether as they take a gigantic step forward in arms control. And they're together
> as they stand in the United Nations against your brutal, naked aggression. So, if
> there's any connection, that's the message that I'd like to see come out of all this.[41]

Rhetorically, Bush constitutes the Soviet Union as the undeniable adversary,
even employing god and devil terms. However, this adversary seems to have
had a change of heart. Although Bush acknowledges the distinctiveness of
both the nations, he emphasizes their new-found community. Together, they
stand against a new evil, Saddam, whose "brutal, naked aggression" emerges
in dialectical opposition to the forces of good in the New World Order. Bush
thus makes persuasive appeals to win the support of as many nations as possible, including former adversaries. By fashioning a sense of consensus and
predicting the desired outcome as the inevitable response, Bush establishes
identification with the former adversary against the new adversary. As Kenneth Burke explains, "identification is affirmed with earnestness precisely because there is a division. . . . If men were not apart from each other, there
would be no need for the rhetorician to proclaim their unity."[42] By forging an
identity amid the apparent disparity, Bush's rhetoric emerges as a viable alternative to the "absolute communication" that would be possible only if "men
were wholly and truly of one substance."[43]

Bush's rhetorical vision of the New World Order cannot be understood
apart from the context of the United Nations. American leadership and the
validation of the Security Council guided him past the first experiment of the
New World Order. Bush's description of the New World Order and what it
should look like resonates with the U.N. Charter. He describes it as "the
dream of a world in which major powers worked together to ensure peace; to
settle their disputes through cooperation, not confrontation."[44] However, the
difficult question that Bush and his New World Order might have to respond
to is: whose New World Order is it? Although Saddam's conduct was repre-
hensible, the difficult question to answer is whether Iraq deserved to lose over

150,000 of its soldiers, not counting civilian casualties, for the act of one mad dictator. Although one can commend Bush for the principles entailed in the New World Order; the interpretation of its meaning is possible only through comparing its principles with the U.N. Charter. Bush's recurring motifs, consistent with the overall peacekeeping mission of the United Nations, include the following:

- *Peace:* opportunity for peace, new era of peace, enduring peace, United Nations, a peacekeeping force, and quest for peace

- *Justice:* the pursuit of justice, justice for all

- *Strong/weak:* the strong respect and protect the weak

- *Rights:* rights of the individual, human rights

- *Freedom:* commonwealth of freedom, shared responsibility for freedom

- *Partnership of nations:* consultation, cooperation, collective action, united world response

- *Rule:* rule of law, no rule by force, no rule of the jungle

- *Fair play, security, Soviet and American forces working together:* nations prosper and live together

- *Elimination:* of war, of violence

- *Democratic values and new era:* post–Cold War, no threat of terror, reduced and controlled arsenals[45]

Yet the downside is that both the United Nations and the emerging international system under the New World Order display an elitist bias. The powerful nations in the Security Council enjoy veto power, which means that invariably the smaller nations will be under the dominance of the more powerful nations in the United Nations.[46] The same appears to be the case under the New World Order, where there is only one superpower.

AMERICA AND THE NEW WORLD ORDER: HISTORICAL PARALLELS

What is the role of the United States in the New World Order? There are two predominant schools of thought: interventionists and isolationists. One of the more radical versions of the interventionist philosophy is best expressed by Charles Krauthammer:

> The center of the world is the unchallenged superpower, the United States at-
> tended by its Western allies. . . . American preeminence is based on the fact that
> it is the only country with the military, diplomatic, political and economic assets
> to be a decisive player in any conflict in whatever part of the world it chooses to
> involve itself. . . . We are in abnormal times. Our best hope for safety in such
> times, as in difficult times past, is in American strength and will—the strength
> and will to lead a unipolar world, unashamedly laying down the rules of the
> world order and being prepared to enforce them. Compared to the task of de-
> feating fascism and communism, averting chaos is a rather subtle call to great-
> ness. It is not a task we are any more eager to undertake than the great twilight
> struggle just concluded. But it is just as noble and just as necessary.[47]

This position implies that America must carry the burden of policing the
world. America stands at the epicenter of the world, and its policies and behavior should therefore serve as guideposts. Although this position has been
oversimplified and overstated by dissenting scholars, the basic assumption behind the interventionist stance is that the United States, as the world's leading
nation both economically and militarily, will inevitably consent to world leadership. As William A. Rusher notes, "It may be that it [America] will consent
to leadership only reluctantly: will have 'greatness thrust upon it.' But it cannot, it seems to me, escape its destiny."[48]

The isolationist thesis, in contrast, argues that America might decline due
to an "imperial overstretch" if it attempts to intervene in international conflicts and overspend its resources.[49] Jeane J. Kirkpatrick observed, "The time
when Americans should bear such unusual burdens is past. With a return to
'normal' times we can again become a normal nation—and take care of pressing problems of education, family, industry and technology. We can be an independent nation in a world of independent nations."[50] The isolationists
argue that America cannot afford the risk of splurging its resources on some
foreign cause that might be tangential to American national interest. Both interventionists and isolationists present compelling pictures of America's relationship with the rest of the world.

Many U.S. presidents have defined their political philosophy with regard
to America's role in the world. On the one hand, there was the idea of "American exceptionalism"—that America exemplified the ideals of the New World
and thus was destined to "lead the old world from a discredited international
system to a new order."[51] The philosophy of American exceptionalism was reflected in Jeffersonian diplomacy, which espoused the intrinsic merit of American ideals. America represented the "City on a Hill" that shone as a beacon for
the rest of the world. When the rest of the world gazed at this shining city, it
would learn by precept from this new nation. The Jeffersonian tradition was

adopted in the twentieth century by Woodrow Wilson and Franklin Roosevelt and has never really been abandoned since. Wilson articulated the intrinsic goodness present in American ideals such as freedom, and the expansion of freedom across the world thus became his central preoccupation through his notion of collective security and the League of Nations. "It is absolutely necessary," Wilson held, "that a force be created . . . so much greater than the force of any nation now engaged or any alliance hitherto formed or projected that no nation, no probable combination of nations, could face or withstand it."[52] To Wilson, the collective security system was a better alternative for accomplishing the goals of worldwide peace. The old balance-of-power system was an "old and evil system" that had to die; it was thus important to "do away with the old order and establish a new one."[53] Under the umbrella of the League of Nations, the United States would have a unique role to play. Wilson suggested that Americans would act as the "custodians of the spirit of righteousness, of the spirit of even-handed justice, of the spirit of hope which believes in the perfectibility of the law and the perfectibility of human life itself."[54] Wilson stressed that the success of a new international order would depend on the willingness of the United States to take a leadership role in the global system.[55] Similarly, Franklin Roosevelt justified U.S participation in concert with other powers to bring the world out of anarchy. As he described it, the so-called "Four Policemen—the United States, Great Britain, the Soviet Union, and China would have the responsibility to impose order on the rest of the postwar world bombing anyone who would not go along."[56]

On the other hand, there was the Hamiltonian tradition that "eschewed grand ambitions, retaining a belief in military force and preparedness while pursuing a foreign policy tied to limited national interests."[57]

President Bush is an internationalist, following in the footsteps of Wilson; a salient feature of the president's diplomatic rhetoric is underpinned by his insistence on America's role in spreading the gospel of freedom across the globe. The route to freedom may or may not entail traversing the bloody path of war. Under any circumstances, however, aggression must be punished, even if doing so implies a self-contradictory position, of using one evil to combat another. As Bush observed at the beginning of the Gulf War, "every act of aggression unpunished . . . strengthens the forces of chaos and lawlessness that, ultimately, threatens us all."[58] The Wilsonian tradition that the "indivisibility of peace" is inextricably intertwined with U.S security is reinforced in Bush's New World Order rhetoric.[59] Thus, one of the means of safeguarding U.S security consists of disciplining nations that rupture the status quo and upset American plans of furthering the policy of global pacification.

Although the policy of global containment during the Cold War was a worthwhile goal, the depiction of the United States as global policeman became increasingly problematic in a post–Cold War world. Bush thus had to dispel the misconceptions that the international community might have by rhetorically projecting his interpretation of the events during the Gulf War as being synonymous with the interests of the free world. Furthermore, Bush found himself in a rhetorical double bind over what constituted a proper response to Saddam's invasion. On one hand, American passivity might outrage the segment of the international community that looked to the United States as the chief arbiter of world peace. On the other hand, American military intervention would be interpreted by many both in the United States and overseas as a sign of naked aggression. So Bush had to rhetorically depict his view of the New World Order as being the ultimate goal of diplomacy and the only realistic possibility of world peace. In other words, it became a matter of both expediency and rhetorical necessity for Bush to paint Saddam as the enemy of the New World Order. The call to war thus arose out of a rhetorical impulse of meekness, justice, and self-defense, as opposed to rank belligerence. Bush claimed, "This was a war thrust upon us, not a war that we sought. But naked aggression, such as we have seen, must be resisted if it is not to become a pattern. Our success in the Gulf will bring with it not just a new opportunity for peace and stability in a critical part of the world but a chance to build a new world order based upon the principles of collective security and the rule of law."[60] The remarkable ability of the president to portray this rhetorical vision of solidarity against the common enemies of the New World Order helped the United States to look blameless at least momentarily in the eyes of the international community. The war that was "thrust on us" was fought not by the United States alone but by the international community as a whole. America's involvement with the war arose out of a deep necessity to protect the New World Order. Like Armageddon, the battle lines were drawn both rhetorically and militarily. The forces of good were ready to wage war against the forces of evil. America, although on the side of good, nevertheless had to rally the forces of light to support its cause. The United Nations supported the American cause in hastening the birth of the New World Order. Bush noted, "So, part of this new world order has been moved forward by a United Nations that functioned. We might have still been able to stand up and come to the assistance of Kuwait—the United States. I might have said to hell with them, it's right and wrong, it's good and evil, he's evil, our cause is right; and without the United Nations, sent a considerable force to help. But it was enhanced—it is far better to have this collective action where the world—not just the Security Council but the whole General Assembly stood up and condemned it."[61]

Defeating Saddam was a necessary prelude to realizing the New World Order. The concert of nations involved in the Gulf War emerged as a corrective against the expansionist tendencies of Iraq. The expansion of freedom through war was rhetorically legitimated over the expansion of tyranny through annexation. The blossoming of the New World Order under the vision and leadership of the United States would make the rest of the world value the principle of collective security. Bush's rhetoric operated under the assumption that world peace and the collective security of nations required strong American leadership. The United States had the economic strength, military might, and moral will to take up the position of leadership and usher in an era of collective security among the nations. As Arnold Wolfers explains, "promotion of the idea of collective security has created a psychological situation in which the United States cannot turn its back on the concept, not because of what collective security can accomplish . . . but because of what millions of people . . . believe it may accomplish in time. Collective security has come to be the chief symbol of hope that . . . a community of nations will develop in which there will be no more war."[62]

The burden of shouldering this responsibility fell heavily on America. The combined aspirations of millions had to be borne by America, no matter how distant and remote the cause. From a more pragmatic point of view, collective security provided a better alternative to the perpetual tensions of the Cold War in spite of the cold comfort afforded through the "balance of power." Bush jumped on this opportunity and gave life to a nonexisting New World Order as the path that the nations of the world should take to pursue peace and prosperity.

The goals of the New World Order could only be accomplished by a concert of nations. However, the reality of international politics shows that more often than not, the powerful would rule over the weak. Even if a climate of egalitarian politics exists, the nation with more resources inevitably ends up leading. Bush continued in this tradition and exercised the belief that American leadership in a coalition-based war to free one country from another nation would only enhance the image of the United States in the eyes of the world. Said Bush, "I think because of what's happened we won't have to use U.S forces around the world. I think when we say something that is objectively correct—like don't take over a neighbor or you're going to bear responsibility—people are going to listen. Because I think out of all this will be a new-found—let's put it this way: a reestablished credibility for the United States of America."[63]

WHERE DID BUSH GO WRONG?
THE PROBLEM OF DEFINITION

The New World Order happens to be one of those grand phrases that can either inspire devotion or cause instant revulsion. Bush took pains to explain both to the American public and to his international audience that the purpose of the New World Order was to fulfill the historic vision of the United Nations.[64] However, he never specified the parameters under which his rhetorical vision would be implemented. The Gulf War was just one of the initial phases. In his own words, "I'm not talking here of a blueprint that will govern the conduct of nations or some supranational structure or institution. The new world order does not mean surrendering our national interests. It really describes a responsibility imposed by our successes. It refers to new ways of working with other nations to deter aggression and to achieve stability, to achieve prosperity, and, above all, to achieve peace."[65] On one hand, Bush's attempt to spell out the goals of his vision is praiseworthy; on the other hand, Bush did not explain how to get there or define in his own words what the vision was. The lack of a definition made Bush vulnerable to attack from all sides. White House Press Secretary Marlin Fitzwater, when queried about the definition of the New World Order, responded: "Well, I don't think it [the New World Order] ever really got defined. I think he [Bush] saw it as a structure where America would have to be defining its role during the next four years of his presidency. . . . He never tried to lay it out. The problem with that, of course, is that it leaves a vacuum of definition that others can jump in and fill so that people like Pat Buchanan can say that the New World Order means you are turning America's security over to the United Nations."[66]

From Fitzwater's response, it seems likely that Bush would have attempted to define the New World Order and America's role in this new forum in a more systematic way during the second term of his presidency. Yet the lack of definition subjected Bush to severe criticism from both the right and the left. The "vacuum of definitions" created a rhetoric of default, in which a proliferation of definitions created by others became the dominant lenses through which Bush's vision of the New World Order was perceived. Bush's acts of rhetorical omission, in other words, transposed what could have been a unifying rhetorical idiom, the New World Order, into a free-for-all of interpretive utterance.

From the right, Pat Robertson in his influential book *The New World Order* made the equation between the locution and apocalyptic world domination, spearheaded by the Antichrist.[67] Robertson suggests that Bush's endorsement of the New World Order was inadvertently fulfilling the wishes of a "tightly knit cabal whose goal is nothing less than a new order for the human race under the domination of Lucifer and his followers."[68] Robertson employs his "mastery of the rhetorical question as a device for instilling arguments in the reader's mind."[69] For example, he asks: "Is George Bush merely an idealist or are there plans now under way to merge the interests of the United States and the Soviet Union in the United Nations—to substitute 'world order' power for 'balance of power,' and install a socialist 'world order' in place of a free market system?"[70] Robertson screams conspiracy; the New World Order would not only diminish America's sovereignty but also usher in a world government in which an influential few would control everything. "A single thread runs from the White House to the State Department to the Council on Foreign Relations to the Trilateral Commission to secret societies to extreme New Agers. There must be a new world order. It must eliminate national sovereignty. There must be a world government, a world police force, world courts, world banking and currency, and a world elite in charge of it all."[71]

Pat Buchanan's thesis is quite different from Robertson's, yet the common thread in their arguments is that globalism would undermine the sovereignty of America.[72] Buchanan more specifically castigates Bush for his "open borders, open trade" policy. Buchanan summarized his differences with Bush as follows: "[Bush] is a man of graciousness, honor and integrity, who has given a lifetime to his nation's service. But the differences between us are now too deep. . . . He is a globalist and we are nationalists. He believes in some Pax Universalis; we believe in the Old Republic. He would put America's wealth and power at the service of some vague New World Order; we will put America first."[73] Buchanan's economic nationalism, based on the philosophy of "America First," decried the New World Order since the locution smacked of globalist agendas that would ultimately undermine America's sovereignty. Buchanan's vision considered America a fortress, and presented a rhetorical vision of America looking inward. Much of Buchanan's ire was directed against NAFTA, and he looked upon this organization, to borrow Kissinger's phrase, as the "architecture of a new international system . . . a step toward the new world order."[74]

From the left, one of the most vociferous critiques of Bush's New World Order comes from Noam Chomsky. First, Chomsky presents two visions of the New World Order: one proclaimed by the developing countries as an order based on justice, equity, and democracy; and the second, proclaimed by the developed countries (Northern Hemisphere), which celebrates the triumph of Western values. According to Chomsky, "it is George Bush's call for a 'new world order' that resounded, not the plaintive plea of the South, unreported and unheard. The reaction to the two near-simultaneous calls for a New World Order reflects, of course, the power relations. The timing of the two calls is fortuitous, coming at the five hundredth anniversary of the voyages that set in motion the European conquest of the world, establishing Churchill's rich men in their well-appointed habitations while bringing 'dreadful misfortunes' to the victims of 'the savage injustice of the Europeans.'"[75] Chomsky's penchant for hyperbole is well illustrated in his depiction of Bush's vision as a celebration of European conquests; nonetheless, his position that the New World Order represents the aspirations of the industrialized West over the rest of the world is an apt summary of the leftist interpretation of Bush's vision.

Given this backdrop, where did Bush go wrong? His failure to clarify or define the meaning of the New World Order was a rhetorical blunder. A definition of the phrase might have helped to dispel some of the misconceptions associated with the term. The answer perhaps lies in what Fitzwater hypothesized, that the vision would be developed during the second term of his presidency. But time was not on Bush's side. There was to be no second term. To Bush, "the Gulf War put this new world to its first test."[76] Fortunately or unfortunately, it also turned out to be the last test, because there was no programmatic development of this idea beyond the construction of the Gulf War coalition. The world never got to see what the New World Order would look like. Ironically, the end of Bush's term coincided with a phase in world history in which the ominous shadows of the Cold War permanently faded away, yet it was a phase in which the birth pangs of the "New World Order" merely produced a stillborn child.

Although one could make a compelling argument that Bush's lack of definition could work in his favor insofar as he could modify or alter his vision in response to the situation, numerous instances, as illustrated above, negate the case for strategic ambiguity. It would have been more productive if Bush had spelled out his vision of a New World Order as a fulfillment of the United Nations Charter in a more explicit manner. The New World Order would have become much more than a grand and empty abstraction if Bush had enunciated concrete steps as to how his administration, in conjunction with the United Nations, intended to promote freedom and democracy throughout the world. Such a blueprint would have solidified an otherwise grandiose locution that ironically failed to live up to its promise.

NOTES

1. Bush, "Address before a Joint Session of the Congress on the Cessation of the Persian Gulf Conflict," Box 191, Speech File Drafts, White House Office of Speech Writing, OA 8486, 3/6/1991, George Bush Presidential Library, College Station, Texas (hereafter cited as Bush Library).

2. Ibid.

3. George Bush, "Remarks by the President and Secretary of State James A. Baker III at Swearing In Ceremony," Box 1, Speech File Drafts, White House Office of Speech Writing, OA 2771, 1/27/1989, Bush Library.

4. Murray Edelman, *Political Language: Words That Succeed and Policies That Fail* (New York: Academic Press, 1977), 16.

5. Martin J. Medhurst, "Afterword: The Ways of Rhetoric," in *Beyond the Rhetorical Presidency*, ed. Martin J. Medhurst (College Station: Texas A&M University Press, 1996), 219.

6. Dan Jahn, "Memorandum for Tony Snow: Presidential References to the New World Order," Box 191, Speech File Drafts, White House Office of Speech Writing, OA 8486, 6/26/1991, Bush Library.

7. The Charter of the United Nations of June 26, 1945, as amended by the General Assembly Resolution 1991, in *The Charter of the United Nations: A Commentary*, ed. Bruno Simma (Oxford: Oxford University Press, 1994), xix.

8. Richard Falk, Samuel S. Kim, and Saul H. Mendlovitz, eds., *The United Nations and a Just World Order*, Studies on a Just World Order, No. 3 (Boulder, Colo.: Westview Press, 1991).

9. Ibid., 2.

10. Ibid., 3.

11. David Jablonsky, *Paradigm Lost? Transitions and Search for a New World Order* (Westport, Conn.: Praeger, 1995), 64.

12. Ibid., 70.

13. Ibid., 22.

14. Falk, Kim, and Mendlovitz, eds., *United Nations and a Just World Order*, 3.

15. "Excerpts from President's Speech," *New York Times*, September 27, 1988, 6.

16. George Bush, "Inaugural Address," January 20, 1989, online document available at: <http:www.csdl.tamu.edu/bushlib/papers/1989/89012000.html>

17. Stephen R. Graubard, ed., *Exit from Communism* (New Brunswick, N.J.: Transaction Publishers, 1993).

18. Zbigniew Brzezinski, *The Grand Failure* (New York: Scribner's, 1989), 252.

19. Lea Brilmayer, *American Hegemony: Political Morality in a One-Superpower World* (New Haven: Yale University Press, 1994).

20. George Bush, *National Security Strategy of the United States, 1991–1992* (New York: Brassey's, 1992), 7.

21. Bush, "Remarks by the President and Secretary of State James A. Baker III at Swearing In Ceremony."

22. George Bush, "Remarks and a Question-and-Answer Session at a Meeting of the Economic Club in New York," in *Public Papers of the Presidents of the United States, 1991, Book 1* (Washington, D.C.: U.S Government Printing Office, 1992), 117–27.

23. George Bush, "Address before a Joint Session of the Congress on the State of the Union," January 28, 1992, online document available at: <http://www.csdl.tamu.edu/bushlib/papers/1992/92012801.html>

24. Thomas Kane, "Foreign Policy Suppositions and Commanding Ideas," *Argumentation and Advocacy* 28 (1991): 80–90.

25. George Bush, "State of the Union 1991," *Vital Speeches of the Day* 56 (1989–90): 674–75.

26. Martin J. Medhurst, "Eisenhower's Rhetorical Leadership," in *Eisenhower's War of Words: Rhetoric and Leadership,* ed. Martin J. Medhurst (East Lansing: Michigan State University, 1994), 291.

27. George Bush, "Address before the 45th General Assembly of the United Nations in New York City," Box 191, Speech File Drafts, White House Office of Speech Writing, OA 8486, 10/1/1990, Bush Library.

28. George Bush, "Remarks at a Meeting of the Economic Club of New York," Box 191, Speech File Drafts, White House Office of Speech Writing, OA 8486, 2/6/1991, Bush Library.

29. George Bush, "Interview with Middle Eastern Journalists," Box 191, Speech File Drafts, White House Office of Speech Writing, OA 8486, 3/8/1991, Bush Library.

30. Ibid.

31. Simma, ed., *Charter of the United Nations: A Commentary,* xx.

32. Bush, "Interview with Middle Eastern Journalists."

33. Brilmayer, *American Hegemony,* 169.

34. Ibid.

35. George Bush, "Address before a Joint Session of the Congress on the Persian Gulf Conflict and the Federal Budget Deficit," Box 191, Speech File Drafts, White House Office of Speech Writing, OA 8486, 09/11/1990, Bush Library.

36. Ibid.

37. George Bush, Address before the 45th General Assembly of the United Nations in New York City," Box 191, Speech File Drafts, White House Office of Speech Writing, OA 8486, 10/1/1990, Bush Library; Bush, "Address before a Joint Session of the Congress on the Persian Gulf Conflict and the Federal Budget Deficit."

38. U.N. Charter, Chapter VII, Article 39, in Simma, ed., *Charter of the United Nations: A Commentary,* xxvi.

39. Simma, ed., *Charter of the United Nations: A Commentary,* xxvi.

40. Brilmayer, *American Hegemony.*

41. George Bush, "Remarks and an Exchange with Reporters Following a Discussion with Prime Minister Margaret Thatcher in Paris, France," Box 191, Speech File Drafts, White House Office of Speech Writing, OA 8486, 11/19/1990, Bush Library.

42. Kenneth Burke, *On Symbols and Society,* ed. Joseph R. Gusfield (Chicago: University of Chicago Press, 1989), 181–82.

43. Ibid., 182.

44. George Bush, "Remarks at Maxwell Air Force Base War College in Montgomery, Alabama, April 13, 1991," Box 191, Speech File Drafts, White House Office of Speech Writing, OA 8486, 4/13/1991, Bush Library.

45. Jahn, "Memorandum for Tony Snow: Presidential References to New World Order."

46. Noam Chomsky, *World Orders: Old and New* (New York: Columbia University Press, 1994).

47. Charles Krauthammer, "Unipolar Moment," in *Rethinking America's Security: Beyond*

Cold War to New World Order, ed. Graham Allison and Gregory F. Treverton (New York: W. W. Norton, 1992), 296–98, 306.

48. William A. Rusher, *Conservative Chronicle,* January 1, 1991.

49. Paul Kennedy, *The Rise and Fall of Great Powers: Economic Change and Military Conflict from 1500 to 2000* (New York: Random House, 1987).

50. Jeane J. Kirkpatrick, in *The New World Order: Opposing Viewpoints,* ed. David L. Bender and Bruno Leone (San Diego, Calif.: Greenhaven Press, 1991), 76.

51. Jablonsky, *Paradigm Lost?* 65.

52. James Brown Scott, ed., *President Wilson's Foreign Policy* (New York: Oxford University Press, 1918), 248.

53. Ray S. Baker and William E. Dodd, eds., *The Public Papers of Woodrow Wilson: War and Peace,* 6 vols. (New York: Harper, 1927), 1:342, 2:234–35.

54. Ibid., 3:147–48.

55. Jablonsky, *Paradigm Lost?*

56. John Lewis Gaddis, *Strategies of Containment: A Critical Appraisal of Post-War American National Security Policy* (New York: Oxford University Press, 1982), 10.

57. Jablonsky, *Paradigm Lost?* 66.

58. Robert W. Tucker, "Brave New World Orders," *New Republic* 206, no. 8 (February 24, 1992), 26.

59. Jablonsky, *Paradigm Lost?* 66.

60. George Bush, "Remarks on the Observance of National Black History Month," Box 191, Speech File Drafts, White House Office of Speech Writing, OA 8486, 2/25/1991, Bush Library.

61. Bush, "Interview with Middle Eastern Journalists."

62. Arnold Wolfers, *Discord and Collaboration* (Baltimore: Johns Hopkins University Press, 1962), 197.

63. Bush quoted in Robert W. Tucker and David C. Hendrickson, *Imperial Temptation: The New World Order and America's Purpose* (New York: Council of Foreign Relations Press, 1992), 153.

64. Bush, "Address before a Joint Session of Congress on the Cessation of the Gulf War Conflict," Box 191, Speech File Drafts, White House Office of Speech Writing, OA 8486, 3/6/1991, Bush Library.

65. Bush, "Remarks at Maxwell Air Force Base War College in Montgomery, Alabama."

66. Marlin Fitzwater, interview with Wynton Hall, December 10, 1998, 1:00 P.M. (Eastern Time).

67. Pat Robertson, *The New World Order* (Dallas: Word Publishing, 1991).

68. Ibid., 37.

69. James Arnt Aune, *Selling the Free Market* (New York: Guilford Press, 2002), 238.

70. Robertson, *New World Order,* 58.

71. Ibid., 6.

72. Patrick J. Buchanan, *The Great Betrayal: How American Sovereignty and Social Justice Are Being Sacrificed to the Gods of the Global Economy* (Boston: Little, Brown, 1998).

73. Ibid., 260. Buchanan outlines his manifesto of economic nationalism by attacking NAFTA and Bush's New World Order, especially in chap. 14.

74. Ibid., 264.

75. Chomsky, *World Orders,* 7–8.

76. Bush, "Address before a Joint Session of Congress on the Cessation of the Gulf War Conflict."

CHAPTER 6

Political Truancy: George Bush's Claim to the Mantle of "Education President"

HOLLY G. MCINTUSH

Public sentiment is everything. With public sentiment nothing can fail, without it nothing can succeed.
Abraham Lincoln

When George Bush campaigned in 1988 to be the "education president," he left people wondering, "But what are his actual goals?" Four years later, following two major legislative initiatives, two secretaries of education, a governors' summit, and countless ceremonial speeches, that question remained unanswered. Was Bush simply trying to place education on the legislative agenda? Or was he really interested in enacting specific proposals? In either case, it seems that Bush failed in his effort to be *known as* the education president. His speeches proposing specific legislation were not well publicized, and his ceremonial speeches and photo ops left the public cold—feeling as if his campaign pledge was simply an attempt to capture votes. Yet there is a Bush record on educational issues, and an examination of that record reveals that he did pursue reform. However, as a Republican who believed in a limited role for the federal government, he faced a challenge. Bush failed in his attempt to be known as the education president for two reasons: first, because his goals and the desires of the nation were incompatible; and second, because his campaign lacked focus.

THE EDUCATION PRESIDENCY

Until recently, education has always been of marginal concern to presidents. From George Washington forward, two major motifs have emerged in presidential rhetoric about education policy. First, education is always linked to other issues and concerns. Second, education is viewed as primarily the responsibility of state and local governments.

Most often, education has been seen as a means to an end, rather than an end in itself. As education policy analyst Janet Kerr-Tener notes, "When education has appeared as a top priority, it has often done so as a handmaiden to other pressing national concerns."[1] Francis Keppel, U.S. commissioner of education from 1962 to 1965, noted four themes that have advanced education policy. The first theme, seen in the rhetoric of Presidents Washington through Jefferson, is that education is a means to break down factions and create a national identity. From the Civil War through Theodore Roosevelt's administration, education policy relied on the theme of incorporating new citizens (immigrants and former slaves) into active citizenship. Starting with Teddy Roosevelt and going through World War II, we can find the third theme: education as a means to economic development and a tool in international rivalries. The fourth theme, education as a right of all citizens as citizens, was first promoted by Franklin Roosevelt.[2] These same themes also underlie the rhetoric of the postwar presidents.

While virtually every president talked about education, they worked from the premise that while the nation has an *interest* in education, state and local governments have *responsibility* and *control* of education policy. Thomas Jefferson believed that a constitutional amendment was necessary before the federal government could even become involved in education policy. However, beginning with Franklin Roosevelt, and escalating with Lyndon Johnson, the federal government has played an increasing role in education policy, justifying its actions through the four social interests outlined by Keppel.

With the end of World War II and the beginning of the Cold War, presidents began to take new interest in education policy. Franklin Roosevelt's administration undertook two initiatives related to the war that had drastic implications for higher education. The first was the use of universities to conduct scientific research for the war effort; the second was the G.I. Bill. The motivation behind the G.I. Bill was a fear that the nation's economy could not support all the young men returning from war. Rather than have them immediately face high unemployment rates, the federal government provided funds for them to go to college. After the war, President Truman focused on university education. He appointed the Zook Commission on Higher Education and then sent proposals for college financial aid to Congress in 1949, as recommended by the commission's report.[3]

While Presidents Roosevelt and Truman made changes in higher education to aid the war effort, Dwight Eisenhower promoted education legislation to help win the Cold War. Motivated by the Soviet launchings of Sputnik I and II in 1957, Eisenhower sent the National Defense Education Act (NDEA) to Congress. This legislation emphasized math, science, and foreign languages in an attempt to defend the nation through economic and technical advances.[4] As Keppel, who oversaw administration of the NDEA during his tenure as commissioner of education, noted, "We were supposed to beat the Soviets with science teaching and the teaching of foreign languages."[5]

During the Kennedy and Johnson administrations, the focus shifted from increasing international competition to decreasing domestic competition. Legislation was aimed at elementary and secondary education in attempts to give African Americans and the poor a more equal economic and social foothold. Lyndon Johnson, a former schoolteacher, had a personal dedication to education reform. During the Johnson administration, Congress passed several pieces of education legislation, including the Elementary and Secondary Education Act of 1965, Head Start, and the National Teacher Corps. Johnson's education commissioner, Harold Howe II, summed up the president's commitment to education reform: "Committee chairmen in the Congress were continually practically harassed by Lyndon Johnson, who knew the details of much of this legislation vastly better than many of the bureaucrats trying to get it through. . . . The core of his personal interest in all this was his own commitment to poor and disadvantaged people in the United States. He believed that education was the instrument by which they could be helped to pick up themselves by their own bootstraps and move themselves ahead economically in the society."[6] Johnson, against the recommendation of his advisers, also took his concern for education reform to the public in a separate education address, in which he emphasized the importance of education and "freedom from ignorance" as a right of all Americans.[7]

Following the efforts of Kennedy and Johnson, Congress embraced education as an issue and began to take the initiative on education legislation. Samuel Halperin and David L. Clark note that "congressional action on behalf of education legislation and appropriation had been so strong that the budget of the old Office of Education multiplied fourfold *after* Johnson left the presidency. So the efforts of the Nixon and Ford administrations were, by and large, directed at holding that line."[8]

Carter also faced a zealous Congress, backed by lobbying from the National Education Association (NEA). He spent the first two years of his administration trying to get Congress to spend *less* money on education. Then he inserted a new issue into the debate: the creation of the Department of Education. During the 1976 presidential campaign, Carter promised the NEA that he would create a cabinet-level department. By following through on his campaign promise, Carter was able to satisfy education advocates from within and outside Congress, while directing their attention to debates over how the department should be organized, rather than fighting over how much federal spending should be increased.[9]

President Reagan was committed to cutting federal spending on education. During fiscal years 1981 and 1982, Reagan achieved education budget cuts nearing 20 percent. He also transformed many programs into block grants, thus giving responsibility for education reform back to the states.[10] One of the most influential reports to come out of the Reagan administration was *A Nation at Risk: The Imperative for Educational Reform,* variously described as a "best seller," and a "well-crafted doomsday document," which claimed that American students were graduating from high school with a poorer education than their parents had received and were not prepared to compete in a global economy.[11] Reagan and his education secretary William Bennett took advantage of the alarm caused by *A Nation at Risk* to shift the focus of education reform to issues that were more in line with Reagan's ideology. Some analysts still argue that the administration's biggest achievement in education was shifting how the nation talked about reform. Discussion in the Reagan years focused on state and local government, and concerns about how education influences economic productivity, rather than on issues of equal access and social welfare. Reagan had originally promised to eliminate the newly formed Department of Education, which he termed a "bureaucratic monstrosity"; however, the administration eventually decided that this would cost more time, money, and effort than it was worth.[12]

Even while Reagan was urging devolution to the states, he was advancing the idea that the nation has a stake in education reform. The idea that presidents and Congress should be concerned with education policy has become firmly ensconced in our political culture, as noted by Kerr-Tener: "Judging by the last 45 years, education and presidential politics have, like an old married couple, grown rather accustomed to one another. Every president since Harry Truman has paid tribute to education. . . . Education as a subject for rhetorical pieties ranks right up there with jobs, motherhood, and apple pie."[13] George Bush was aware of education's saliency to the public. He responded to the public outcry for education reform that came with *A Nation at Risk* by campaigning to become "the education president," a phrase he first used on January 6, 1988, in a speech at Manchester, New Hampshire.

GEORGE BUSH AS "THE EDUCATION PRESIDENT"

From the beginning, political commentators, analysts, and fellow politicians were cynical about Bush's campaign promise. This cynicism was well expressed in the following aphorism: "In some ways you might think of the term 'education president' as something of an oxymoron, like 'military intelligence,' 'jumbo shrimp,' 'Vice President Quayle.'"[14] The reasons for this cynicism varied. Some Democrats charged that it was simply an attempt to garner votes and that Bush never really cared about education. Pat Williams, Democratic congressional representative and chair of the Education and Labor subcommittee on postsecondary education, told *CQ Weekly Report* that he suspected education was simply the "issue *du jour*" and that Bush's strategy consisted solely of ceremonial photo opportunities.[15] Others, such as Denis Doyle, education policy analyst at the Hudson Institute, expressed a more general doubt that there could ever be an education president because of the primacy of state and local control. Still others thought that Bush's ideology would keep him from spending enough money to satisfy the public and education lobbyists. Phil Kuntz, *CQ Weekly Report*'s education reporter, keyed on the challenge facing Bush: "As a fiscally conservative Republican, Bush likely never will propose enough to satisfy the nation's education establishment and its powerful Democratic allies in Congress. While Republicans on Capitol Hill will always sing his praises, the pragmatic Bush probably won't satisfy many conservatives outside Congress who want more radical change than he's likely to attempt."[16]

While commentators were skeptical that Bush's campaign promise was more than just that, the public had faith in their new president. Several polls taken near the beginning of his administration measured the public's belief that George Bush would achieve education reform. When asked in a Gallup poll if he would be able to improve educational standards, 74 percent answered yes.[17] Similarly, a CBS News/*New York Times* poll asked the question, "Do you think George Bush will or will not be able to significantly improve education in this country?" and found that 62 percent answered "will" while only 30 percent answered "will not."[18]

Even though history has not recognized George Bush as the education president, there is substantial evidence to support his sincerity. While in office, Bush sent two major initiatives to Congress, held an education summit with the governors to establish national education goals, and initiated an ongoing partnership with the governors to achieve those goals. An examination of Bush's views on education policy and his major efforts to achieve those ends shows a president who was initially dedicated to reform. His initial attempts, however, were to no avail and Bush's efforts dwindled during the second half of his term. Bush failed to become known as the education president despite the early endeavors because his actions lacked focus and were not adequately linked to the goals set forth in 1990 or to the reasons the public was urging reform.

Bush's Education Philosophy

George Bush was "a conservative in the classical Tory tradition of public service."[19] He was a moderate who did not believe in government activism. Political scientist George Edwards described Bush's governing philosophy as one of "prudent stewardship, practicing a politics of moderation, but not one that was oriented toward laying the groundwork for significant changes in domestic policy."[20] George Bush did believe that social problems should be actively eliminated, but this should be achieved through community service rather than government action. This theme can be seen throughout his political life. In 1964 Bush responded positively to the idea behind Lyndon Johnson's Great Society programs: "A better life for all, elimination of poverty and disease, fair play in civil rights and domestic tranquility on all fronts." However, Bush doubted "that a great society can or should be built solely by the federal government—or any government."[21]

Bush's reaction to education reform was much the same as his reaction to the War on Poverty. He believed that education was a local responsibility and required the involvement of state and local governments, businesses, and entire communities. He wanted the federal government to talk about education reform and help lift restrictions to allow the states to enact reform; however, he did not want the federal government to issue more regulations or spend more money. His views on education are best expressed in the following excerpt, included in countless responses to citizens' letters, signed by him or by members of his staff: "I believe that there is an appropriate role for the Federal Government to serve as a *catalyst* for innovation, accountability, and choice throughout the education system . . . Education Secretary Lamar Alexander and his team will be working with the Nation's Governors, with educators, with the private sector, and with Americans in all walks of life to advance our goals. However, to make America's schools the best in the world, concerned citizens like you will have to be involved."[22] Notably absent from the list of entities with which the administration will work is the Congress.

The public's views on education were quite different, and the Bush administration was well aware of the discrepancy. In a September 12, 1989, memo to the president, Roger B. Porter, assistant to the president for economic and domestic policy, cited the results of the twenty-first annual Gallup poll on education. Gallup had asked the public what issues in education reform mattered most and why. Results showed that most Americans cited economic reasons for wanting their children to have a better education (33 percent, job opportunities/better job; 25 percent, better life; and 15 percent, financial security). In order to give their children a quality education, Americans desired "national goals and standards for education (70 percent), national public school curricula (69 percent), and national testing programs to measure achievement (77 percent)."[23] Eighty-three percent thought that something needed to be done to improve schools in poorer communities, and 80 percent favored more state and/or federal assistance so that finances would not keep students who were admitted to college from attending.[24]

As these results show, the public wanted the federal government to become more involved and to spend more money—the very things that George Bush hoped to avoid. From the beginning, therefore, Bush's views and public opinion about education reform were on a collision course. As education scholar James Guthrie noted, "It is difficult for presidents to lead where no one wants to follow."[25] But George Bush did not simply give up after learning the poll results. He still went forward with attempts to bring about his own brand of education reform.

Bush's Education Initiatives

Education reform was listed among George Bush's goals from the beginning of his presidency. In a February 9, 1989, prime-time address to a joint session of Congress on the administration's goals, Bush spoke about the importance of education reform, carrying on Reagan's theme that we must have reform in order to compete in a global economy: "But the most important competitiveness program of all is one which improves education in America. . . . In education, we cannot tolerate mediocrity. I want to cut that dropout rate and make America a more literate nation, because what it really comes down to is this: The longer our graduation lines are today, the shorter our unemployment lines will be tomorrow." This very pragmatic approach is commensurate with the public's views as expressed in the Gallup poll. Bush then goes on to introduce more specific proposals:

> So, tonight I'm proposing the following initiatives: the beginning of a $500 million program to reward America's best schools, merit schools; the creation of spe-

cial Presidential awards for the best teachers in every State, because excellence should be rewarded; the establishment of a new program of National Science Scholars, one each year for every Member of the House and Senate, to give this generation of students a special incentive to excel in science and mathematics; the expanded use of magnet schools, which give families and students greater choice; and a new program to encourage alternative certification, which will let talented people from all fields teach in our classrooms. I've said I'd like to be the "Education President." And tonight, I'd ask you to join me by becoming the "Education Congress."[26]

While Bush explicitly links the reasons for reform to the economy, he leaves the audience free to make the connection between his specific proposals and the economic impact. He never spells out how his programs will directly help American students compete in the job market, leaving himself vulnerable to the attack that he is simply embracing vague goals with no substantive reform.

In April 1989 Bush officially sent his "Educational Excellence" initiative to Congress. In his transmission message to Congress and on fact sheets delivered to the press, Bush listed four principles as the driving force behind the legislation: (1) excellence and success; (2) helping those in financial need; (3) choice and flexibility; and (4) accountability. The bill contained seven separate initiatives supposedly aimed at fulfilling these principles. But, once again, the president did not lay out the links between his proposals and the four themes, nor did he connect the four themes to the public's economic concerns.[27]

While the bill was presented in such a way as to appear broad and vague enough not to cause much controversy, it still drew fire from both ends of the political spectrum. Liberal education interest groups criticized the plan for not allocating enough money.[28] Some congressional Democrats, such as Senator Claiborne Pell, chairman of the Senate subcommittee on education, actually praised the ideas contained in Bush's package; however, they were not willing to cut funding to existing programs in order to fund the new legislation. Augustus F. Hawkins, chair of the House education committee, was not as open to the president's proposal. He told *CQ Weekly Report*, "This legislation has no future on Capitol Hill, since the president is attempting to strip programs long supported by Congress to pay for new initiatives of questionable value."[29] While Democrats complained about the lack of funds, Republicans criticized the Bush initiative for spending too much and not including a private school tuition voucher program.[30] As the *San Diego Tribune* noted, Bush's conciliatory approach was actually doing more harm than good: "Welcome to George Bush's world of political fence-straddling, where the White House frequently compromises itself into a no-win situation."[31]

When the Senate subcommittee began to negotiate the bill, it was quickly amended and reworked. The subcommittee version passed the Senate with a vote of 92 to 8, after suffering a cut of over $100 million of Bush's initiatives aimed primarily at elementary and secondary education and receiving an increase of twice that amount in provisions aimed at higher education.[32] The House delayed even considering the legislation until 1990. When it did take up the bill, the debate was characterized by intense partisanship.

While Democrats and Republicans were battling it out in Congress, Bush called the nation's governors together for an education summit on September 27–28, 1989. This was a high-profile, public relations–rich move by President Bush. The week before the event, *CQ Weekly Report* stated:

> The 24-hour event is the first time a president has called the governors together to discuss education, and only the third time a president has ever called them together on a single issue.
>
> For that reason, it's a dangerous move at a crucial time for education policy. Hopes and expectations are running high that the event will be substantive, and the nation's parents appear hungry for action.[33]

Following the summit, Bush and the governors issued a joint statement announcing two broad reform objectives of flexibility and accountability and expressing their intent to set national performance goals for the nation's school systems by 1990.[34]

Overall, the public was not impressed with the summit. Education professionals reiterated the theme that the federal government should invest more money in education. They viewed the event as a media opportunity for Bush and the governors that would not necessarily help bring about real reform.[35] *Washington Post* staff writer Jim Naughton called into question the substantive value of the summit. He noted the short length (ninety minutes) of the three policy meetings and argued that "the governors could be said to have 'met' with the president in the same sense that the tens of thousands of people who crammed his inaugural balls could be said to have 'partied' with him." He questioned "how the summit could be simultaneously 'historic' and uneventful."[36]

The governors' summit was not simply a media event, however. It led to the adoption of national education goals and the creation of a "National Education Goals Panel," which in turn gave rise to an ongoing partnership between the federal government and the nation's governors. In Bush's January 31, 1990, state of the union address, he unveiled the six national performance goals, which were officially adopted by the governors' association the next month:

• By the year 2000, every child must start school ready to learn.

• The United States must increase the high school graduation rate to no less than 90 percent.

• In critical subjects—at the fourth, eighth, and twelfth grades—we must assess our students' performance.

• By the year 2000, U.S. students must be the first in the world in math and science achievement.

• Every American adult must be a skilled, literate worker and citizen.

• Every school must offer the kind of disciplined environment that makes it possible for our students to learn—and every school in America must be drug free.[37]

House Speaker Tom Foley criticized the goals as mere rhetoric because the president did not call for significant budget increases: "While I commend the President for his desire to be known as 'the education President,' I question whether he can achieve that goal by proposing a meager 2 percent increase in the Federal spending on Education. The simple fact is we don't have a 2 percent education problem in this country. The education gap is much more daunting."[38] After the announcement of the goals, Representative Hawkins sent a letter to President Bush informing him that on March 7, 1990, the House subcommittee on elementary, secondary, and vocational education had voted to further delay consideration of the Education Excellence Act of 1989 because they wanted to first learn how the earlier bill fit in with the goals announced by the president in the state of the union address.[39] Led by Hawkins, House Democrats then proposed a bill entitled "Equity and Excellence in Education Implementation Act." Hawkins told *CQ Weekly Report,* "Having a set of goals for achievement in education is quite laudable. But, as most first-year management students know, having goals without a plan to achieve them is not very useful."[40] Like the bill the Senate had passed the term before, the House Democrats' bill included parts of several other pieces of legislation before Congress, called for large budget increases, and was aimed at meeting the goals Bush promoted.[41] Eventually, the education bills died in the Senate in 1990 when members of Bush's own party threatened to filibuster.[42]

Despite Hawkins's claims of inactivity, Bush did not just mention the goals in the state of the union address and then forget about them. In order to achieve these goals, which were set by the administration and members of the National Governors' Association Task Force on Education, with input from business leaders and professional educators, Bush established a National Education Goals Panel, consisting of cabinet members, governors, business leaders, and White House officials, to "measure and monitor progress towards these goals."[43] To those ends, each year the administration issued a "Report to the Nation's Governors" on the administration's progress. To develop the report, members of the president's staff solicited information from each of the departments and compiled a list of what each was doing to promote the achievement of the administration's goals.[44]

In 1991 George Bush reinvigorated his drive to become the education president by appointing former Tennessee governor Lamar Alexander to be education secretary. In December 1990 Bush had requested a resignation from former Department of Education head Lauro F. Cavazos, who was "viewed as ineffective by members of Congress, White House officials, and the education community."[45] Lamar Alexander, in contrast, "gained wide attention [as governor] . . . for pushing a major education initiative through a Democratic-controlled legislature."[46] Furthermore, Alexander had already shown interest in helping to develop a national education reform strategy. In December 1989, a full year before Cavazos was asked to resign, Alexander had sent chief of staff John Sununu a copy of a letter in which he discussed possible strategies for the president to use in promoting reform.[47] In January 1991, after having been nominated for secretary of education, Alexander sent a memo to the president in which he expressed support for the six goals laid out by the president and the governors, and stated, "I see my job as helping you become the Education President." Part of that plan included advocating a "state of education" address, similar to the one given by President Johnson. However, the suggested remarks by Alexander were taken by Bush to be recommendations for points to be made in the 1991 state of the union address.[48]

In early 1991 Bush sent his second initiative to Congress. Dubbed "America 2000," this initiative was based on the objectives laid out in the governors' summit. It included plans to set national standards and tests, an initiative that promoted state government experiments with school choice plans, a "flexibility" plan allowing schools to disregard federal regulations in attempts to improve students' achievement, grants for "merit schools" and "governor's academies," merit pay for teachers, and establishment of "New American Schools."[49] President Bush unveiled the plan in his April 19 "Address to the Nation on the National Education Strategy."

In this address Bush made the first concerted effort to refute the argument promoted by Democrats and education lobbyists and adopted by much of the nation—that the solution to America's education problems lay in more federal funding. He refuted this in two ways. First, he attacked the underlying premise that spending more money would improve the nation's education system. "Let's stop trying to measure progress in terms of money spent. We spend 33 percent more per pupil in 1991 than we did in 1981—33 percent more in real constant dollars. And I don't think there's a person anywhere, anywhere in the country, who would say that we've seen a 33-percent improvement in our school's performance."[50] Aware that his new proposal could also be attacked for not mandating enough federal involvement, Bush also negated the premise that the federal government can improve the education system. "People who want Washington to solve our educational problems are missing the point."[51] Bush sought to overthrow these minor premises so that the conclusion reached would not be that the federal government should spend more on education to benefit society, because under this conclusion, Bush's education proposal would not make the grade.

Therefore, Bush provided his own major premise as a replacement: individual involvement and responsibility are necessary and sufficient to improve schools. "Dollar bills don't educate students," Bush proclaimed. "Education depends on committed communities." And "what happens here in Washington won't matter half as much as what happens in each school, each local community, and yes, in each home." George Bush created an enthymeme whose conclusion fit his ideology: "We who would be revolutionaries must accept responsibilities for our schools. . . . It's time we held our schools—and ourselves—accountable for results." Bush ended his address by appealing to "all Americans to be Points of Light in the Crusade that counts the most: the crusade to prepare our children and ourselves for the exciting future that looms ahead."

Lamar Alexander recognized the importance, for the success of Bush's education policy, of defeating the liberal argument for more federal money and replacing it with a sense of volunteerism. "In an America 2000 Community, individual action and community commitment are fundamental to the creation of better schools. We need to get this part of the America 2000 strategy out in front of the public," he said.[52] Bush's chance to be known as the education president rested on the public's acceptance of this premise. If the public agreed, it would be satisfied that Bush had indeed been a "catalyst" for change. If not, it would continue to view his campaign promises and ceremonial speeches as "empty rhetoric."

Reaction to Bush's second initiative was mixed. Some viewed it as a desperate move to prevent being charged in the 1992 campaign with having broken his earlier promise to become the education president.[53] Education lobbyists offered reserved praise for the proposal as substantive reform. Some questioned the setting of national tests, concerned that the federal government's role in education might become too large. Others backed all the proposals but complained that the initiative did not allocate enough money to meet the goals.[54]

Once again, Democrats in the House and Senate criticized the president's plan for not allocating enough money, and countered with a plan of their own, aimed at meeting Bush's goals, that included some of his original initiatives. Both bills included provisions for higher education that the administration opposed. The inclusion of a school choice initiative sparked much controversy. While the House bill included the school choice initiative, the Senate refused to accept it. The administration threatened to veto the bill over both the school choice exclusion and the inclusion of large increases in funding for higher education.[55] During negotiations, *CQ Weekly Report* quoted a Bush aide as saying, "We're not going to eat a whole bunch of stuff in higher ed that we don't like just to get some stuff that's marginally important."[56] Bush's more adamant and controversial stand on education was considered to be election cycle politics, and caused many Democrats to stand even firmer against compromise. Senator John Kerry, Democrat from Massachusetts, said, "If he intends to veto everything, we ought to put out things that demonstrate the differences between him and us. You're going to see a lot more of that."[57] However, by the time the House and Senate conference committee agreed on a bill, neither party was happy. In the end, Bush's second chance for substantial education legislation was stopped, like the first, by a Republican filibuster.[58]

THE EDUCATION PRESIDENT?

At the end of four years, was President Bush viewed as the education president? Not by many. An editorial in *U.S. News and World Report* stated that Bush had been the education president "only in the sense that Herbert Hoover was the prosperity president."[59] In a review of the major candidates' stances on different issues, *Technology Review* said that while "George Bush has talked more about education" than Bill Clinton or Paul Tsongas, he "has accomplished little."[60] Bush's efforts to become known as the education president failed because they lacked focus and were not adequately linked to the goals set forth in 1990 or the reasons the public was urging reform.

In his reports to the governors Bush drew upon any program being administered by any department that was somehow related, however remotely, to the six education goals. Many of the initiatives had been in place long before the goals were established. He then used this as evidence that he was truly making progress toward improving education. But by including so much information, Bush actually undermined the efforts of his administration. As education secretary Lauro F. Cavazos said in reference to the first annual report to the governors, "The document is a hodgepodge of material that does not seem to have a focus under each of the goals."[61] The need for focus was a theme reiterated by several presidential advisers and friends of the administration, yet it was never really heeded.

Further, Bush did not adequately link the administration's activities to the reasons given for reform. Recognizing that parents' desires for their children to have a good education stemmed from their desire for their children to be economically stable, Bush latched on to this as a reason for America to attempt reform. Particularly in the April 18, 1991, "Address to the Nation," he referred to the necessity of a good education system in order for America to compete in a global economy. However, in that same address, Bush did not then link the six goals to job preparation, nor did he connect his proposals to the six goals. He should have explicitly laid out how meeting these goals would improve America's economy and then told the public how his proposals directly advanced these goals. As a Tory, he of all people should have known that promoting reform for reform's sake is not sufficient.

Even so, George Bush's commitment to education reform was substantial when compared with that of the other postwar presidents. Bush, however, was going against the grain of public opinion by advocating volunteerism and steering clear of more federal spending and/or regulation. While he attempted to overcome these rhetorical hurdles by refuting the premise that federal involvement was the solution to the nation's education problems, he did not articulate his position often enough or clearly enough. The nation would only have accepted his new premise if it could have seen a link between the president's arguments and improved economic status. The public failed to perceive such a link. In the end, Bush's ideology and lack of rhetorical focus doomed his chances to be known as the education president.

NOTES

1. Janet Kerr-Tener, "Presidential Politics and Educational Commissions," in *The Presidency and Education,* ed. Kenneth W. Thompson (New York: University Press of America, 1990), 82.

2. Francis Keppel, "From Washington to Johnson," in *Presidency and Education,* ed. Thompson, 1:6–8.

3. Ibid., 8–9.

4. Samuel Halperin and David L. Clark, "Some Historical and Contemporary Perspectives," in *Presidency and Education,* ed. Thompson, 1:19; and Kerr-Tener, "Presidential Politics," 82–83.

5. Keppel, "From Washington to Johnson," 10.

6. Harold Howe II, "LBJ as the Education President," in *Presidency and Education,* ed. Thompson, 1:102.

7. Ibid.

8. Halperin and Clark, "Some Historical and Contemporary Perspectives," 21.

9. Ibid.; Kerr-Tener, "Presidential Politics," 81.

10. Halperin and Clark, "Some Historical and Contemporary Perspectives," 24.

11. Ibid., 25; Kerr-Tener, "Presidential Politics," 86; National Commission on Excellence in Education, *A Nation at Risk: The Imperative for Educational Reform* (Washington, D.C.: U.S. Government Printing Office, April 1983).

12. Halperin and Clark, "Some Historical and Contemporary Perspectives," 24–25; Kerr-Tener, "Presidential Politics," 86–87.

13. Kerr-Tener, "Presidential Politics," 79–80.

14. Edward Fiske, "George Bush as the Education President," in *Presidency and Education,* ed. Thompson, 1:122.

15. Phil Kuntz, "Bush Puts Focus on Schools with Words, Not Money," *CQ Weekly Report,* September 23, 1998, 2459.

16. Ibid., 2458.

17. Gallup Poll, January 24–26, 1989, cited in George C. Edwards III, "George Bush and the Public Presidency: The Politics of Inclusion," in *The Bush Presidency: First Appraisals,* ed. Colin Campbell, S.J., and Bert A. Rockman (Chatham, N.J.: Chatham House Publishers, 1991), 143.

18. CBS News/*New York Times* poll, January 12–15, 1989, cited in Edwards, "George Bush and the Public Presidency," 143.

19. Herbert S. Parmet, *George Bush: The Life of a Lone Star Yankee* (New York: Scribner's, 1997), 118.

20. George C. Edwards III, "Evaluating the Bush Presidency: The Travails of a Tory," *American Review of Politics* 14 (1993): 183–95.

21. Bush, quoted in Parmet, *George Bush,* 116.

22. Letter, George Bush to Fred R. Williams, May 8, 1991, Doc. Number 249707, WHORM: Subject File, Bush Presidential Records, George Bush Presidential Library (hereafter cited as Bush Library), College Station, Texas. Emphasis added. There were several letters in the Education Subject files that contained this paragraph. For more examples, see also Box 28, Folder [269000–272999] [2] and Box 29, Folder [275648–275741].

23. President Bush did establish national education goals for the state and local governments to reach; however, he was leery of establishing any national programs, such as curricula or tests, that would increase direct federal involvement or spending.

24. Memo, Roger B. Porter to George Bush, September 12, 1989, "Public Attitudes toward Education Reform Initiatives," WHORM: Subject File, Bush Presidential Records, Bush Library.

25. Quoted in Kerr-Tener, "Presidential Politics," 90.

26. George Bush, "Address on Administration Goals before a Joint Session of Congress," February 9, 1989, Public Papers of the President. Available online at: <http://www.csdl.tamu.edu/bush/cgi/>.

27. George Bush, "Message to the Congress Transmitting Proposed Legislation on Educational Excellence," April 5, 1989, Public Papers of the President. Available online at: <http://www.csdl.tamu.edu/bush/cgi/>.

28. Miller, "Fence Straddling," *San Diego Union-Tribune,* April 29, 1989, B14.

29. "Bush Education Proposal Draws Fire on Hill," *CQ Weekly Report,* April 8, 1989, 763.

30. Kuntz, "Bush Puts Focus on Schools," 2460.

31. Miller, "Fence Straddling," B14.

32. "Bush Plan Pared, OK'd by Panel," *CQ Weekly Report,* July 22, 1989, 1870; Phil Kuntz, "President's School Aid Package Revamped by Senate Panel," *CQ Weekly* Report, July 15, 1989, 1791; Jill Zuckman, "Senate Passes Much-Revised Bush Schools Initiative," *CQ Weekly Report,* February 10, 1990, 389.

33. Kuntz, "Bush Puts Focus on Schools," 2458.

34. "Joint Statement on the Education Summit with the Nation's Governors in Charlottesville, Virginia," September 28, 1989, Public Papers of the President. Available online at: <http://www.csdl.tamu.edu/bush/cgi/>.

35. Lucia Mouat, "First, Say Leaders, the Nation Must Agree on Educational Goals," *Christian Science Monitor,* September 27, 1989, 14.

36. Naughton, in *Washington Post,* September 29, 1989, D1.

37. George Bush, "State of the Union," *CQ Almanac,* January 31, 1990, 18–20.

38. Thomas S. Foley, quoted in Associated Press, "Education: Bush Criticized on Schools," *New York Times,* February 28, 1990, B8.

39. Letter, Augustus F. Hawkins to George Bush, March 7, 1990, Doc Number 120860, WHORM: Subject File, Bush Presidential Records, Bush Library.

40. Quoted by Jill Zuckman, "Democrats Put Up Bill to Meet National Goals Set by Bush," *CQ Weekly Report,* March 31, 1990, 1001–2.

41. "Bush's Education Proposals Unfulfilled," *1990 CQ Almanac,* 610–15; Jill Zuckman, "Measure Grows as House Gives Bush a Lesson in Addition," *CQ Weekly Report,* July 21, 1990, 2317.

42. "Bush Initiative OK'd by Senate Committee," *1989 CQ Almanac,* 193–94; "Bush Education Proposals Unfulfilled," *1990 CQ Almanac,* 610–15.

43. George Bush, "Statement on the Establishment of the National Education Goals Panel," July 31, 1990, Public Papers of the President. Available online at: <http://www.csdl.tamu.edu/bush/cgi/>.

44. Memo, Ede Holiday to George Bush, May 8, 1991, "Cabinet Promotion of the American 2000 Strategy," Doc. No. 236633SS, WHORM: Subject File, Bush Presidential Records, Bush Library.

45. "Cavazos Is Forced Out," *CQ Weekly Report,* December 15, 1990, 4143.

46. "Alexander Named to Education Job," *1990 CQ Almanac,* 614.

47. Letter, Lamar Alexander to Paul H. O'Neill, December 21, 1989, Doc. No. 100181, WHORM: Subject File, Bush Presidential Records, Bush Library.

48. Memo, Lamar Alexander to George Bush, January 11, 1991, Doc. No. 209533S, WHORM: Subject Files, Bush Presidential Records, Bush Library.

49. George Bush, "Message to Congress Transmitting America 2000 Legislation," April 19, 1991, Public Papers of the President. Available online at: <http://www.csdl.tamu.edu/bush/cgi/>.

50. George Bush, "Address to the Nation on the National Education Strategy," April 18, 1991, Public Papers of the President. Available online at: <http://www.csdl.tamu.edu/bush/cgi/>.

51. Ibid.

52. Letter, Lamar Alexander to Lawrence P. Peduzzi, June 19, 1991, Doc No. 233000–235999, WHORM: Subject File, Bush Presidential Records, Bush Library.

53. Richard Benedetto, "Critics See Politics in Education Plan," *USA Today,* April 19, 1991, 4A.

54. Dennis Kelly, "Bush Hopes to 'Re-Invent' Education," *USA Today,* April 19, 1991, 1A;

Bill Lambrecht, "Will It Make the Grade? Teachers, Politicians Evaluate Bush's Plan for US Schools," *St. Louis Post-Dispatch,* April 19, 1991, 1C.

55. "Hill Counters President's Education Plan," *CQ Weekly Report,* September 7, 1991, 2561.

56. Quoted in Zuckman, "Democrats Challenge," 2561.

57. John Kerry, quoted in "President's Mastery of Veto Perplexes Hill Democrats," *CQ Weekly Report,* July 27, 1991, 2045.

58. Jill Zuckman, "Dead Again: School Reform Done In by Both Sides," *CQ Weekly Report,* October 3, 1992, 3052.

59. Mortimer B. Zuckerman, "A Thousand Points of Slight," *U.S. News and World Report,* August 24, 1992, 72.

60. Edwin Diamond and Jane Newman, "The Candidates and the Issues," *Technology Review* 95, no. 4 (May 1992): 26–33.

61. Memo, Lauro F. Cavazo to Ede Holiday, Assistant to the President and Secretary of the Cabinet, July 26, 1990, "Draft Report to the Governors on the National Goals," ED Box 17, Folder [135000–161999], Bush Library.

CHAPTER 7

Prudence, Procrastination, or Politics: George Bush and the Earth Summit of 1992

MARTÍN CARCASSON

During the 1988 campaign George Bush dubbed himself the "Environmental President."[1] Four years later, in June 1992, Bush was asked to put his environmentalist label on the line at the 1992 United Nations Conference on the Environment and Development (also known as UNCED, the Rio Conference, or the Earth Summit) in Rio de Janeiro, Brazil.[2] As *Time* magazine noted in an article entitled "Summit to Save the Earth," "the so-called Earth Summit, more than two years in the making, will be the largest and most complex conference ever held—bigger than the momentous meetings at Versailles, Yalta, and Potsdam. Those summits carved up empires, drew new borders and settled world wars. The agenda for the Earth Summit is more far reaching: it sets out to confront not only the world's most pressing environmental problems—from global warming to deforestation—but poverty and underdevelopment as well."[3] Despite these very high global expectations, the conference turned out to be a monumental failure from which the international environmental movement has seemingly yet to recover.[4]

The worldwide frustration and anger over the failure of the conference were clearly directed at the Americans. The United States, it was frequently reported, not only forced the "watering down" of one major agreement (the climate change convention), but remained the only industrialized nation in the world that refused to sign a second (the biodiversity convention). The denunciation of the United States in general and of President Bush in particular in the national and international press was overwhelming. The negative press actually compounded the damage, because the media focused on the U.S. positions and the reactions to them, rather than on the environmental issues themselves. Adam Rogers, for example, argued that "America-bashing" was considered "one of the few consistent activities during the Earth Summit."[5] A *New Republic* article even described the media atmosphere as exhibiting a "Satan America spin."[6] The United States was labeled as "the evil empire," a "party pooper," the "black knight of the green movement," "the forces of darkness," and "the prime villain" of the international environment, while Bush was called "the Antichrist," "Uncle Grubby," the "Grinch who stole the eco-summit," "cranky Uncle Scrooge," and "eco-wimp."[7]

The criticism was not limited to environmentalists and representatives from developing countries, but rather came from all sources:

- *American allies:* Environmental Minister Klaus Topfer of Germany said, "What we see emerging in the United States is something like 'ecologism'—fear of a new Communism hidden behind ecology."[8]

- *American citizens:* It was reported that "thousands of US citizens in Rio marched in protest carrying signs saying 'You're embarrassing U.S.'"[9]

- *American media:* A *Newsweek* article opined that "it is a mark of how far America has drifted from environmental leadership that those 'extremes' [which Bush had refused to join] include Britain and Germany."[10]

- *Political opponents:* Senator Al Gore was the leader of a delegation of U.S. senators at the conference, and was highly vocal throughout, while Democratic presidential hopeful Bill Clinton was frequently in the press attacking Bush's holdout, arguing that he would sign all the documents.[11]

Bush's address at the conference worked only to increase the opposition's ire. Ernst Ulrich von Weizsäcker wrote that "the USA found itself isolated in an unprecedented way, just three years after the collapse of Communism and a little more than a year after the Gulf War. . . . President Bush's speech at Rio was a masterpiece of environmental pretentiousness; he did not really address any of the global environmental problems caused in large part by his country, but instead boasted about domestic pollution control which had little to do with UNCED's agenda. Seemingly, the speech did not even impress the electorate at home to which it was, of course, mainly addressed."[12] In the end, it was clear that the entire Rio experience was a public relations disaster for Bush, one that threatened, in the words of the *Wall Street Journal,* to "undercut his standing in one area where voters still have confidence in him: foreign affairs."[13] A few months later, Bush lost the presidential election to Clinton and Gore, thereby completing one of the fastest falls from popularity in presidential history.[14]

This chapter examines the situation Bush faced at the Earth Summit and seeks to evaluate both his decisions and his rhetoric surrounding and explaining those decisions. The most popular explanation of the significant gap between the "environmental president" of 1988 and the "eco-wimp" of 1992 simply charges Bush with acting out of political expediency. Bush's environmental transformation is thus explained as an opportunistic change in electoral strategy: in 1988 Bush pursued the environmental vote; in 1992 he evidently decided he did not need to or could not afford to court it. Bush administration officials dismissed such election pressure and explained that the harsh criticism was simply due to a "failure of rhetoric" on the part of Bush and his advisers.[15] They thereby differentiated the *decisions* made, which were deemed to be legitimate, from the *explanations* of them, which were admitted to be poor.

I argue that both these accounts have merit but are limited. Close analysis of the rhetorical situation encompassing the Bush presidency, the Earth Summit, and the 1992 election reveals substantial reasons for Bush's chosen rhetorical path. Specifically, I argue that the root of Bush's rhetoric and decision making concerning Rio resides in his philosophies of government, the environment, and rhetoric. These philosophical principles worked against a proactive stance at Rio, and their influence was magnified when considered in conjunction with the structural constraints of the situation—namely, the uncertainty of global science, the economic recession, and the pending election. I argue that the election *influenced,* but clearly did not *dictate,* his strategy. Due to these conditions, Bush's decision not to sign the various documents was not unexpected and cannot be considered purely political or pernicious. Nonetheless, Bush's attempts to justify his position or at least deflect some of the criticism were not very successful; that they were flawed lends support to the administration's "failure of rhetoric" claims.[16]

The analysis presented in this chapter is informed by Chaim Perelman's and Robert Beiner's perspectives on rhetoric and political judgment, respectively. Perelman's rhetorical view is focused heavily on a concern for audiences. In *The New Rhetoric,* he and Olbrechts-Tyteca write that "knowledge of those one wishes to win over is a condition preliminary to all effectual argumentation. . . . and an orator wishing to persuade a particular audience must of necessity adapt himself to it."[17] Without this precaution, a rhetor often succumbs to the error of imagining an audience "to be susceptible to the same arguments that persuaded him."

Following the work of Aristotle, Immanuel Kant, and Hannah Arendt, Beiner wrote, "When understanding is placed at the service of judgment it requires the free exercise of imagination, in particular, the ability to imagine how things look from a position that we do not in fact occupy. Judgment may require us to make the effort to understand those whose point of view we do not share and which we may indeed even find highly distasteful. Disagreement does not release us from the responsibility to understand that which we none the less reject; if anything, it rather heightens this responsibility."[18] The insights of these two theorists can be brought together in an attempt to judge the decisions of the Bush administration, the rhetoric accompanying those decisions, and the rhetoric of those hoping to criticize or influence the administration.

If rhetorical criticism is considered an endeavor that seeks to judge how well rhetors are able to choose the "available means of persuasion in a given instance," Beiner's insights into judgment are clearly relevant, especially when considering public policy issues that typically are subject to numerous constraints.[19] Critics must attempt to "imagine how things look from a position that we do not in fact occupy" in order to render such a judgment. Such "enlarged mentality" is useful to critics not only to better understand the perspective and choices of the rhetor, but to better understand, and perhaps subsequently adjust, their own perspective.[20] Criticism, in other words, can be considered as part of a broader political dialogue, especially when such criticism considers contemporary social controversies. In this endeavor critics should exhibit what Richard W. Paul characterizes as "critical thinking in the strong sense."[21]

If activism is an endeavor that seeks to judge, and on some level to influence, the decisions of political actors, it must do the same. If activists truly hope to influence the targets of their protests, they would be well served in considering the viewpoints of their targets and adjusting their arguments accordingly. Such adjustment should not be total, of course, as rhetors should seek the ideal mean between the comparable ends of principle and pragmatism, dogma and relativism, or scientism and emotivism.[22] Such is the aim of Aristotle's *phronesis*.[23] It is also the spirit of Donald Bryant's description of the function of rhetoric as represented in the tension between "adjusting ideas to people and people to ideas."[24]

The chapter begins with a brief review of historical circumstances leading up to the Earth Summit, then goes on to an examination of Bush's philosophical convictions and structural constraints as they relate to the conference. Having established the rhetorical situation from Bush's perspective, I examine Bush's rhetorical strategies within those constraints, and explain why they were reasonable from his perspective and aggravating from the environmentalist perspective.

EARTH SUMMIT BACKGROUND

The Earth Summit was considered critical to the international environmental movement because it brought together developed and developing countries, and provided a forum to confront difficult issues such as poverty, overpopulation, and global warming. These issues can only be truly confronted in such international forums, because the magnitude of the problems transcends national boundaries. Indeed, a critical issue of the global environmental movement is the diminution of the national-international distinction. Stephen Hopgood identified two dimensions of this decline: one of autonomy (loss of effective control), and the other of sovereignty (loss of authority).[25] The transnational aspect of environmental problems—that nations must share the same air, ocean, and atmosphere, and that pollution tends to drift—erodes autonomy, while the creation of international government bodies and the signing of international treaties and conventions impair national sovereignty.

Leading up to the conference, the divide between the so-called developed North and developing South was evident. The southern Group of 77 (G77) countries tended to focus on the *development* aspect of the U.N. Conference on Environment and Development, while the industrialized countries emphasized the *environment*. Ernst Ulrich von Weizsäcker described the conflict as a chasm between the global haves and the have-nots: "From the Southern perspective, the UNCED . . . was devoted to development, global inequalities, and their links with the environment. . . . The South has tended to define the UNCED agenda as a strategy for overcoming poverty and reversing the global economic inequalities. Environmental questions would in this interpretation be subordinated to global economic issues. This view almost invariably leads to a repetition of Indira Gandhi's famous statement twenty years ago at the Stockholm UN Conference on the Human Environment, that 'poverty is the biggest pollution.'"[26] Since the difficulties of the North-South split are best exemplified through the debates concerning global warming, I will summarize the issue.

Global warming is clearly a transnational issue that tends to inflame passions as sovereign countries argue over the extent of the problem, who is to blame for it, who should be responsible for the solutions, and what those solutions should be. The North's consumption patterns and industrial infrastructure are currently the main source of the emissions, with the United States, despite having only 5 percent of the world's population, contributing 25 percent of the world's emissions.[27] The South owns most of the sprawling rainforests that act as "sinks" for the greenhouse gases. Unfortunately, these same forests are one of the South's critical resources: they are cleared to make room for agriculture, they are harvested to sell as exotic woods, and they are consumed as a primary, and dirty, source of fuel. The North, suddenly keenly aware of these environmental dangers, is calling for the South to conserve the resources the world needs. The South, struggling to match the standard of living enjoyed by the North, demands the sovereign right to exploit its own resources to achieve the North's lifestyle. As stated by a Malaysian diplomat during the conference: "we are certainly not holding our forests in custody for those who have destroyed their own forests and now try to claim ours as a part of the heritage of mankind."[28]

As the South develops, the situation is likely to worsen. In the future, the developing countries—unless the North volunteers resources and clean technologies—will go through the same "dirty" economic phases the North passed through decades ago, and will then contribute a majority of the global pollution. An article in the *Economist,* published in 1989, captures this new dynamic vividly:

> As economic growth has accelerated, and as more countries, with more people, have joined in, so its environmental side-effects have increased. . . . the environment is what poor countries live off. Typically, primary production—farming, forestry, fishing, mining—accounts for more than a third of their GNP, more than two-thirds of employment, and over half their export earnings. Their natural resources are their main assets. From them, they must feed a billion more mouths every 13 years. . . . *As the poorer countries industrialise, buy cars, get richer, their capacity for damage will overtake that of the rich world—because they have more people.* China alone, by burning its dirty coal and making polluting refrigerators, could torpedo everybody else's efforts to stop the build-up of atmospheric carbon and damage to the ozone layer.[29]

In other words, what is done within U.S. borders is immaterial if something is not done concerning developing countries like China, Malaysia, and Brazil. It is becoming exceedingly clear that the poorer southern countries are (somewhat understandably) more concerned with their short-term survival than with long-term environmental consequences. Simply put, if a nation's people cannot eat, the fortunes of their great-grandchildren do not seem so critical.

In this context, the post–Cold War Earth Summit seemed to represent a unique and important global opportunity to confront and deliberate about these difficult environmental issues. The United States, at once the world's richest, most powerful, most polluting, and most environmentally conscious nation, would clearly have to play an important role. Environmentalists approached the unprecedented meeting with high expectations. These expectations were quickly dashed, thanks to the negative American stances on the official treaties.[30]

With the concept of international sovereignty still in its relative infancy, conferences such as these serve primarily as symbolic events. Though the occasional international document is legally binding, most of the documents are simply pledges, and much of the conference's power is derived from the momentum and awareness produced by public statements presented during the conference and the normative pressure they can create. They seem to rely on national pride, as countries seek to show the world that they have their priorities in order (or, alternatively, countries are shamed when they do not). Organizers of the Earth Summit thus hoped to bring international environmental issues to the forefront of worldwide agendas. Unfortunately, the primary issues that many felt needed to be discussed at the conference—North-South relations, poverty, overpopulation, lifestyles, climate change—were hardly discussed. The necessary optimistic approach based on international collaboration was trumped by the negatives of Bush's lonely stand against the world. Due in part to the American actions and the predominant international reaction to them, the momentum, sense of urgency, and spirit of cooperation that environmentalists hoped could have been fostered at Rio never developed. Indeed, the opposite message was sent to the world, and the dominant competitive, growth-based economic paradigm was simply reinforced as even the world's richest country argued that it would not make sacrifices that were seen to be necessary and critical.

The vehement attacks on Bush seem to imply that if only Bush had consented to the hopes of environmentalists, the Earth Summit, as well as the future, could have been very different. From the environmentalist perspective, the United States would have led the international community at Rio, and would have pushed its allies and the developing countries to make the necessary sacrifices for the environment. Bush would have used the "bully pulpit" to lead the American people and a worldwide audience to reconfigure the dominant economic, development, conflict paradigm to one focusing on the environment, sustainable development, and worldwide cooperation—a true global village. The world's wealthiest nation and most powerful leader would set a "positive" example and add to, rather than detract from, the symbolic power of the conference. The conference, rather than focusing on negatives, would have reveled in the promise of the future. Environmentalists perhaps imagined Bush signing the various documents proudly, as John Hancock fearlessly signed the Declaration of Independence. Bush would invoke his own frequently uttered phrase concerning the "New World Order," and would begin a new age of global prosperity and global stewardship. In the process, he would be able to overcome the difficulty of constructing a viable foreign policy consensus in the post–Cold War period, as the world restructured itself around the concept of sustainable development.[31] All nations would finally come together to fight the common enemies: poverty, inequality, environmental degradation, and the fears of ecological catastrophe.

Environmentalists might argue that such a strategy could have salvaged Bush's failing reelection bid, as the American people once again would see their president leading the world to a glorious victory (instead of seeing him universally condemned). Bush, in other words, would finally discover a "vision," harness the power of his incumbency, charm the "soccer moms," and solidify his legacy as the president presiding over not only the fall of communism, but also the rise of unprecedented international cooperation for the sake of the planet.

With this environmentalist dream in mind, the anger directed toward Bush for "ruining" the conference seems justified. Many environmentalists simply could not understand why Bush would (in their opinion) sacrifice the world to appease American corporations or win conservative votes. To these environmentalists, the issue seemed very simple, and the consensus for action seemed overwhelming. The United States, after all, was the only nation steadfast against emission targets and timetables, and the only industrialized nation not to sign the biodiversity convention. American environmentalists, used to being in the forefront of the world's environmental movement, suddenly found their nation pushing the world in the opposite direction. Bush was thus scapegoated as the one critical hurdle to positive action.

The rhetorical situation that Bush faced was much more complex than that assumed by most environmentalists and the media, in part because the idealistic "environmentalist dream" I outlined above considers the situation from only one perspective. To construct an alternative view of the rhetorical situation, I will turn now to an examination of Bush's philosophical convictions.

THE BUSH PHILOSOPHY

If Bush's political ideology, environmental ethic, and rhetorical perspective are considered, the administration's "failure to lead" in Rio could easily have been predicted. Each of these three factors worked against Bush providing the proactive, international leadership environmentalists had hoped he would exhibit in Rio. Each of these aspects of the Bush presidency would be considered deficiencies by some (especially environmentalists) and positives by others (conservatives). The point here is not to judge whether Bush's philosophy was "right" or "wrong," but rather to better understand how his philosophy affected the decisions surrounding Rio.

Bush's Political Philosophy

Bush was considered primarily a conservative, Tory-style politician who worked best reacting to problems rather than advocating proactive policies. As Bert A. Rockman wrote in an essay on Bush's leadership style, "a Tory's view of the world is imbued with skepticism about alterations to the status quo; it embodies the precept that doing nothing more likely is better than doing something."[32] This ideology did not fit well with environmental issues, which require a certain amount of faith and vision to address proactively, due to the numerous unknowns involved.

As an economic conservative, Bush was also very reluctant to jeopardize American jobs for uncertain causes. Like most economic conservatives, Bush was optimistic about the power of the market to alleviate numerous problems, including problems concerning the environment. Bush initially believed that by releasing American ingenuity (and not restraining it with unnecessary regulations), new technologies could be developed to counter any ill effects of economic growth. Bush was thus able to tie together the economic, the scientific, and the environmental. For example, in 1991 Bush said, "Recent world events make it clear that free markets and economic growth provide the firmest foundations for effective environmental stewardship. People tend to forget that environmental stewardship is a high-tech business, and it requires great ingenuity and insight. Science and technology give us tools for cleaning up our environment and keeping it clean. They help us identify our problems precisely and develop efficient solutions. Our genius will open up new frontiers of clean energy: nuclear power, solar power, geothermal power, and others that exist only in the imagination of our dreamers and innovations." In other words, Bush rhetorically employed science as an environmental savior. Later in that same speech Bush solidified his point of view, saying, "We want to use science to help us solve our chief environmental problems. . . . Good science hastens our progress toward a cleaner environment, and we ought to use it to our best advantage."[33] In other words, the needs of the economy and the market prevailed over the needs of the environment, because eventually the economy would produce technologies that would fix the environment (if it were actually broken). This logic was evident in Bush's Earth Summit address, when he explained: "Twenty years ago, some spoke of limits to growth. Today we realize that growth is the engine of change and the friend of the environment."[34] From Bush's perspective, economic growth and innovation were the means to the end of environmental progress; therefore, to convince him to agree to curtail economic growth through regulations for the sake of the environment was clearly a difficult sell.

The concept of "prudence" was also very important to Bush. Prudence calls for leaders to be rational and careful with their decisions, to wait until enough evidence is presented, and to balance carefully all the available exigencies. As we will see, the uncertainty of global science and various concerns about the agreements led Bush directly into the position of using the uncertain science as a justification for inaction based on a call for prudence.

Bush's Environmental Ethic

A review of Bush's environmental rhetoric from the beginning of his 1988 campaign also affords some insight into the Rio decisions.[35] The inconsistency of the "environmental president" ruining the Earth Summit seems evident, but Bush was rather consistent concerning his environmental rhetoric throughout his term. From the beginning, Bush exhibited an environmental ethic that was more accurately conceived as a nationalistic conservation that called for environmental protection, rather than an international perspective that endorsed environmental improvement and difficult changes or sacrifices.

His emphasis on the merging and balancing of economic and environmental goals was also consistent throughout his presidency, and simply took center stage in Rio. Considering the economic recession, a shift toward a focus on improving the economy rather than improving the environment was logical and consistent for Bush at that time. He typically focused on national environmental issues, such as clear air, clean water, and the preservation of national parks and forests, rather than on global issues, such as poverty, overpopulation, and global warming. His focus on the same national issues at the Earth Summit should not have been surprising. Rather than serve as a world leader, Bush focused on his role as American leader, and focused primarily on the national, rather than international, interest.[36]

Bush's Nonrhetorical Presidency

The final philosophical aspect of the Bush administration that worked as a constraint against positive action for the environment in Rio was his personal aversion to persuasion and rhetorical methods. Not only was Bush not particularly skilled in the art of oratory, especially in comparison to his predecessor and successor, but he also disliked the potential influence that it carried. Mark Rozell, examining Bush's antirhetorical presidency, wrote that Bush's staff described Bush as a "pragmatic leader, not a rhetorical one," who "genuinely disliked the rituals of politics" and was "more committed to substance than symbolism."[37] George Will wrote that Bush "discounts rhetoric because he discounts persuasion of the people."[38] By all accounts, Bush rejected the notion of the rhetorical presidency and its "vision thing," and did not approve of using the presidency as a bully pulpit to convince the American people and/or Congress to act in any particular way. This personal belief was critical during the Earth Summit because Bush was likely unaware of or unconcerned with the symbolic nature of the conference.

This last point should not be underestimated. The environmentalist's dream presented earlier, and the positive implications it presupposed, was based on Bush's ability to realize and take advantage of the *rhetorical* potential of the international conference. The decision to sign or not sign the documents had both pros and cons. Not only were most of the advantages to signing the document in the rhetorical realm, but they also required rhetorical skill to achieve. *Both the means and the ends of the conference, therefore, depended on a skill and viewpoint that Bush generally dismissed as inappropriate.* The advantages of not signing were primarily concrete—such as retaining the flexibility of national action rather than submitting to the constraints of international regulations. Simply put, Bush was focused on the concrete substance of the actual convention documents, while the press and other international critics were more focused on the overall "message" sent by the conference. Neither side seriously considered the viewpoint of the other, which explains at least in part the highly polarized atmosphere between them.

An examination of Bush's strategy makes it clear that he believed he was doing the right thing. He believed his reservations about the documents were legitimate, and he seemed to be comfortable knowing (or at least believing) that the United States would remain environmentally proactive without regard to or enforcement of strict international regulations. His decisions, in other words, were clearly and logically within the realm of Bush's philosophy, without even considering the structural constraints of the election and the economy.

THE STRUCTURAL CONSTRAINTS ON ACTION

Though the analysis thus far has already sought to explain the actions of Bush and the administration in the failure surrounding the Rio conference, several structural realities existed that must be considered as well—namely, the uncertainty of global science, the recession, and the 1992 presidential election. These structural issues magnified the philosophical constraints concerning environmental activism that have already been examined.

Uncertainty of Science

The first factor that underlies the American position is the uncertainties in the science concerning international environmental issues. Though significant consensus has formed concerning the increase in greenhouse gases in the atmosphere, questions concerning their effect and possible treatments are still highly disputed. Add to such controversies the high cost of proposed solutions, and the uncertainty of whether such solutions would be successful, and significant barriers to actions begin to form. Bush, following his philosophy of prudence, reacted to the intense debate among scientists concerning global warming by calling for caution. Under the banner of "prudence," Bush called for increased funding for scientific research on climate change. This tactic merged well with Bush's optimism concerning the market and science as environmental saviors. To environmentalists, such prudence seemed timid procrastination at best, and willful deceit at worst, while to Bush it was prototypical conservative leadership. Once again, neither side seemed to consider the perspective of the other.

Bush's stance on science was evident as early as his addresses to the Intergovernmental Panel on Climate Change in Washington, D.C., in April 1990. The panel was preceded by a series of scientific reports warning about the dangers of global warming. Included in those reports was an appeal by the Union of Concerned Scientists, endorsed by 49 Nobel laureates and 700 members of the National Academy of Sciences, that urged Bush to take action immediately.[39] The scientists, agreeing that more research was necessary, nonetheless argued that uncertainty was "no excuse for complacency."[40] Despite the growing evidence, Bush disappointed the panelists from ten European countries by continuing to urge prudence: "Our responsibility is to maintain the quality of our approach, our commitment to sound science, and an open mind to policy options."[41] In all the various environmental venues leading up to the Earth Summit, Bush, clearly influenced by skeptics such as John Sununu, consistently disappointed proactive scientists by calling for more research rather than bold action.[42] "Talking points" distributed among White House advisers before the Earth Summit emphasized that "scientists disagree about global warming" and explicitly stated that the president would not sign an agreement "based on unsound science or greenhouse guesswork."[43]

For environmentalists, the problem lies in the possibility that the science will not be clear until it is too late for positive action to affect irreversible processes. The idealistic American belief in science, which showed no sign of decline during the Clinton years, is thus seen as a perilous stimulant to procrastination.[44] Of course, the appeal to uncertain science is not unusual in such issues. John McCormick argued that "inconsistent and incomplete scientific data has been repeatedly quoted by governments and industries opposed to action on environmental problems."[45] Often the issue hinges on the difference between prevention and cure, with governments hesitating to commit major funding to the prevention of future problems, often preferring to "wait" until the scientific data are more concrete. In a study of various international environmental issues, Porter and Brown concluded that "scientific evidence has helped galvanize international action on some issues (acid rain and ozone depletion) but has been secondary or irrelevant in other issues (whaling, hazardous waste trade, tropical deforestation, Antarctic minerals, and trade in African ivory).[46] Science is clearly a critical issue in international debate regarding global warming, and from Bush's "Tory" perspective—right or wrong—it should not have been surprising for him to act as he did in Rio.

Economic Troubles

The second major constraint involved the recession that affected the United States in the summer of 1991. Considering that the environment and the economy are typically considered in competition, despite the notion of sustainable development, the recession was obviously a deterrent to positive action by the Bush administration.[47] The recession, and the rise in unemployment it caused, highlighted the assumed negative effects of environmental policy on American industry and business, and in many ways forced Bush to lean even more toward the economic side.

It would be understandably difficult for Bush to have sold to the public during a recession the notion of massive subsidies to developing countries and the sacrifice of American jobs. Perhaps the American people wanted Bush to lead the world at Rio and make strong rhetorical flourishes, but when it came to finding the funds to support the treaties and enforce the regulations they required, Bush perhaps assumed the support would likely wane. Bush saw himself making the necessary tough decisions to protect both the American economy and the environment, rather than simply acquiescing to public pressure based on what he considered bad information.

The 1992 Election

The effect of the American presidential election on the thinking of the Bush administration toward the Rio documents was discussed openly at the Rio conference. Maurice Strong, the organizer of the Rio conference, was said to believe that "holding a high-profile environmental gathering in an American election year would be advantageous."[48] Organizers thus purposely scheduled the conference to correspond with the American election, in the hope that the environmentally conscious public would force environmental concessions. Unfortunately, the conference organizers did not consider the possibility of a recession, combined with a three-party presidential race. As the conference neared, organizers realized the strategy had failed miserably. Tommy Koh, chair of the conference's main working session, expressed his disappointment the day after Bush's speech, muttering that "this will teach the United Nations not to hold a conference in an American election year."[49]

The 1992 campaign represented a significant change from the 1988 campaign. In 1988 Bush had attacked his opponent on the environment, citing Dukakis's poor record as governor, and had used the environment as an issue to win back more moderate voters alienated by Reagan's stark antiregulation administration.[50] In 1992 the situation was very different. Although Clinton had "an atrocious environmental record" as the governor of Arkansas, he was very vocal before and during the conference in expressing his support for the documents.[51] The decision to add Gore to the Democratic ticket was Clinton's "redemption" for his past environmental sins. The Bush team had to realize they could not "out-green" the Democrats for the environmental vote. Although Clinton had not yet chosen Gore as his running mate by the time of the conference, the positive press that Gore received as a stalwart Democratic environmentalist at the Earth Summit was clearly a concern to the Bush administration. One book that reviewed the proceedings of the Earth Summit included a section on Gore's conference activities entitled "Will the *Real* Environmental President Please Stand Up?"[52]

To make matters worse for Bush, Perot was pushing for the conservative, probusiness votes that Bush had been able to take for granted in 1988. Suddenly Bush had to shift his strategy and, according to the *New York Times,* cater more to "the political base of party loyalists and Reagan Democrats that swept two Republicans into the White House, and who are now being seduced by the pro-business oratory of Ross Perot."[53] Stephen Hopgood argued that Perot also gave the skeptics in the White House another angle to attack the environmental proposals: "They [the conservatives in the White House] were able to argue strongly that in a three-way contest the Republican party had to play to its base which meant supporters who were largely anti-regulation and pro-business, as well as being less sympathetic (although often not *un*sympathetic) to the environmental movement."[54] The decision by the administration to "take full election-year advantage of his uncomfortable new role, in which he is seen by many as global environmental spoilsport . . . [and] playing to the hilt the role of global maverick," was pushed by aides to the president who believed the display of "a brand of tough leadership . . . [would] play extremely well at home, especially in an election that features the tough-talking Mr. Perot."[55] Partly in response to these conditions, the conservative faction in the White House began to gain greater influence over the president as the election neared, a situation that only compounded the constraints surrounding proactive environmental policy.[56]

All these factors combine to show that Bush had little political incentive to be proactive in Rio. Even if Bush did personally believe the documents should have been signed, it would not have been politically viable for him to do so. Cynicism aside, politicians must "save their seat" before they can "save the world." Interestingly, polling research is rather inconclusive concerning these issues. In a series of *USA Today* polls published in June 1992, almost 60 percent of the respondents felt Bush should sign the treaty, and almost 40 percent believed global warming was a "major threat to civilization."[57] Yet opinion poll research discussed within the Bush White House revealed a high concern for environmental issues in general—even when compared to economic needs—but little application of this concern in voting decisions.[58] So while the environmentalists had hoped the election would stimulate Bush's environmentalism, it seems clear that in 1992 just the opposite occurred.

BUSH'S RIO STRATEGY AND THE "FAILURE OF RHETORIC"

At the Earth Summit, Bush was attacked for allowing wayward political aspirations to dominate his decision making. I have argued thus far that an alternative examination of the situation reveals significant reasons—both abstract philosophical convictions and concrete structural constraints—that must be considered when judging Bush's actions. One might argue that either group of factors, the philosophical or the political, would have been sufficient without the other to explain Bush's actions. Taken together, the constraints seem overwhelming. This poses the question: Why, if he had such good reasons, was he unable to explain them to his detractors?

The Bush administration's positions on the various documents were well known before the summit actually began, as negotiations had been going on throughout the previous two years. As the conference neared, the public attacks on Bush grew, and he began to respond to the criticism in various ways.

Overall, the administration's defense was composed of three interrelated tactics: the recitation of positive information concerning the American environmental record; the launch of a counter-offensive to give the impression of strength and resolve; and a focus on the dissociation between global rhetoric and American action. It seems evident that these strategies were primarily targeted to the core Republican voters, and thus tended to further alienate those national and international audiences connected to the Earth Summit.

The American Record

All the defenses centered on a recitation of the American environmental record. This tactic was essentially the typical political maneuver of standing behind one's record, labeled in apologic theory as "bolstering."[59] The use of this tactic disclosed an interesting international paradox: the United States was the world's environmental "leader" in two important ways. It was simultaneously the *world's foremost protector* of the environment and the *world's foremost polluter* of the environment. An article in *USA Today* on the day of Bush's Rio speech outlining the American record captured the irony of the situation rather clearly. The article reported that while the United States was the first industrial nation to limit pollution, it was also the world's worst greenhouse gas producer (over 20 percent of all CO_2), and, of course, the only industrialized country at Rio to oppose emission targets. The United States had pioneered concepts of wilderness preserves and national parks, but had lost 90 percent of its ancient forests and more than half of its 221 million acres of wetlands in the lower forty-eight states. The recycling industry is among America's fastest growing industries, but Americans generate twice the amount of garbage per person produced by Western Europeans or Japanese. Lastly, U.S. research spending on conservation and renewable resources rose from $324 million in 1989 to $540 million in 1992, but the United States is also the leading consumer of energy per capita in the world.[60]

Aware of their positive environmental leadership, and evidently oblivious to their negative leadership, Bush and various administration officials continuously referred to the American environmental record in the days leading up to the conference. Talking points instructed administration officials that the United States "currently spends more than any other nation in controlling pollution and protecting the environment," and "has the most advanced environmental laws and performance of any nation on earth, having spent $800 billion since 1981."[61] These talking points rarely mentioned the negative aspects of the American environmental record (just as the administration's environmental critics rarely conceded the positive aspects, while focusing solely on the negative).

Several members of the administration also reacted to the global criticism with bitterness. Bush's advisers seemed to be asking, "We spend and do more than anybody, so how can they be attacking us?" According to Russell Frye, Americans "rightly feel that they have paid a price for being environmental leaders, and it is difficult to accept criticism of America's stance on environmental issues from other countries."[62] For example, a handwritten note scrawled on the margins of an early draft of Bush's departure statement from Andrews Air Force Base suggested the inclusion of the following passage: "Without the U.S. economy, over the last half century there would be no Marshall Plan, no common defense against totalitarian regimes in Europe, as well as Asia, and certainly a lot less food and aid for the developing world— albeit that there would be less carbon dioxide in the atmosphere."[63] John Sununu made the point that the United States was "spending about $1.3 billion [a year] for programs dealing with global warming impacts. We'd love many of the other countries of the world who are so militant on this issue to come even close to matching this level of research funding."[64]

Bush himself continuously referenced America's "global leadership" in the speeches he made before and during the conference. In his conference speech Bush, obviously cognizant of the criticism that had been levied against him and his administration, squarely faced his critics, saying:

> Let's face it, there has been some criticism of the United States. But I must tell you, we come to Rio proud of what we have accomplished and committed to extending the record on American leadership on the environment. In the United States, we have the world's tightest air quality standards on cars and factories, the most advanced laws for protecting lands and waters, and the most open processes for public participation. Now for a simple truth: America's record on environmental protection is second to none. So I did not come here to apologize. We come to press on with deliberate purpose and forceful action. Such action will demonstrate our continuing commitment to leadership and to international cooperation on the environment.

Despite such clear appeals, Bush's invocation of American leadership was likely counterproductive to his environmental critics. Obviously, the Bush administration chose to focus on the positive leadership, while the rest of the world was focused on either the general negative leadership or the specific abandonment of leadership at Rio. For example, when Bush mentioned America's record being "second to none" during his conference address, a "ripple of

laughter" was heard in the delegates' room where the speech was being simul-
cast.[65] In reality, neither extreme perspective—top protector or top polluter—
was a fair evaluation of American environmental efforts.

The Best Defense is a Good Offense

As the criticism continued to mount despite references to America's environmental record, Bush went further on the offensive. On June 11, two days
before Bush was scheduled to speak at the conference, a reporter asked the
president whether he expected "other countries to try to beat up" on him in
Rio. The president's answer was clear:

> It doesn't matter. It doesn't matter. We are the United States. We are the leader in
> the environment. We've got a good record. Most of the groups that are criticiz-
> ing are from the United States, I think. But that's all right; I've been there before.
> I'm going to represent the people on this visit and do it firmly in putting forward
> the best environmental record that any country has. . . . we are not going to act
> like we have an open checkbook and that people are going to come in and tell us
> how much money to spend. We can't do it. We're trying to protect the taxpayer
> here through this balanced budget amendment, and I will protect the tax-
> payer down there in Rio.[66]

The next day, Bush delivered one last message from Andrews Air Force Base
as he prepared to leave for Brazil. The story remained the same: he reaffirmed
the decision not to sign the biodiversity convention, despite the "many governments and many individuals from the U.S. and other nations" that had
"pressed" him to sign. In the end, he pledged that "if the United States has to
be the only nation to stand against the bio-diversity treaty as now drawn,
so be it."[67]

Stephen Hopgood argued that such comments represented part of a
planned strategy to "go on the offensive by promoting its [America's] isolation
as a sign of leadership and integrity. Electoral strategists began to see advantages in a kind of 'imperial defiance.'"[68] The attack tactic was consistent with
the argument that Bush was purposefully stubborn concerning the negotiations on the biodiversity convention in order to appear resolute in his convictions. For example, a *Washington Post* editorial printed before Bush's speech
suggested that "on environmental policy in this political season, President
Bush clearly would rather have an issue than an agreement. The administration has shown little interest in compromise on the treaties now before the
United Nations' conference in Rio de Janeiro. Instead, Mr. Bush has set up

sharp-edged disagreements in which he affects a stand as the adamant defender of American businesses and jobs against the assaults of environmental 'extremists.'"[69] The *New York Times* made a similar claim, writing that "the Bush administration went out of its way to appear obstructionist, even when its underlying positions were reasonable."[70]

The Bush campaign team seemed to believe that a principled stand for American interests (and especially "taxpayers") against international pressure would impress voters, especially those who felt Bush had ignored domestic issues as a result of his focus on foreign affairs. Hopgood claimed that "campaign strategists also found some solace in Bush's new role as a 'global maverick' which they believed would show him as a tough leader unafraid of being isolated on a point of principle. This would play well against Ross Perot, they thought."[71] Clayton Yeutter clearly approved of the administration's isolated position, evidenced by his sending letters of congratulations to the American negotiators of the climate convention, extolling how the negotiations were "the United States versus the rest of the world, and the U.S. won. What a marvelous achievement, and what a testimony to your preparation, patience, and basic negotiating skills."[72]

Evidently to supplement the strategy, the Bush administration never clearly explained its opposition to the various documents, though there were several points where the objections were clearly valid. One of the primary American concerns with the climate change convention was its focus on carbon monoxide (of which the United States was the primarily emitter) rather than on methane (which European countries primarily emitted), though both gases contributed to global warming. The document, in other words, was rather biased against the United States in some ways.

Other important issues centered on the problems with the monetary structure, the transfer of technology, and intellectual property rights in the biodiversity treaty.[73] Bush also had some valid objections to these concerns, and the United States had the right to a different point of view than was held by the rest of the world. American corporations, not government, were responsible for many of the innovations in biotechnology, and allowing open trade of hard-earned technological advances would obviously affect the financial incentives for these companies to push for innovation (and thus would hinder the market forces Bush praised so often). Due to the American dominance of the biotechnology market, the documents required much greater sacrifice from the United States than any other nation. In addition, by signing the documents, Bush would be relinquishing American control to an intergovernmental agency—a course that to him, as a conservative, would be imprudent.

The administration was never able to explain these reservations well. Indeed, thanks to the "global maverick" strategy, it never systematically attempted an explanation. Without an alternative explanation, the press simply focused on the political pressure from conservatives, American biotechnology firms, and Quayle's Council on Competitiveness as the reasoning behind the unpopular decisions. Such a strategy thus added to the polarization and misinformation.

Whether or not the strategy was effective with American voters, it certainly solidified the hostility toward Bush in Rio. The media clearly focused on the attacks on Bush rather than on his stand for the American taxpayer. The tactic enraged the audiences at the Earth Summit, who felt Bush's stance was arrogant, making a bad situation even worse.

RHETORIC VERSUS ACTION

The bitterness stemming from the perceived undue criticism and the strategy of emphasizing the "global maverick" image led to an extraordinary, thinly veiled attack on U.S. allies. Several advisers believed that in order to reap the political windfall, allies such as Germany and Japan had agreed to conventions they could not possibly adhere to, and which they did not have any real intention of fulfilling. According to Bush's science adviser, D. Allan Bromley, it seems the distrust of global environmental rhetoric began in Bush's first year. Bromley, attending a conference in the Netherlands, was told by "the head of one of the major European delegations" that the agreement being discussed was "only a piece of paper and they don't put you in jail if you don't actually do it." In his memoirs, Bromley goes on to explain: "This attitude, time and again, makes it extraordinarily difficult for the United States to participate in international meetings, because, as a matter of principle, we believe that when we commit formally to a course of action we must be prepared to follow through on it."[74] The concept that the United States must stick to its "principles," rather than succumb to the temptation of empty rhetoric, surfaced often in the statements leading to the conference.

Understandably, administration officials never explicitly accused their allies of dishonesty. Several White House documents instructed administration officials to emphasize the comparison of American "action" to the "rhetoric" of other countries. A document entitled "Talking Points on the Earth Summit" claimed that "while other nations may talk a good game, the United States is unparalled in world environmental leadership."[75] Another document, entitled "UNCED Talking Points," offered that "the U.S. has matched rhetoric with action. . . . We are encouraging other nations to join us in this effort. We are leading by example." Yet another report maintained that "the U.S. rhetoric in the run-up to UNCED may not have matched that of many other nations, but our actions have surpassed theirs."[76] On May 30 Bush, after explaining his stand on the Rio documents, said: "When the United States makes a commitment, it has to keep it. And we do that. Our word is pretty good, and it should be."[77] The unstated conclusion to his statement was perhaps something to the effect of "unlike our friends in Germany and Japan."

At a June 10 "off the record" briefing held in Rio, this tactic took center stage in a remarkable session. Administration officials clearly revealed the administration's belief that their allies, unlike the United States, were indulging in empty rhetoric that had not been and would not be backed up by positive action:

> The irony is that in the run up to the UNCED Summit, and even at the Rio meeting itself, it is probably true that the United States' rhetoric has not matched that of many other countries. But we feel it's ironic because the United States' actions have, in fact, surpassed . . . that of most other countries. . . . We've all along said that actions speak louder than words. . . . There's been too much focus on rhetoric and not enough on actions. . . . It has been very easy for some countries to make a rhetorical commitment to targets and timetables or to their alleged leadership when, in fact, they have not been home legislating and actually taking actions that will reduce greenhouse gas emissions.[78]

Members of the press asked to allow the comments to be put on the record, due to their profound claims, but the administration officials refused to do so.

Within this context, the rhetoric/action distinction was both an attack and a defense. The administration defensively argued that the actions of the United States surpassed its rhetoric, and attacked the allies for utilizing rhetoric to disguise legislative deficiencies. Bush's philosophy of rhetoric obviously applies here. The argument was that Bush had simply been unable—or, perhaps more appropriately, unwilling—to talk as good a game as the other countries, primarily because he, unlike the others, actually planned on living up to his promises. Administration officials explicitly admitted to such a rhetorical failure, saying, "So it may be—the point I would make is that to the extent the United States has had a failure, it's been a failure of rhetoric and not a failure of action."[79] This distinction was also evident in Bush's conference address, as he continuously emphasized the need for "action" in comparison to "words," "concern," and "intentions."[80] The rhetoric-action distinction was even more evident in a section of the speech that was removed just before delivery. A draft faxed to the White House the day before the speech included this less subtle point: "If the world is to tackle the complex environmental challenges ahead, we need less emotion, and more deliberate purpose. Less divisive rhetoric, and more unified action."[81]

Thus, while admitting to a *rhetorical* failure, the Bush administration was simultaneously refuting the substantive attacks concerning its *actions,* and attacking the rhetorical successes but substantive failures of other nations. This dissociation between rhetoric and action clearly fit within Bush's favoring of substance over style. An author from the *New Republic,* evidently agreeing with the argument, even wrote, "Perhaps it's refreshing to hear that, for a change, the White House bungled the symbols while handling the substance."[82]

Bush evidently hoped the American people would perceive the same dissociation between rhetoric and action or, following his "global maverick" strategy, was unconcerned with the misunderstanding. But Bush failed to understand that the power of the conference was primarily a rhetorical power, not a substantive one. *Bush's failure of rhetoric, in other words, was likely more fatal to the hopes of the conference—and thus the movement—than any failure of action.* Again, thanks to his philosophical perspective discounting rhetoric, Bush likely never grasped this important point. He simply believed that he had good reasons not to sign the documents as they were and that the negative perception of the United States was misguided, and thus felt he could leave it at that.

CONCLUSION

This chapter has examined the rhetorical situation President Bush faced at the Earth Summit and has sought to consider more systematically the president's rhetoric and decision making from his perspective. Despite the heavy global criticism of Bush's decisions concerning the conference, I argue that Bush's typical philosophical assumptions, reinforced by various structural constraints of the specific situation, made the probability of a proactive stance from the White House rather unlikely. In addition, I argue that Bush's strategy and rhetoric surrounding the conference issues were likely counterproductive to appeasing his environmental critics, and thus are somewhat to blame for the level of criticism. Bush relied on a dissociation between rhetoric and action that was a misreading of the symbolic nature of the conference.

An analysis of these additional exigencies and constraints helps explain not only why Bush chose to defy the world in Rio, but also why the international environment continues to be a nonissue in U.S. presidential politics, despite continued economic success and persistent warnings, and evidence concerning issues such as global warming and overpopulation. Since the Earth Summit, American environmental leadership has continued to be sluggish.

President Clinton did eventually sign the biodiversity convention, and he outwardly supported the more stringent climate change treaty negotiated at the Kyoto conference in 1998, which reinstated the specific targets and timetables that were removed from the Earth Summit document. However, Clinton never submitted the treaty for congressional ratification (knowing it would not be approved), and expended very little political capital pushing its acceptance, despite public approval and growing scientific evidence.[83] Before the 1992 election Gore wrote in his bestselling book *Earth in the Balance*—a book ridiculed within the Bush White House—that "bold and unequivocal action" must be taken so that the environment becomes civilization's "central organizing principle."[84] Nevertheless, during the 2000 election, even Gore shied away from global environmental issues.[85] George W. Bush, on the other hand, attacked the Kyoto treaty, saying "it would cost American jobs."[86] Shortly after taking office in 2001, the newly elected president sent a letter to four Republican senators explaining that he had reversed his campaign position on the reduction of emissions from power plants due to "important new information," and announced his rejection of the Kyoto treaty.[87] Overall, it seems clear that the American president will continue to avoid the international environmental crisis rather than confront it.

NOTES

1. For an examination of the differences and similarities between the Reagan and early Bush administrations on environmental policy, see Norman J. Vig, "Presidential Leadership: From the Reagan to the Bush Administration," in *Environmental Policy in the 1990s,* ed. Norman J. Vig and Michael E. Kraft (Washington, D.C.: Congressional Quarterly Press, 1990), 33–58.

2. In December 1989 the U.N. General Assembly passed a resolution to hold a second major conference on environment and development (the first was the historic Stockholm conference in 1972). Preconference meetings (precoms) were held in Nairobi (August 1990), Geneva (March and August 1991), and New York (March 1992). By the time the U.N. Conference on Environment and Development convened, twenty years to the day after the Stockholm conference, its scope had been narrowed to several major issues. Major works examining the Earth Summit include the following: Steve Lerner, ed., *Beyond the Earth Summit: Conversations with Advocates of Sustainable Development* (Bolinas, Calif.: Common Knowledge Press, 1992); Caroline Thomas, ed., *Rio: Unraveling the Consequences* (Portland, Ore.: Frank Cass, 1994); Irving M. Mintzer and J. Amber Leonard, eds., *Negotiating Climate Change: The Inside Story of the Rio Convention* (Cambridge: Cambridge University Press, 1994); Stanley P. Johnson, ed., *The Earth*

Summit (Boston: Graham and Trotman/Martinus Nijhoff, 1993); and Ranee K. L. Panjabi, *The Earth Summit at Rio: Politics, Economics, and the Environment* (Boston: Northeastern University Press, 1997). Other recent and useful sources concerning global environmentalism in general include Gareth Porter and Janet Welsh Brown, *Global Environmental Politics* (Boulder, Colo.: Westview Press, 1991); Joyeeta Gupta, *The Climate Change Convention and Developing Countries: From Conflict to Consensus?* (Boston: Kluwer Academic Publiishers, 1997); Ian H. Rowlands, *The Politics of Global Atmospheric Change* (New York: Manchester University Press, 1995); Matthew Paterson, *Global Warming and Global Politics* (New York: Routledge, 1996); Ernst Ulrich von Weizsäcker, *Earth Politics* (Atlantic Highlands, N.J.: Zed Books, 1994).

3. Philip Elmer-Dewitt, "Summit to Save the Earth," *Time,* June 1, 1992, 42.

4. As I will argue below, conferences such as these must be considered primarily as symbolic events that seek to springboard other actions, both national and international. Both the documents and the rhetoric that emerged from the Earth Summit were disappointing to environmentalists, and were insufficient to spark considerable environmental action or raise international environmental issues to a higher point on legislative agendas. Consider, for example, that the Kyoto conference, held in 1998, focused on many of the same issues—albeit in a background of stronger evidence of global warming—but was still unable to garner significant progress and commitments. A Kyoto document requiring emission reductions and stabilization has yet to be ratified by the U.S. Congress, and public discussion of the issue at this point seems negligible. Neither the Republican nor Democratic presidential candidates for the 2000 election focused on international environmental issues. See Jay Branegan, "Is Al Gore a Hero or a Traitor," *Time,* April 26, 1999, 67; Todd Ackerman and R. G. Ratcliffe, "Bush Blasts Global Environmental Plan," *Houston Chronicle,* September 2, 1999, 3A.

5. Adam Rogers, *The Earth Summit: A Planetary Reckoning* (Los Angeles: Global View Press, 1993) 74.

6. "Rio-Con," *New Republic,* July 6, 1992, 7.

7. See Charles P. Alexander, "On the Defensive," *Time,* June 15, 1992, 35; Sharon Begley, "The Grinch of Rio," *Newsweek,* June 15, 1992, 30; *Newsweek,* June 22, 1992; Stephen Hopgood, *American Foreign Environmental Policy and the Power of the State* (New York: Oxford University Press, 1998), 191; Mark Dowie, *Losing Ground: American Environmentalism at the Close of the Twentieth Century* (Cambridge, Mass.: MIT Press, 1995), 167; Albert Gore, "Success for World, Failure for Bush," *USA Today,* June 5, 1992, 13A. According to a U.S. Information Agency special report that surveyed foreign media reaction to Bush's preconference positions, international commentators "vented their frustration" and were "dismayed" at Bush's stances, calling them "narrow and backward," and predicting they would result in Bush incurring a "serious risk of seeing his country in the role of the great international villain of ecology." See USIA Special Report, Foreign Media Reaction, "Dark Clouds Gather over Rio-92," April 1, 1992, Bush Presidential Archives, Office of Policy Development, T. Gorman files, Global Warming and UNCED, file 4, OA/ID 07667.

8. Paul Lewis, "U.S. at the Earth Summit: Isolated and Challenged," *New York Times,* June 10, 1992, A8.

9. Hopgood, *American Foreign Environmental Policy,* 191.

10. Sharon Begley, "The Grinch of Rio," 30. Begley went on to write, "This week more than 100 heads of state or government will attend the last two days of the extravaganza. The climate-control and biodiversity treaties will get enough signatures to go into effect, and the would-be architect of the new world order will have had little to do with it. Bush had put his own twist on the adage 'Think globally, act unilaterally.'"

11. In an article for *USA Today* published on June 15, 1992, Gore described the Earth Summit as "a monumental failure of leadership on the part of George Bush." He described the

mood at the conference as "one of astonishment and sorrow rather than anger. Virtually every nation was looking to him to provide the vision so necessary in the first years of the post–Cold War era. With American ideas—political and economic freedom—ascendant throughout global civilization, people everywhere were anticipating leadership from our president. What they got was a leadership vacuum—one which Japan and Germany moved quickly to try to fill. . . . President Bush promised them [the American people] once that he would be both the environmental president and the foreign-policy president. At the Earth Summit, he was neither." Gore was actively on the attack, appearing on television news shows and granting interviews during the conference. For information on Bill Clinton's criticism, see, for example, Edwin Chen, "Clinton Blasts Bush for U.S. Holdout," *Los Angeles Times,* June 13, 1992, A23.

12. Weizsäcker, *Earth Politics,* 170.

13. Rose Gutfield and John Harwood, "President's Clumsy Handling of Earth Summit Results in a Public-Relations Disaster for Him," *Wall Street Journal,* June 15, 1992, A14.

14. See Jack W. Germond and Jules Witcover, *Mad as Hell: Revolt at the Ballot Box, 1992* (New York: Warner Books, 1993).

15. An unnamed "senior administration official" used this terminology to explain the negative press leading up to the Earth Summit at a press briefing in Rio. See "June 10 Press Briefing," Bush Presidential Archives, Press Files, Administration Files, Box 138, "Earth Summit (1)" folder.

16. But this judgment must remain rather tentative, due to the political "maverick" strategy his advisers sought to create for him. It seems clear the administration wanted to appear rather obstructionist, in order to give the strong impression that Bush was fighting for the American taxpayer against international pressure. The failure of rhetoric, in other words, may have been strategic. These issues are considered later in this chapter.

17. Chaim Perelman and L. Obrechts-Tyteca, *The New Rhetoric: A Treatise on Argumentation,* trans. John Wilkinson and Purcell Weaver (Notre Dame, Ind.: University of Notre Dame Press, 1969), 20–21.

18. Robert Beiner, *Political Judgment* (Chicago: University of Chicago Press, 1983), 177.

19. Aristotle, *On Rhetoric: A Theory of Civic Discourse,* trans. George A. Kennedy (New York: Oxford University Press, 1991), 36.

20. Beiner discussed Kant's "maxim of enlarged thought" in *Political Judgment,* 51.

21. Paul argued that critical thinkers in the strong sense have "developed abilities that aid them in overcoming their minds' natural tendencies to reason egocentrically and sociocentrically" and "grasp both strengths and weaknesses in opposing modes of thought." See Paul, "Critical Thinking in the Strong Sense and the Role of Argumentation in Everyday Life," in *Argumentation: Across the Lines of Discipline, Proceedings of the Conference on Argumentation 1986,* ed. Frans H. van Eemeren, Rob Grootendorst, J. Anthony Blair, and Charles A. Willard (Providence, R.I.: Foris Publications, 1987), 379.

22. See Wayne Booth, *Modern Dogma and the Rhetoric of Assent* (Chicago: University of Chicago Press, 1974).

23. Much has been written concerning Aristotle's notion of *phronesis,* or practical wisdom. Beyond Aristotle's own writings in the *Politics, Rhetoric,* and *Nicomachean Ethics,* see Alasdair MacIntyre, *After Virtue: A Study in Moral Theory,* 2d. ed. (Notre Dame, Ind.: University of Notre Dame Press, 1984); Robert Beiner, *Political Judgment;* Thomas B. Farrell, *Norms of Rhetorical Culture* (New Haven: Yale University Press, 1993).

24. Donald Bryant, "Rhetoric: Its Function and Its Scope," *Quarterly Journal of Speech* 39 (1953): 401–24, reprinted in *Essays on the Rhetoric of the Western World,* ed. Edward P. J. Corbett, James L. Golden, and Goodwin F. Berquist (Dubuque, Iowa: Kendall/Hunt, 1990), 41.

25. Hopgood, *American Foreign Environmental Policy,* 4.

26. Weizsäcker, *Earth Politics,* 3.

27. Information from U.S. Environmental Protection Agency. See the agency's Web site: <www.epa.gov/globalwarming/climate/intro.html>.

28. Cited in Tarla Rai Peterson, *Sharing the Earth: The Rhetoric of Sustainable Development* (Columbia: University of South Carolina Press, 1997), 59.

29. "Costing the Earth: The Politics of Posterity," *Economist,* September 2, 1989, 1 (emphasis added).

30. See Rogers, *Earth Summit.*

31. For an examination of Bush's and Clinton's attempts at establishing a new rhetorical conception of foreign policy, see Mary E. Stuckey, "Competing Foreign Policy Visions: Rhetorical Hybrids after the Cold War," *Western Journal of Communication* 59 (1995): 214–27.

32. Rockman, "The Leadership Style of George Bush," in *The Bush Presidency: First Appraisals,* ed. Colin Campbell, S.J., and Bert A. Rockman (Chatham, N.J.: Chatham House, 1991), 25.

33. "Remarks at an Environmental Agreement Signing Ceremony at the Grand Canyon, Arizona," September 18, 1991, *Public Papers of the Presidents of the United States,* available online at <www.presidentialrhetoric.com>.

34. "Address to the United Nations Conference on Environment and Development in Rio de Janeiro," June 12, 1992, Public Papers, 1992.

35. Bush's primary environmental success, considered one of his few domestic victories, was the 1990 Clean Air Act, which focused on domestic air quality. A review of Bush's major addresses on the environment throughout his presidency reveals the preference for domestic environmental issues. Bush invoked global issues only to specific audiences. See "Remarks at the Opening Session of the White House Conference on Science and Economics Research Related to Global Change," April 17, 1990; "Remarks at the Closing Session of the White House Conference on Science and Economics Research Related to Global Change," April 18, 1990; "Remarks to the Intergovernmental Panel on Climate Change," February 5, 1990; "Remarks at an Environmental Agreement Signing Ceremony at the Grand Canyon, Arizona," September 18, 1991; "Remarks and an Exchange with Reporters Prior to Discussions with United Nations Secretary-General Boutros Boutros-Ghali," May 12, 1992; "White House Statement on the Establishment of the Inter-American Institute for Global Change Research," May 15, 1992; "Remarks and a Question-and-Answer Session with the Agricultural Community in Fresno, California," May 30, 1992; "Remarks on Departure for the United Nations Conference on Environment and Development," June 11, 1992; "Address to the United Nations Conference on Environment and Development in Rio de Janeiro, Brazil," June 12, 1992. All speeches from the presidency of George Bush are available on-line through the George Bush Presidential Library at: <http://www.cdsl.tamu.edu/bush>.

36. Ironically, Bush was typically considered to be a president who focused on foreign affairs to the detriment of domestic issues. The Earth Summit is one case in which Bush focused on domestic issues to the detriment of the international views.

37. Mark Rozell, "In Reagan's Shadow: Bush's Antirhetorical Presidency," *Presidential Studies Quarterly* 28 (1998): 136, 127. Journalist Maureen Dowd also labeled Bush the "antirhetorical President"; see "The Language Thing," *New York Times,* July 29, 1990, 32.

38. Will, "It's Not Modesty, It's Arrogance," *Washington Post,* October 12, 1990, A21.

39. See "More Groups Address Climate Change," *Science News,* February 10, 1990, 95. Other reports included an EPA study concerned with the "migration" of trees northward due to warming trends and the impending rise in sea level, and a report from the International Energy Agency that identified economic and technological options for reducing emissions.

40. Colleen Shannon, "Washington Washout: Global Warming," *Chemistry and Industry,* February 19, 1990, 88.

41. "Remarks to the Intergovernmental Panel on Climate Change," February 5, 1990, Public Papers, 1990.

42. A focus on the need and benefit of "sound science" was repeated throughout the Bush presidency. Practically every speech listed in note 35, above, for example, mentioned the phrase. For commentary on Sununu, see John Sununu, "The Political Pleasures of Engineering: An Interview with John Sununu." *Technology Review,* August/September 1992, 24–25; Maureen Dowd, "Who's Environmental Czar, E.P.A. Chief or Sununu," *New York Times,* February 15, 1990, A1.

43. "Talking Points on the 'Earth Summit,'" Bush Presidential Archives, Dorrance Smith files, Media Affairs, OA/ID 08292.

44. Clinton also linked environmental progress to his belief in the free market. In October 1997 he called for the "unleashing [of] the full power of free markets and technological innovations to meet the challenge of climate change," and proposed a package of "strong market incentives, tax cuts, and cooperative efforts with industry." His plan was designed to "play to our strengths—innovation, creativity, entrepreneurship." "Remarks by the President on Global Climate Change," October 22, 1997, Public Papers, 1997.

45. McCormick, *Reclaiming Paradise: The Global Environmental Movement* (Bloomington: Indiana University Press, 1989), 89.

46. Porter and Brown, *Global Environmental Politics,* 104.

47. For examination of the issues surrounding economic-environment issues and sustainable development, see Peterson, *Sharing the Earth;* Herman E. Daly and John B. Cobb, Jr., *For the Common Good: Redirecting the Economy toward Community, the Environment, and a Sustainable Future* (Boston: Beacon Press, 1989).

48. Hopgood, *American Foreign Environmental Policy,* 143.

49. Cited in Peterson, *Sharing the Earth,* 71.

50. Vig, "Presidential Leadership."

51. Dowie, *Losing Ground,* 177.

52. Rogers, *Earth Summit,* 78–83.

53. Wines, "The Earth Summit," *New York Times,* June 11, 1992, A1.

54. Hopgood, *American Foreign Environmental Policy,* 173.

55. Wines, "Earth Summit," A1.

56. The administration's conservative turn was characterized in an article in the *New York Times* as follows: "The President has recently adjusted his dialogue to stress disgust with environmental advocates and his insistence that curbs on pollution and development will not come at the cost of jobs. . . . The conservatives, mostly in Vice President Dan Quayle's office and in economic policy posts, have captured the high ground and Mr. Bush's favor in many recent debates. They are backed by other conservative strategists . . . who see environmental policy as a way for Mr. Bush to win back Western conservatives who are deserting him." Those conservative victories included the decision not to reduce the logging of primary-growth forests in Oregon, the breaking of Bush's no-net-loss pledge on wetlands, and the significant relaxation of some of the new Clean Air Act's regulations. Wines, "Earth Summit," A1.

57. Polling data acquired online through Odum Institute's "Public Opinion Poll Question Database." The cited USA Today polls are located at <ftp://ftp.irss.unc.edu/pub/search_results/POLL. .18Mar2005.10.21.33.txt>, specifically questions 8 and 11.

58. Various polling data on environmental attitudes were discussed within the Bush White House, according to archival data. On July 16, 1992, Roger B. Porter wrote a memo to Bush reporting on Time Mirror polls. The polls were highly pro-environment. For example, one ques-

tion asking respondents to choose between "environmental protection" and "economic development" found 64 percent chose the former and only 17 percent the latter. On August 7, 1992, David Struhs from the president's Council on Environmental Quality provided Bush with a report on polling data concerning the environment, writing that "despite the Persian Gulf war and the economic recession," there had been "increasing attention to public opinion on environmental issues." The polls themselves showed that the American people, despite Bush's rhetoric, were comfortable with the need to trade jobs for environmental initiatives, and consistently over 50 percent of the respondents to one survey would be willing to increase their personal income taxes by 5 percent for programs to help clean the environment. Despite these answers, 79 percent of respondents reported they had never voted for or against candidates because of their environmental records. See David Struhs, "Public Opinion Polling on the Environment," August 7, 1992, Bush Presidential Archives, Subject File NR, Box 10, Folder 8; Roger B. Porter, "Public Opinion on the Outdoors and the Environment," Bush Presidential Archives, Subject Files NR, Box 10, Folder 10.

59. See B. L. Ware and Wil Linkugel, "They Spoke in Defense of Themselves: On the Generic Criticism of Apologia," *QJS* 59 (1973): 273–83; William Benoit, *Accounts, Excuses, and Apologies: A Theory of Image Restoration Strategies* (New York: SUNY Press, 1995).

60. *USA Today,* June 12, 1992. The cited source was the 1992 Information Please Environmental Almanac, compiled by World Resources Institute. Other, contradictory data exist. For example, in total dollars the United States gave more aid to developing countries than any other developed nation, but as a percentage of GNP, it gave only .21 percent, which was far below countries such as Norway (1.17), France (.79), Canada (.44), Germany (.42), Italy (.32), Japan (.31), and Britain (.27), and below the U.N. goal of .7 percent. See "Rio Conference on Environment and Development," *Environmental Policy and Law* 22 (1992): 217.

61. "UNCED Talking Points," Bush Presidential Archives, David Bradford, CEA, UNCED, file 2, OA/ID 07929; "The Bush Record on Environmental Issues at UNCED," Bush Presidential Archives, Media Affairs, Maria Eital Sheehan files, Rio Summit, OA/ID 06813.

62. Russel S. Frye, "Uncle Sam at UNCED," *Environmental Policy and Law* 22 (1992): 343.

63. This specific comment appeared on a copy of the draft sent originally to Holiday. The comments seem to match the handwriting on the memo of Paul Korfonta. Document located in the Bush Presidential Archives, Speech Files, Box 154, "Departure Statement, Rio Summit, Andres AFB" File.

64. See Sununu, "Political Pleasures of Engineering."

65. Rogers, *Earth Summit,* 174.

66. Bush, "Remarks and Exchange with Reporters Prior to a Meeting with Congressional Leaders," June 11, 1992, Public Papers, 1992.

67. Bush, "Remarks on Departure."

68. Hopgood, *American Foreign Environmental Policy,* 192.

69. "The 'Environmental President,'" *Washington Post,* June 7, 1992, C6.

70. "The Road from Rio," *New York Times,* June 15, 1992, A18.

71. Numerous other examples could be cited. For example, an anonymous adviser was quoted in the *New York Times* as having said: "Japan's out there killing whales and running driftnets, for God's sake, while we've got the world's toughest environmental laws and we're twisting ourselves into knots over how many jobs to abolish to save a subspecies of an owl. And these guys presume to lecture us about environmental responsibility?" See Hopgood, *American Foreign Environmental Policy,* 193.

72. Letter from Clayton Yeutter to Robert Reinstein, May 13, 1992, Bush Presidential Archives, Subject Files, NR-NR, Box 9, File 7. A similar letter in the same folder was written

to Robert Zoellick and read: "It was the United States versus nearly all the rest of the world, and our fundamental viewpoint prevailed."

73. An editorial by Clayton Yeutter appearing in the June 12, 1992, issue of the *Washington Post* defended Bush's objections to the biodiversity treaty. Also see "Rio-Con," *New Republic,* July 6, 1992, 7.

74. Bromley, *The President's Scientists: Reminiscences of a White House Science Advisor* (New Haven: Yale University Press, 1994), 145.

75. "Talking Points on the 'Earth Summit,'" Bush Presidential Archives, Dorrance Smith files, Media Affairs, OA/ID 08292.

76. June 1, 1992, Bush Presidential Archives, Council of Economic Advisors files, David Bradford Files, UNCED file 2 of 3, OA/ID 07929; "The Bush Record on Environmental Issues at UNCED," Bush Presidential Archives, Maria Eitel Sheehan files, Media Affairs, "Rio Summit" folder, OA/ID 06813.

77. George Bush, "Remarks and a Question-and-Answer Session with the Agricultural Community in Fresno, California," May 30, 1992, Public Papers, 1992.

78. June 10 Press Briefing, Bush Presidential Archives, Press Files, Administration Files, Box 138, "Earth Summit (1)" folder. The administration also felt that both developing and developed countries were unfairly making the United States out to be the scapegoat for all the world's problems. During the same press briefing, it was said that "there is a variation of this idea [dependency theory in economics] which is what I refer to as the 'Amerika school,' spelled with a K. And that basically is that, forget what the record says, just blame the United States." Simply put, the United States was suffering undue criticism merely because it was "a convenient target."

79. June 10 Press Briefing, Public Papers, 1992.

80. Consider the following excerpts: "We've not only seen the concern, we share it. We not only care, we're taking *action.* We come to Rio with an *action* plan on climate change." "Let us join in translating the words spoken here into concrete *action* to protect the planet." "We come to press on with deliberate purpose and forceful *action.* Such *action* will demonstrate our continuing commitment to leadership and to international cooperation on the environment." "When our children look back on this time and this place, they will be grateful that we met at Rio, and they will certainly be pleased with the intentions stated and the commitments made. But they will judge us by the *actions* we take from this day forward. Let us not disappoint them." See "Address to the United Nations Conference on Environment and Development in Rio de Janiero," June 12, 1992, Public Papers, 1992 (emphasis added).

81. Speech draft located in Bush Presidential Archives, Science and Technology files of D. Allan Bromley, folder title "Environmental UNCED Visit of President and Mrs. Bush to Rio de Janiero, June 13, 1992," OA/ID 08713.

82. "Rio-Con," *New Republic,* July 6, 1992, 7.

83. A January 1998 Harris poll reported that 86.7 percent of respondents believed global warming was "very serious" or "somewhat serious." Numerous stories have mentioned the disconnection between worldwide public concern and presidential indifference to the issue. See, for example, William K. Stevens, "Meterologists Say Earth Temperature Hottest Ever in '98," *Houston Chronicle,* December 12, 1998, 2A; William K. Stevens, "Scientists Warn against Ignoring 'Serious' Global Warming Problem," *Houston Chronicle,* January 29, 1999, 17A; Dick Thompson, "Capitol Hill Meltdown: While the Nation Sizzles, Congress Fiddles over Measures to Slow Down Future Climate Change," *Time,* August 9, 1999, 56–59. Of course, strong opposition to the global warming evidence continues to surface also. For a valuable source for global warming skepticism, visit the Climate Change Resources Web site: <www.cei.org/gw.html>.

84. In a short study dated August 6, 1992, and entitled "Al Gore and *Earth in the Balance*," the unnamed author attacked the "cramped" and "radical" nature of the book. The author mentioned that there "are all sort of errors," noting that "poking fun at his rhetoric is almost too tempting." Bush Presidential Archives, Subject File NR, Box 11, Folder 1.

85. Albert Gore, *Earth in the Balance: Ecology and the Human Spirit* (New York: Houghton Mifflin, 1992), 269. For commentary on Gore's environmental retreat, see Branegan, "Is Al Gore a Hero or a Traitor," 67; and David A. Ridenour, "Times When Gore's Hypocrisy Is Just Breath-taking," *Houston Chronicle,* September 2, 1999, 33A.

86. Quoted in Ackerman and Ratcliffe, "Bush Blasts Global Environmental Plan," 3A.

87. George W. Bush, "Text of a Letter from the President to Senators Hagel, Helms, Craig, and Roberts," March 13, 2001. Document available online: <www.whitehouse.gov>.

CHAPTER 8

George Bush and the Religious Right

AMY TILTON JONES

Beginning with the 1976 presidential campaign season, the Religious Right became a presence in national politics, aligning with the Republican Party in 1980 to elect Ronald Reagan.[1] Religious conservative voters who once supported fellow evangelical Jimmy Carter decided by 1980 that he had become politically too liberal and that they had no legitimate chance of enacting their legislative agenda under a Carter administration. Since that time this facet of the Republican Party has become the most powerful in terms of voter mobilization. Therefore, most candidates believe that they must cater to the Religious Right if they hope to be successful in their bid for the Republican presidential nomination.[2] The members of the Religious Right do not yet have the power to dictate who the candidate or winner will be in any given campaign, but no one has won the Republican presidential nomination since 1980 without their support. Today's Religious Right is a large, multifaceted, and legitimate force within the Republican Party that "combines lobbying muscle—it played a major role in defeating the Clinton health plan—with a stunning ability to cultivate and harvest voters at election time, mainly by distributing some 60 million voter guides and congressional scorecards through 65,000 churches."[3]

The vote-getting power of the Religious Right does not come without a price, however. Religious conservative leaders who have rallied support around a candidate and helped him or her get elected fully expect substantial thank-yous in the form of legislation and the appointment of religious conservatives to key positions in the administration.[4] In other words, the Religious Right will support a worthy candidate with millions of voters on election day, but once in office the politician must be able to deliver on promises made during the campaign. Jimmy Carter failed to fulfill the expectations of Christian and religious conservatives. Even Reagan and Bush did not always fulfill religious conservatives' expectations for evangelical appointments to the new administration. Their calls for profamily and anti–alternative lifestyle legislation often went unheeded. This is where the Religious Right's disillusionment with the Republican Party began during the Bush administration, and it eventually caused trouble for the president in his bid for reelection in 1992.

The Religious Right is composed of many religiously conservative people and organizations. While all hold basic profamily, prolife beliefs, the way they choose to get their collective message "out there" is as varied as the many groups and organizations themselves. Group members of the larger religious conservative movement include the Christian Broadcasting Network, the Family Research Council, Focus on the Family, Concerned Women for America, American Family Association, and Christian Voice. Members of the Religious Right also include Christian journalists, such as Cal Thomas and Marvin Olasky; religiously based periodicals; famous preachers and pastors, such as Charles Stanley and D. James Kennedy; professors in public and private universities; lobbyists, carrying the message and agenda of the various Religious Right organizations to Capitol Hill and beyond; and motivational speakers, such as Doug Wead, on the business circuit.

Through their various positions in society, religious conservatives present a generally united ideology to their listeners, viewers, congregations, constituents, students, and political representatives. The Religious Right believes in family values, defined as including increased availability and affordability of childcare services, the autonomy of religious-based schools and daycare centers, use of vouchers to attend private/ religious schools, bigger tax breaks for families with children, textbook and library censorship, the annihilation of pornography, and the overall preservation of the traditional family. In support of these positions, the Religious Right staunchly opposes alternative lifestyles and any type of gay/lesbian rights organizations, including civil rights organizations that are seen as too liberal or accepting of "un-Christian-like" behavior or ideologies, such as the National Organization for Women (NOW), and the American Civil Liberties Union (ACLU). However, the Religious Right is most known for its unwavering, "tenacious opposition to abortion, gay rights, and sex education."[5]

To have access to the voting power of religious conservatives, a candidate must be unwavering in his or her support of these issues. This was the beginning of the problems for President George Bush. The biggest lightning rods in the relationship between the Bush administration and the Religious Right were abortion and gay rights. Bush was known for changing his stand on abortion throughout his political career, and some on the Religious Right disagreed with his view as president that abortions could be acceptable in cases of rape or incest, or if the life of the mother was in danger.[6] On the issue of gay rights, Bush was also seen as wavering in his position against more rights for homosexuals by allowing leaders of gay and lesbian rights organizations to attend ceremonies at the White House and by involving homosexual groups with the publicity surrounding the April 1990 signing of anti–hate crime legislation. This wavering led many members of the Religious Right to vocalize their belief that Bush was becoming too moderate for their continued support.[7]

How did George Bush rhetorically mediate the competing needs of keeping the Religious Right in the Republican camp while at the same time preventing it from taking control of the party, or from dictating candidates and policy? Through the analysis of primary and secondary sources, archival research at the George Bush Presidential Library, and interviews with members of the Bush administration and religious conservatives, I hope to shed light on this question.

THE PRE-PRESIDENTIAL YEARS

As the vice president for eight years, George Bush was the natural choice to be Ronald Reagan's successor. The Religious Right had a large role in electing Bush, as it had in both of Reagan's victories. In the 1988 election this produced a campaign that was "charged with religious language and sanctified causes."[8] Even though George Bush had learned to speak, however haltingly, the language of the Religious Right in his bid for the presidency, the first three years of his administration put a strain on the relationship between Bush and religious conservatives.

As the 1988 campaign approached, the leaders and membership of the various organizations that make up the Religious Right were lukewarm about supporting Bush as the Republican nominee. For the most part, the disagreement rested on the perception that Bush did not seem to be as ideologically in tune with religious conservatives as Reagan had been.

The most notable ideological disagreement concerned Bush's past positions on abortion. Bush, throughout most of his political career, had taken a prochoice stance. As a presidential candidate, Bush opposed abortion on demand, but believed allowances should be made in cases of rape or incest, or if the life of the mother was in danger. Although his friend Jerry Falwell agreed with Bush on the stipulation about the life of the mother, many members of the Religious Right, including Patrick Buchanan, opposed abortion under any and all circumstances. Even so, the Religious Right fell in line behind the Bush candidacy.

THE BUSH ADMINISTRATION

Although the Religious Right helped elect George Bush, once in office Bush intentionally sought to minimize its influence in his administration. One member of the Religious Right, Doug Wead, was named special assistant to the president, but he was the only senior member of the staff with direct ties to the Religious Right. Bush, who was never comfortable speaking about controversial social issues, nevertheless adopted part of Reagan's strategy for dealing with the Religious Right. He tried to talk his way into their good graces.

In 1989, Bush's first year in office, he spoke on the subject of abortion twenty-three times. These references to one of the Religious Right's key issues mostly took the form of letters to Congress about upcoming legislation, or disapproval of how Congress had voted on a bill dealing with the issue of abortion.[9] These position statements usually reiterated Bush's belief that adoption could and should replace the practice of abortion, and then moved on to the next topic with little new discussion on the abortion issue. For example, in his remarks to a 1989 March for Life Rally, Bush said: "We are concerned about abortion because it deals with the lives of two human beings, mother and child. . . . And I think when it comes to abortion there's a better way: the way of adoption, the way of life."[10]

Throughout 1989 Bush often stated and restated his position on the abortion issue, but only within clearly demarcated limits. In a letter to congressional leaders, he urged them to "protect the lives of America's unborn children," and noted that if he were presented with a bill that appropriated funds for any type of abortion other than cases when the life of the mother was in danger, he would veto it.[11] Bush focused his solution on adoption, and rarely called for new legislation. Abortion and adoption were often subsumed in Bush's rhetoric under the ever-widening umbrella of "family values." In opening a memorandum on adoption, for example, Bush stated, "The foundation of our nation is the American family, protector of our most valuable yet vulnerable resource—our children." Then he went on to say, "Everyone wins in adoption."[12]

Though Bush spoke regularly about abortion during the first year of his administration, that practice dropped drastically in his second year. In 1990 Bush spoke on the issue of abortion only twelve times. These references and speeches were mostly to press groups and in question-and-answer sessions—not to groups that could initiate or affect legislation. In 1991 the frequency of Bush's comments on abortion increased slightly, to seventeen references. However, these speeches continued to be to press groups and citizens at large, not to anyone directly related to the legislative process. Never did Bush put the full weight of his office behind the Right to Life movement's primary goal of a constitutional amendment to ban abortion.

NATIONAL ENDOWMENT FOR THE ARTS

While Bush's lack of involvement or interest in the abortion wars was always bothersome to the Religious Right, it was his handling of the National Endowment for the Arts funding debacle that first caused a serious rift with his religious allies. This first test of how he would implement his ideology was compounded by insistence from religious conservatives that he take a hard-line stance against funding of indecent art, and attempts by members of his administration to shield the president from those pressures.

The controversy revolved around artworks that were featured in exhibits that had received federal money from the National Endowment for the Arts. Andres Serrano came under fire by religious conservatives in 1989 for one of his pieces that featured a crucifix submerged in a container of urine. Members of the Religious Right termed this "sacrilege," and said exhibits like these were not art.[13] However, Serrano defended his work, stating that he too was a Christian and that he did not mean anything sacrilegious by the exhibit, provocatively titled "Piss Christ." Serrano explained further, "My work reflects ambivalent feelings about religion and Christianity . . . of being drawn to Christ but resisting organized Christianity."[14]

The second controversy involved an exhibit of photographs by Robert Mapplethorpe. The Mapplethorpe exhibit was objectionable to members of the Religious Right because it was seen as pornographic, again something that religious conservatives did not view as art. Conservatives objected to several photographs in the Mapplethorpe exhibit "The Perfect Moment." Among the objectionable photos were a picture "of a man with his penis protruding from a polyester suit and a girl with her dress lifted partway."[15]

The Religious Right objected to the funding of what they considered clear examples of pornography and homoeroticism. They believed that "grants to artists should include restrictive language forbidding obscenity, and that the NEA should be done away with entirely."[16] Besides being disgusted and offended by certain works in the Serrano and Mapplethorpe exhibits, the members of the Religious Right were upset over the "refusal by the Bush Administration to endorse restrictions on the content of Federally financed arts programs."[17] Furthermore, this controversy was seen as "the first major test of the President's ability to keep ardent conservatives as happy members of his party."[18] At the end of the controversy, "religious conservatives responded angrily to Mr. Bush's announcement that the Administration would not support their call for legislation to deal with what they consider objectionable art."[19]

The Bush administration response—clearly seen as inadequate by the Religious Right—was twofold. First, John Frohnmayer, the chair of the NEA, defended the Mapplethorpe and Serrano exhibits as being examples of artistic expression. Furthermore, Frohnmayer stated, "Art cannot avoid being offensive and confrontational, especially when it breaks new ground or presents new ideas of what art is."[20] He also inadvertently hinted that the Religious Right's objections to the exhibits did not represent the average American's viewpoint by stating that "what offends one will not necessarily offend another."[21] The NEA also saw the Religious Right as unfairly targeting Mapplethorpe as representative of the NEA, and feared that the negative publicity might adversely affect the NEA's health.[22] In the aftermath of the Mapplethorpe and Serrano controversy, the Senate Appropriations Committee stepped in and placed a ban on NEA grants to two art groups that were connected with the organization of the exhibits in question. This legislation was passed and implemented, thus creating a five-year ban on funding despite the fact that the Mapplethorpe exhibit posted record-breaking attendance marks.[23]

Bush's personal response also fell under close scrutiny by the Religious Right. When asked about controversies such as the National Endowment for the Arts funding investigation, Bush responded in a vague manner, using religious rhetoric. Bush stated, "There is a fundamental understanding that we are one nation under God, that we have great respect for religious diversity, and that as we see the social problems of the day we return more and more to the importance of the family."[24] Bush was not shy about stating his objection to the exhibits of work by Serrano and Mapplethorpe, calling the pieces "sacrilegious, blasphemous depictions that are portrayed by some to be art." But he was not as quick to call for tough restrictions on future NEA grants. Instead, Bush said he had faith in Frohnmayer, whom he had appointed to run the NEA, and that he supported whatever decisions Frohnmayer made and implemented.[25] Frohnmayer stood behind his statements that all good art will eventually offend someone, but ultimately resigned his post a year and a half later, after it became clear that his stance was hurting George Bush.[26]

The conflict over how Bush handled the NEA funding controversy was the beginning of the disillusionment between the Religious Right and the Bush administration. Religious conservatives were upset with Bush for not taking a stronger rhetorical stance. They wanted him to call for legislation that would impose restrictions on what artists could do with federal grant money. They were also upset at the way the Bush administration handled the news of the pending Mapplethorpe and Serrano exhibits. According to Doug Wead, White House liaison for religious issues, he and David Demarest, the director of communications, knew about the exhibits two months before they opened. But Wead was instructed not to "bother the President" with the information.[27] As a result, President Bush had to answer questions about the exhibits from angry leaders of the Religious Right when he had not been briefed by his advisers about how to answer their questions adequately. Therefore, Bush appeared not to know about or have control over what was happening in his own administration.

TALKING TO THE RELIGIOUS RIGHT

Annual speeches to the National Religious Broadcasters and the National Association of Evangelicals gave Bush the opportunity to talk directly to large segments of the Religious Right. The National Religious Broadcasters (NRB) is perhaps the most important part of the Religious Right in terms of reaching the general public. Notable members of this group include Pat Robertson of television's *700 Club,* Reverend Billy Graham, Robert Schuller, Charles Stanley, John Hagee, Paul Crouch of the Trinity Broadcasting Network, and James Dobson of *Focus on the Family.*

George Bush addressed the NRB annual convention several times during his tenure as vice president and president of the United States. As president, he spoke to the NRB in 1990, 1991, and 1992. He missed the scheduled 1989 appearance because of a last-minute attack of laryngitis.[28] These three addresses illuminate some of the rhetorical battles that began to take place between Bush and the Religious Right. As one of the public-focused factions of the Religious Right, the NRB openly admitted that it supported Bush's ideology less strongly than Reagan's. However, the early relationship between the Religious Right and Bush was cordial, though not close. One noted member, Reverend Billy Graham, was a good friend of Bush and had delivered prayers at the 1989 inauguration. This friendly tone is clearly present in the 1990 speech. In the 1991 speech to the NRB, Bush tries to begin mending the relationship that had been splintered by several incidents, particularly the perception by the Right that Bush was getting soft on the issue of gay rights.[29] This speech also fell during the beginning of the Gulf War. Bush uses his 1991 address to get the Religious Right on his side for the war effort. Therefore, it is not surprising that Bush uses terms familiar to religious conservatives, speaking of morality and the idea of a "just war." This rhetorical stance demonstrated to the religious conservatives that Bush was familiar with their language and beliefs. And Bush's rhetoric seemed to have worked when, shortly after his address, the NRB board passed a resolution "to wholeheartedly stand in prayer and in support of our president and government . . . as they do all that is necessary, though costly, to bring genuine peace in the Middle East."[30]

Bush's 1992 address to the NRB focused on ideology, an ideology that not so coincidentally mirrored that of the Religious Right. On the brink of his reelection bid, and following his sweeping victory in the Gulf, Bush continued to repair the ideologically torn relationship between his administration and the conservative wing of the party that he would need in November. This speech was more policy-laden than the previous two efforts, as it focused on the "Weed and Seed" program, an effort aimed at reducing crime in poor areas of large cities and simultaneously spurring economic growth.[31] My analysis focuses on the continuum created by these three addresses—the strategies employed in one text and absent from the others, the behind-the-scenes strategies that governed the drafting (and in some cases repeated redrafting) of the speeches to the National Religious Broadcasters.

1990 SPEECH TO THE NATIONAL RELIGIOUS BROADCASTERS

The 1990 NRB speech deals with the issue of ideology, but contains a whole page of jokes before turning to issues such as the religiosity of America, abortion, and family values. The presence of jokes is a marked difference between this speech and the other two speeches that Bush delivered to the NRB during his tenure as president. George Bush often utilized humor and self-depreciation in his rhetoric, but in the opening paragraphs of the 1990 NRB speech, he deploys religious humor to "warm up" his audience. The jokes are lighthearted and fairly humorous. The idea of including religiously based jokes in the NRB speech was the biggest topic of discussion between speechwriters and advisers in the weeks before the address.

Drafts of the speech went out to everyone from Wead (to insert proper biblical references) to speechwriters, advisers, and legal consultants to tweak the details and message that the president would deliver to the NRB. Memo after memo streamed back to David Demarest, assistant to the president for communications, and Chriss Winston, chief of speechwriting, advising the interested parties that the selected jokes and general use of humor mixed with religious doctrine "makes us nervous."[32] Wead responded to the draft of the speech with a memo titled "The Psychology of the NRB Speech." The opening line of Wead's cautionary memo reads: "The psychology of this speech is rather tricky."[33] When subsequent drafts still included the string of opening jokes, more memos followed, communicating the dislike of opening such a speech with humor. Roger Porter, chief of domestic policy, wrote: "This is the second time we have seen the two jokes included in the second and fourth paragraphs on page one and we still believe they are inappropriate."[34] Further appearance of the jokes also caused various recipients of the draft to write rationales for why they thought the jokes were offensive and why they should be removed.

One series of jokes read: "In the spirit of the occasion, I want to make two vows. First, I'll be brief. And I know there's a mention in the bible about the burning bush. But I also know—and I say this not with humility but with objectivity—compared to most around here, I'm not that hot a speaker. So, I won't burden you. But the second promise is for those of you way off in the back of the room: I'll try to speak up. Jerry Rose warned me that the agnostics in this room are very bad."[35] In response to these humorous remarks, John Gardner wrote: "I really think this is offensive to Evangelicals. It's hard for me to imagine this audience laughing at the joke, and I would recommend deleting it."[36] Although the joke that Gardner objected to was kept in the final draft of the speech, two notable changes were made. First, the word "vows" in the first line was deleted and replaced by "promises." Because of its role in a religious wedding ceremony, the word "vows" has a stronger religious connotation. Second, the name of the person referred to in the last line of the joke was changed from Jerry Rose to Pat Robertson. There is no evidence as to why these two changes were made. Bush himself was unsure about the use of humor in this speech to the NRB. After learning about the objections to the use of humor in this speech, President Bush went to Wead to ask whether the jokes would be appropriate for the audience in question. Wead believes that Bush had convinced himself that the audience would not laugh at the jokes and was unsure how to react if they did not laugh. In response to this uneasiness, Wead suggested that Bush call Reagan and tell him the joke; if Reagan laughed, the joke should stay. Bush made the phone call, and Reagan laughed at the joke. During the car trip on the way to deliver the speech, Wead coached Bush on how to react if the audience did not laugh. The audience laughed.

Another example of humor in the 1990 NRB speech touches on differences in ideology that writers and advisers deemed possibly offensive. Bush was to say: "Sure, differences exist over sect and theology. Some, for instance, claim the stairway to heaven is climbed through good works. . . . Others think the Pearly Gates welcome only those who like horse shoes and country music."[37] In response to this humor, Gardner advised, "The notion that good works alone lead to salvation was what Protestants (falsely) accused Catholics of believing for centuries. And I don't think the President should even joke about the idea that only people like him will be saved."[38] This humor was removed from the final draft of the speech, but another joke was inserted in its place that met the approval of the majority of the writers and advisers: "I hope you know by now—you know me—I'm an optimist; and after all, last year I had the experience that renewed my faith. I was running out of prayers. I had almost given up. Then a miracle occurred: I caught a fish!"[39] Although this bit of humor could be seen as minimizing the importance of miracles, it did not inadvertently raise ideological problems as the previous joke was thought to do.

Despite the extended debate about the president's use of humor in this speech, most of the jokes still appeared in the final text version, and were included in the text of his speech delivered to the national convention on January 29, 1990. In short, Bush spoke comfortably and amicably to the 1990 convention.

The relationship between Bush and the Religious Right changed between the 1990 and 1991 speeches to the NRB. In April 1990 President Bush invited leaders of gay and lesbian activist groups to a Rose Garden signing of an anti–hate crime bill. Leaders of the Religious Right were outraged that a man their faction had helped to elect appeared to be "getting soft" on the issue of gay rights. In response to this scene, many members and leaders wrote letters of protest to Wead. Wead responded with a letter, typed on official White House letterhead, that denounced the actions by the president and held that Bush's advisers were wrong to have let him invite "such people" into the White House. In July of the same year a press photo showed the presence of two homosexual community leaders at the signing of the Americans with Disabilities Act. After Wead wrote yet another apologetic letter on official letterhead, he was fired.[40] These actions eliminated any direct link between the Bush administration and the Religious Right. This event was the catalyst for the increased disillusionment with Bush by conservative Christians. Although over 80 percent of evangelicals had voted for Bush in 1988, his approval numbers among the same group after Wead's firing dropped off sharply.[41]

1991 Speech to the National Religious Broadcasters

The 1991 address to the National Religious Broadcasters was affected by this strain in the relationship. Humor is absent from this speech. After a brief welcome, Bush addresses the ideological rifts that have developed between the two parties by talking about the values they have in common, rather than the issues upon which they disagree: "Matthew also reminds us in these times that the meek shall inherit the Earth. At home, these values imbue the policies which you and I support. Like me, you endorse adoption, not abortion."[42] Although he identified himself as prolife, Bush also thought that exceptions in the ideology should be made for cases of rape or incest, and if the life of the mother was at risk. Although Jerry Falwell agreed with Bush on these exceptions, the majority of the Religious Right strictly opposed abortion under any circumstances. Bush used this address, by deleting details of his ideology, to draw a common ground between the NRB and the Bush administration.

The latter part of the 1991 NRB speech offers moral justification for Bush's actions in the Persian Gulf, as well as religious justification for why the war was the "moral" thing to do. Bush asked the National Religious Broadcasters to support the effort, and to voice this support to their listeners and viewers on a daily basis. He asked for support across religious lines on the basis of morality by saying: "The war in the Gulf is not a Christian war, a Jewish war, or a Moslem war; it is a just war. And it is a war with which good will prevail. The first principle of a just war is that it support a just cause. Our cause could not be more noble. We seek Iraq's withdrawal from Kuwait—completely, immediately, and without condition; the restoration of Kuwait's legitimate government; and the security and stability of the Gulf."[43] Bush was seeking support from the NRB and the wider public that tuned into its broadcasts. However, this speech also exemplified the use of prudence by Bush. His "practical use of reasoning," as well as case building for his own actions, are more obviously present in this speech than in the 1990 address.[44]

Bush also offered religious reasoning and support for the Gulf War, stating: "The clergyman Richard Cecil once said, 'There are two classes of the wise: the men who serve God because they have found Him, and the men who seek Him because they have not found Him yet.' Abroad, as in America, our task is to serve and seek wisely through the policies we pursue."[45]

1992 Speech to the National Religious Broadcasters

The 1992 speech to the NRB showed a continuance of ideological identification in preparation for the 1992 campaign. Again, humor was absent from the speech, even though the war had concluded and the tone of the speech was accordingly less severe. Bush highlighted his accomplishments in the Gulf and introduced a new initiative that was "right up the alley" of the NRB, the "Weed and Seed" program. This speech was also seen as central to the campaign effort to woo the Religious Right back to the side of the Bush administration. Memos from speechwriters and advisers to President Bush make clear what the administration hoped to accomplish before the conservative audience of the NRB: "Your speech strives to cut through the political vagaries of campaign season by focusing on values—the values that sustain America and that this administration shares with our nation's religious broadcasters. You talk about the sanctity of unborn life, opportunity and empowerment, decency and tolerance, family and choice, the war against drugs, and the power of prayer."[46] Bush's second paragraph dealt with the American victory in the Gulf War and repeated the religious and moral justification that he had offered for the war in the 1991 address. Bush recalled: "A year ago we met in the first week of a struggle to protect what is right and true. And I came before you to talk of what was not a Christian or Jewish war, not a Moslem war. It was a just war. And in the Persian Gulf we fought for good versus evil. It was that clear to me: right versus wrong, dignity against oppression. And America stood fast so that liberty could stand tall."[47] This passage served two purposes: to laud his own accomplishments, but also to present the moral justifications behind those accomplishments. This speech, like the 1991 address, was more serious in tone, contained more biblical and religious references and justifications, and was more ideologically oriented than the 1990 address.

"ON THE ROAD AGAIN": THE 1992 CAMPAIGN

Coming off the first three years of his presidency, George Bush was riding high with astronomical approval ratings following the swift victory in the Persian Gulf. However, in addition to his ongoing woes with the Religious Right, he also faced some general problems with his ideology and record going into the 1992 campaign. First, the economy had been in a slump since March 1991, and even though economists could show that the recession was over and that the country was technically coming out of its economic woes, most voters still felt the pinch of the economic troubles. The second problem hanging over Bush's bid for reelection was his unkept "no new taxes" pledge from the 1988 campaign. Not only did the broken promise hinder discussion on the economy and tax revenues, but it injured Bush's overall credibility when making campaign promises.

As the 1992 campaign season got under way, so did Bush's renewed ideological identification with the Religious Right. For example, from the opening months of 1992 Bush talked about the issue of abortion to anyone, or any organization, that would listen—twenty-one times in 1992, compared to only twelve in 1990 and seventeen in 1991. Audiences for his precampaign abortion rhetoric include question-and-answer sessions, press conferences, national affairs briefings, and, most important, a commencement address at the University of Notre Dame.[48]

Meanwhile, leaders of the Religious Right were publicly voicing their discontent with George Bush, and openly discussing the possibility that they might not support him for reelection. The same leaders publicly questioned Bush's actions and motives. For example, in his 1991 book *The New World Order,* Pat Robertson wrote: "Is George Bush an idealist or are there plans now under way to merge the interests of the United States and the Soviet Union in the United Nations?"[49] The main reasons for this discontent were events from the first three years of the Bush administration that the members of the Religious Right saw as key points where Bush could have upheld their ideology, and might even have called for legislation that would turn some part of their ideology into law, yet had failed to act. Instead of taking advantage of these events, such as the controversy over the National Endowment for the Arts, Bush had allowed the events to control him, thus causing a further rift between his administration and the Religious Right. Religious conservatives were not satisfied with his response to these and other situations.

By the summer of 1992 the Bush camp was in crisis. The Religious Right was contemplating pulling their enormous support base because Bush was not "pushing hard enough on issues."[50] The large approval ratings that Bush enjoyed after the Gulf War had all but evaporated. Furthermore, "the presidential campaign would be fought domestically, on terrain that was becoming increasingly uncomfortable for the incumbent."[51] Bush appeared to want to rest on the victory he had accomplished in the Persian Gulf, but Americans wanted to hear what he planned to do about economic woes, increasing taxes, and family and societal problems at home, issues on which he was characteristically vague. The result was an incumbent candidate who refused to talk about what voters wanted to hear—namely, how he was going to cure their economic woes. He thus seemed out of touch with the everyday American.

Not only was the Religious Right seen as a powerful force when it came to securing votes, but if unsatisfied with the current state of government, it might throw a candidate of its own into the bid for the presidential nomination. For example, until after the conventions in the summer of 1992, Bill Clinton was not seen as the main enemy by the Bush camp. They were instead focused on overcoming the pull of Pat Buchanan, a traditional Catholic, considered to be a close ally of the Religious Right. Mary Matalin, political director of the campaign to reelect Bush, saw the fight for the nomination this way: "We weren't paying much attention to the Democrats at this point: we had enough trouble dealing with Pat Buchanan and figured we'd just let Clinton and Kerrey and Harkin and Tsongas and Brown beat each other up for a while. We'd get involved when the time came."[52] This observation illuminates two points about George Bush and the Religious Right. First, Bush disliked campaigning, especially in 1992. In his bid for reelection, it bothered Bush that he would have to stop governing and start campaigning. He wanted instead to ride the coattails of the Gulf War victory and his subsequent high job approval ratings.[53] Second, the Religious Right had enough clout in the Republican Party that if Bush did not forward their agenda, they would support a candidate who did, as they had done in 1988 when Pat Robertson entered the Republican primaries. This exemplifies one contextual limitation that the Bush administration always had to keep in mind: the need to keep religious conservatives happy or else to be prepared to campaign against a candidate of their choosing in the primaries.

Because Bush needed the Religious Right vote in the general election, some feel that he "overcorrected to the Right," and that the threat of being beaten by Pat Buchanan for the nomination was not a real one.[54] Polls show that most primary voters who voted for Pat Buchanan did so to send a message to Bush about the economy and broken tax promises. However, in dealing with a candidate who did not pose a "real threat," Bush's campaign spent a lot of time countering the accusations and threats to his reelection bid that came from the Buchanan candidacy. This perceived threat, and the need to woo Religious Right voters back to him in the general election, certainly caused Bush and his advisers to "overcorrect" in the case of the 1992 convention.

A KINDER, GENTLER FAMILY-VALUES PARTY
MEETS PAT BUCHANAN

After defeating Patrick Buchanan and other Republicans for the Republican nomination, Bush was ready to sail into the Houston convention. During the planning stages of the convention's speaking schedule, it was decided that unlike all other speeches to be given at the convention, the Buchanan and Robertson speeches would not be run past the writing, delivery, and editing team. Instead, Buchanan and Robertson were both told that they would "get good speaking times if they endorsed Bush in their speeches."[55] Inherent in this deal was the understanding that Robertson and Buchanan would be allowed to speak in prime time without anyone from the Bush camp seeing ahead of time what they planned to say.

Although Buchanan's speech began in a conciliatory manner, and made a statement of unity about the differing factions within the Republican Party, by the end of his address the harsh, embattled tone stood in stark contrast to anything kind and gentle, and was strongly juxtaposed against the convention theme of "family values." For example, speaking of the Bill and Hillary Clinton team, Buchanan stated: "Friends, this is radical feminism. The agenda Clinton & Clinton would impose on America—abortion on demand, a litmus test for the Supreme Court, homosexual rights, discrimination against religious schools, women in combat—that's change, all right. But it's not the kind of change America wants. It's not the kind of change America needs. And it is not the kind of change we can tolerate in a nation that we still call God's country."[56] This speech sparked a backlash from the media, who christened the Right "extremists," and fostered speculation about the "Radical Right" splitting into its own party because it could no longer get along with Republicans.[57] Other journalists dismissed the rhetoric and warned, "The Religious Right must be careful to avoid arrogance and self righteousness when they strive to promote family values."[58] Another negative effect of Buchanan's speech was related to its timing. Buchanan had been given a prime-time speaking slot, right before former president Ronald Reagan. However, when Buchanan took the podium, he was informed that not all three major television networks were going live; NBC had gone off to cover a breaking news story. Insisting that he had to wait until all three networks were carrying his speech live, Buchanan was allowed to stall for fifteen minutes. Although he began speaking as soon as NBC was back to cover the speech, the stalling time pushed Ronald Reagan out of prime time. The result was that the last time Reagan was to speak at a national nominating convention, he was relegated to the late-night slot, and therefore spoke after most Americans had gone to bed.[59]

Other speakers who joined Buchanan in harsh rhetoric were Marilyn Quayle and Pat Robertson. Quayle's speech was supposed to be run by the writing, delivery, and editing team. However, when this group of writers saw her speech draft, there was a "bad reaction." When asked to lighten the tone of her address, Quayle "would have none of that."[60]

Unlike Buchanan's, Quayle's speech was not openly brash; instead, the tone of her speech came from messages that seemed to be implied in certain passages. For example, in reference to Bill Clinton, Quayle stated, "Not everyone joined the counter-culture. Not everyone demonstrated, dropped-out, took drugs, joined in the sexual revolution, and dodged the draft."[61] Although aimed at Clinton and his well-known indiscretions as a younger adult, the comment was vague enough that it could be read as condemning *anyone* who, even briefly, made the mistake of engaging in the listed behaviors. Quayle went on to detail how she and her husband had met, and how they had started their life together. Quayle noted that she and Dan "believed in God, hard work, and discipline. We married. We went to school and to church."[62] Again, the implied message was that you were somehow less of a person if you did not follow the list in the order it was delineated. Quayle also offered her own definition of family values, which included industry, integrity, morality, and respect. Alluding to the Dan Quayle/ Murphy Brown media argument of 1992, she opined: "If only Murphy Brown could meet Major Dad."[63]

Pat Robertson's speech was seen by some as acceptable because "Robertson finally defined for the country just what was meant by all the Republican talk about traditional family values."[64] However, Robertson's credibility was lessened by attacks he had made on Bush in the past. Furthermore, Robertson and other members of the Religious Right never made it clear exactly how "President Bush . . . had evolved into a worthy standard bearer for the Religious Right agenda."[65] Robertson committed the Religious Right to backing Bush during his convention speech, but the commitment came in August 1992—a little more than three months before the election and when Bill Clinton was already ahead in the polls. Robertson stated: "George Bush's vision for America, ladies and gentlemen, is one of faith in God, strong families, freedom, individual initiative, and free enterprise. He believes that the government should be the people's servant and not their master."[66] However, the tone of Robertson's speech was still harsher than many others on the platform.

Part of the weakening effect was caused by the odd juxtaposition of rhetoric at the convention. For example, Buchanan spoke on August 17, denouncing liberalism and declaring a cultural war. However, two days later on the same platform, Mary Fisher spoke to the convention about the issue of HIV and AIDS. Historically considered a "gay disease" by the Religious Right, AIDS was once referred to by Buchanan as "God's punishment for homosexuals." Fisher was trying to plead for tolerance and acceptance of AIDS, not as a "gay disease," but as a human ailment, a disease that can and does strike anyone.[67] Fisher brought to the convention a "family values" message of inclusion—that AIDS was "no longer a disease that just affects homosexuals, minorities, the promiscuous, and IV-drug users, [that] AIDS has entered the American mainstream."[68] Fisher's speech was one of inclusion, a message that called for compassion and understanding. In an effort to open up her party's ideology, she said: "I issue the plea: Set aside prejudice and politics to make room for compassion and sound policy."[69] Although critics and the media lauded Fisher for setting herself "apart from the rancorous demagoguery," they noted that Fisher's speech seemed odd in comparison to speeches on the same night that contained "bizarre references" to "lesbian witchcraft" and "religious wars."[70] The result was a combination of speeches, all on the same platform and all under the theme of "family values," that seemed mutually contradictory. While Fisher asked for tolerance and compassion, Buchanan sent the message that he and the Religious Right would not be tolerant of all people, especially if they were Democrats. With the implication that the Republican Party was the "party of God," what did that make the Democrats?[71]

Another piece of rhetoric that stood in contrast to speeches by Quayle and Buchanan, in particular, was the address given by first lady Barbara Bush. At the beginning of her speech, Mrs. Bush announced that this was not a speech, but a conversation. She began by offering a more inclusive definition of family values, saying that a family is anyone who teaches "integrity, strength, responsibility, caring, love of God, and pride in being an American. Family means putting your arms around each other and being there."[72] This definition was broader than that given by Quayle and did not set out a "checklist" of requirements for being classified as a family. Her speech was well received by both the convention and the media.

Simply stated, the 1992 Republican National Convention was one that thematically lauded family values, morals, and inclusion, but in reality the rhetoric combined contradictions and exclusion. The aftermath of the convention was a mix of speakers standing firm for what they had said, speakers explaining what they had "meant to say," members of the Religious Right holding celebrations, and media pundits pronouncing the Religious Right as too radical to be contained within the traditional two-party system. For example, Marilyn Quayle's speech was attacked for being "widely perceived as a smug, self-righteous, elitist attack by a woman of privilege on the majority of us who have to work and who struggle to juggle jobs and family."[73] Quayle defended her speech, saying that the true message was being distorted by the media and that the message that people heard was not what "she really meant to say."[74] Other members of the Religious Right switched gears quickly in order to engage in "hand-to-hand combat" with the "pro-abortion, pro-homosexual," "five-star liberal Democrat," Bill Clinton.[75] The media called the Religious Right radical and prejudiced, and asserted that religious conservatives were the reason Bush was lagging in the polls. Furthermore, the confrontational rhetoric that was visited upon the Republican convention by religious conservatives was identified as "the same force that has rent asunder Southern congregations for the last decade, spilled into the public courtyard."[76]

Days after the convention closed, members of the Religious Right gathered to "anoint President Bush as their champion in a battle between good and evil."[77] However, after a year of threats that the Religious Right would pull their support from Bush's reelection bid, and days after a rhetorically confusing convention, the statement of support seemed to be just another case of "too little, too late." A little over a week before the election the *St. Petersburg Times* proclaimed that "a strong attempt by the Republican Party to lock in votes of religious conservatives this year has apparently failed."[78] Others held that losing religious conservative voters to Clinton should not be Bush's biggest worry; instead, Republicans should worry about "voters who identify with the Religious Right staying home on Election Day."[79]

CONCLUSION

In the end, Religious Right voters did stay with President Bush. As Chase Untermeyer noted: "The irony is that in looking at the 1992 voting results, the Christian Right was the most loyal element to George Bush."[80] Bush succeeded in reconstituting his base in the Religious Right, but he did so by overcorrecting at the national convention. For three years Bush had failed to recognize the signs of evangelical disillusionment, nearly losing that constituency by the time he got into campaign mode. He ultimately won that support, but the price was a fractured convention that presented an image of social, cultural, and religious division, an image that many Americans found deeply troubling. Had Bush maintained better liaison with the Religious Right and been more attentive to its concerns during his first three years in office, the overcorrection at the last hour would not have been necessary, and more time could have been spent reaching out to Republican moderates, who ultimately deserted George Bush in favor of Bill Clinton or Ross Perot.

NOTES

1. For the purpose of this essay, the terms *Religious Right* and *religious conservatives* will be used interchangeably to refer to the same group of people. The term *religious conservatives* was chosen instead of the more widely used *Christian conservatives* because the former is more in-

clusive; there are a few members of the Religious Right who are not Christian. Furthermore, the term *religious movement* will be used when discussing the history of the Religious Right, and religion in the United States, because religious conservatives have not always been aligned with the Republican Party. For background on the Religious Right see Matthew C. Moen, *The Transformation of the Christian Right* (Tuscaloosa: University of Alabama Press, 1992); Matthew C. Moen, "The Christian Right in the United States," in *The Religious Challenge to the State,* ed. Matthew C. Moen and Lowell S. Gustafson (Philadelphia: Temple University Press, 1992).

2. The Religious Right, and member organizations, also participate in getting religious conservatives elected at the local and state levels. However, for the purpose of this chapter, the focus is on the role of religious conservatives in electing the president of the United States.

3. Richard I. Kirkland Jr., "Today's GOP: The Party's Over for Big Business," *Fortune,* February 6, 1995, 52.

4. Doug Wead, telephone interview with author, January 13, 1999.

5. Richard S. Dunham, "The Religious Right Saddles Up a Trojan Horse," *Business Week,* September 13, 1993, 45.

6. George Bush, "Statement on the Supreme Court Decision on Abortion, June 29, 1992," *Weekly Compilation of Presidential Documents* 28 (1992): 1161. This statement is in reference to the Supreme Court upholding parental consent laws in the state of Pennsylvania. However, the last paragraph of the statement reads: "My own position on abortion is well-known and remains unchanged. I oppose abortion in all cases except rape or incest or where the life of the mother is at stake."

7. Doug Wead, telephone interview with author, January 13, 1999.

8. "Where Is the Religious Right?" *Christian Century,* February 26, 1992, 216.

9. George Bush, "Statement on the Supreme Court's Decision on Abortion, July 3, 1989," *Weekly Compilation of Presidential Documents* 25 (1989): 1021; George Bush, "Letter to Members of the Senate Appropriations Committee on Federal Funding for Abortion, October 17, 1989," *Weekly Compilation of Presidential Documents* 25 (1989): 1559–60.

10. George Bush, "Remarks to the Participants in the March for Life Rally, January 23, 1989," *Weekly Compilation of Presidential Documents* 25 (1989): 110. See also Bush, "Statement on the Supreme Court's Decision on Abortion, July 3, 1989," 1021.

11. George Bush, "Letter to Congressional Leaders on Abortion Funding in the District of Columbia Appropriations Bill, August 2, 1989," *Weekly Compilation of Presidential Documents* 25 (1989): 1203.

12. George Bush, "Memorandum on Adoption, July 24, 1989," *Weekly Compilation of Presidential Documents* 25 (1989): 1150–51.

13. Allan Parachini, "Serrano Answers Congressional Critics," *Los Angeles Times,* August 2, 1989, sec. Calendar, 1.

14. Ibid.

15. Larry Tye, "Of Erotica and a Staid City," *Boston Globe,* April 24, 1990, sec. National/ Foreign, 3. Not all of the Mapplethorpe exhibit came under fire by the Religious Right. Among those photos considered pornography and homoeroticism were also pictures of a pair of hands reaching out to viewers and several self-portraits of the artist.

16. Louise Sweeney, "Federal Endowment for Arts Shaky," *Christian Science Monitor,* April 23, 1990, 8.

17. Michael Oreskes, "Bush Position on Art Group Evokes Protest from Right," *New York Times,* March 23, 1990, A14.

18. Ibid.

19. Ibid. Oreskes goes on to note that the NEA fight of 1990 just added to the feelings of isolation and disillusionment that members of the Religious Right had been feeling.

20. "The NEA and Art That Offends," *Washington Post,* August 11, 1990, A20.

21. Ibid.

22. Patti Hartigan, "Council Member Prepares to Defend NEA Grants in Public," *Boston Globe,* August 3, 1990, sec. Living, 40.

23. Elizabeth Kastor, "Mapplethorpe Exhibit Controversy Continues," *Washington Post,* July 26, 1989, C1.

24. George Bush, "Remarks and a Question and Answer Session with the Magazine Publishers of America, July 17, 1990," *Weekly Compilation of Presidential Documents* 26 (1990): 1102–9.

25. George Bush, "The President's News Conference, March 23, 1990," *Weekly Compilation of Presidential Documents* 26 (1990): 470–76.

26. George Bush, "Letter Accepting the Resignation of John E. Frohnmayer as Chairman of the National Endowment for the Arts, February 21, 1992," *Weekly Compilation of Presidential Documents* 28 (1992): 309.

27. Doug Wead, telephone interview with author, January 13, 1999.

28. "NRB Faces 'Rocky Points' on Convention Eve," *Broadcasting,* January 29, 1990, 45–47.

29. These occurrences include the National Endowment for the Arts debacle, the firing of Doug Wead, and the appointment of David Souter to the Supreme Court (a judge who Bush thought was conservative, but who turned out to vote with the liberal bloc).

30. "NRB '91: Preparing for New World," *Broadcasting,* February 4, 1991, 43.

31. "Weed and Seed Description," 1992 National Religious Broadcasters Speech, Speechwriting, Speech Draft Files, Box No. 1, ID No. 13474, George Bush Presidential Library (hereafter cited as Bush Library).

32. "Memo from Jim Pinkerton to Chriss Winston, January 26, 1990," National Religious Broadcasters Speech, Speechwriting, Speech Draft Files, Box No. 45, ID No. 13518, Bush Library.

33. "Memo from Doug Wead to David Demarest, January 27, 1990," National Religious Broadcasters Speech, Speechwriting, Speech Draft Files, Box No. 1, ID No. 13474, Bush Library.

34. "Memo from Roger B. Porter to Chriss Winston, January 26, 1990," National Religious Broadcasters Speech, Speechwriting, Speech Draft Files, Box No. 45, ID No. 13518, Bush Library.

35. George Bush, "Remarks at the Annual Convention of the National Religious Broadcasters, January 29, 1990," *Weekly Compilation of Presidential Documents* 26 (1990): 140–42.

36. "Memo from John S. Gardner to Chriss Winston, January 26, 1990," National Religious Broadcasters Speech, Speechwriting, Speech Draft Files, Box No. 45, ID No. 13518, Bush Library. Wead speculates that this speech was fairly important for Bush's credibility because he had misquoted a Bible passage in a speech to the NRB as vice president. Doug Wead, telephone interview with author, January 13, 1999.

37. "Cast Draft," National Religious Broadcasters Speech, 1990, Speechwriting, Speech Draft Files, Box No. 45, ID No. 13518, Bush Library.

38. "Gardner to Winston, January 26, 1990," Speechwriting, Speech Draft Files, Box No. 45, ID No. 13518, Bush Library.

39. Bush, "Remarks at the Annual Convention of the National Religious Broadcasters, January 29, 1990."

40. William McGurn, "Dangerous Liaisons," *National Review,* October 1, 1990, 32.

41. Kim A. Lawton, "It's 'Dog Days' in D.C.," *Christianity Today,* September 10, 1990, 60.

42. George Bush, "Remarks at the Annual Convention of the National Religious Broadcasters, January 28, 1991," *Weekly Compilation of Presidential Documents* 26 (1991): 140–42.

43. Ibid.

44. Eugene Garver, "Professionalization of Virtue," in *Aristotle's Rhetoric: An Art of Character* (Chicago: University of Chicago Press, 1994), 5.

45. Bush, "Remarks at the Annual Convention of the National Religious Broadcasters," January 28, 1991.

46. "Memo from Curt Smith for the President through David Demarest and Tony Snow, January 23, 1992," National Religious Broadcasters Speech, Speechwriting, Speech Draft Files, Box No. 128, ID No. 13601, Bush Library.

47. George Bush, "Remarks at the Annual Convention of the National Religious Broadcasters, January 27, 1992," *Weekly Compilation of Presidential Documents* 28 (1992): 165–68.

48. George Bush, "Remarks to the National Association of Evangelicals in Chicago, Illinois, March 3, 1992," *Weekly Compilation of Presidential Documents* 28 (1992): 388–91. See also George Bush, "Statement on the Supreme Court Decision on Abortion, June 29, 1992," *Weekly Compilation of Presidential Documents* 28 (1992): 1161.

49. Pat Robertson, "The Old World Order," in *The New World Order* (Dallas: Word, 1991), 58.

50. John W. Mashek, "Bush Pleads for Faith," *Boston Globe,* August 21, 1992, sec. National/Foreign, 15.

51. Kathleen A. Frankovic, "Public Opinion in the 1992 Campaign," in *The Election of 1992: Reports and Interpretations,* ed. Gerald M. Pomper (Chatham, N.J.: Chatham House, 1993), 111.

52. Mary Matalin and James Carville with Peter Knobler, *All's Fair: Love, War, and Running for President* (New York: Random House, 1994), 7.

53. Herbert S. Parmet, *George Bush: The Life of a Lone Star Yankee* (New York: Scribner's, 1997).

54. Betty Glad, "How George Bush Lost the Presidential Election in 1992," in *The Bush Presidency: Ten Intimate Perspectives of George Bush,* ed. Kenneth W. Thompson (Lanham, Md: University Press of America, 1997), 188.

55. Craig R. Smith, interview with author, December 2, 1998. Smith was a member of the writing, delivery, and editing team, as well as of the official proceedings staff for the 1992 Republican Convention.

56. "Patrick Buchanan at the Republican National Convention," August 17, 1992, online document available at: <http://www.iac.net/~davcam/buchspee.html>.

57. Dunham, "Religious Right Saddles Up a Trojan Horse," 45. Also see Michael Duffy, "Divided They Fall," *Time,* November 16, 1992, 65, for a discussion of the fragmented future of the Republican Party.

58. Darrell L. Bock, "Arrogance Is Not a Family Value," *Christianity Today,* November 9, 1992, 10.

59. Smith, interview with author, December 2, 1998.

60. Ibid.

61. Marilyn Quayle, "Remarks at the 1992 Republican National Convention," on *Great Speeches: Today's Woman,* videotape, Educational Video Group, 1995.

62. Ibid.

63. Ibid.

64. Darrell Turner and Tom Roberts, "Republicans Give Stage to the Religious Right," *St. Petersburg Times,* August 22, 1992, 3E.

65. Ibid.

66. Jerry Urban, "Evangelicals Lining Up for Bush," *Houston Chronicle,* August 20, 1992, B9.

67. "Remarks by Mary Fisher," *Washington Post,* August 25, 1992, Z7.

68. Alan Ebert, "Living with AIDS," *Good Housekeeping,* October 1992, 167.

69. "Remarks by Mary Fisher," Z7.

70. Daniel Shaw, Leslie Laurence, and Laura Fisher, "The Messenger: AIDS Activist, Mary Fisher," *Town & Country Monthly,* December 1992, 90.

71. David M. Timmerman and Larry David Smith, "The 1992 Nominating Conventions: Cordial Concurrence Revisited," in *The 1992 Presidential Campaign: A Communication Perspective,* ed. Robert E. Denton Jr. (Westport, Conn.: Praeger, 1994), 78.

72. Barbara Bush, "Remarks at the 1992 Republican National Convention," on *Great Speeches,* videotape, Educational Video Group, 1993.

73. Susan Douglas and Meredith Michaels, "The Quayles Speak, Then Say, 'Didn't Mean It,'" *Houston Chronicle,* September 21, 1992, A13.

74. Ibid.

75. "The Godly Right Gears Up," *The Economist,* December 5, 1992, 25–26.

76. Ben Smith III, "Religious Right Using G.O.P. to Fashion World It Wants," *Atlanta Journal and Constitution,* September 11, 1992, C2.

77. Roberto Suro, "The Religious Right: Bush Gets Full Support at Religious Gathering," *New York Times,* August 23, 1992, sec. 1, 26.

78. Religious News Service, "Conservative Religious Voters Favor Clinton," *St. Petersburg Times,* October 24, 1992, 3E.

79. Religious News Service, "Bush Renews Courtship of the Religious Right," *Los Angeles Times,* August 15, 1992, sec. Metro, 4.

80. Chase Untermeyer "Personnel and the Selection Process," in *Bush Presidency,* ed. Thompson, 101.

CHAPTER 9

Economically Speaking:
George Bush and the Price of Perception

WYNTON C. HALL

James Carville's ubiquitous slogan, "It's the economy, stupid," became the Achilles' heel of the Bush reelection effort. The Democratic mantra resonated with American voters because of the perceived weakness of the U.S. economy. In 1992 the rhetorical situation Bush found himself in was riddled with difficulties.[1] The president faced the arduous task of voyaging between the Scylla of declining economic perceptions and the Charybdis of rising political realities. Presidents governing during economic downturns face one central challenge: they must appear to be aware of and attentive to the electorate's concerns, while not calling unnecessary or excessive attention to economic conditions. David Demarest, Bush's director of White House communications, remembers the many difficult conversations he had with the president on this very challenge: "I talked with the president a lot about that quite frequently. That is a *very* complicated problem! He [Bush] understood quite clearly that the economy was not as bad as people were making it out to be. However, for him to say that made it sound like he is out of touch. And if he said that the economy is really in the pits and 'I feel your pain' . . . it exacerbates it."[2] In 1992 President Bush failed to meet this challenge.

Bush's economic rhetoric, throughout his presidency, suffered from a poorly developed sense of *ethos* on economic issues, a disconnect with current perceptions by voters, and unfavorable framing and priming by the media.

This chapter proceeds in three movements: First, a review of literature on issue salience, the media's impact on voters, and political perception is offered. Next, three key rhetorical texts are examined to form the basis of the rhetorical analysis: the New York Economic Club speech delivered on February 6, 1991; the Detroit Economic Club "Agenda for American Renewal" speech delivered on September 10, 1992; and the second presidential debate, held on October 15, 1992, in Richmond, Virginia. These speech texts are chosen for three specific reasons: First, taken together, they offer insight into the linear progression of Bush's rhetorical decision making. Second, they represent pivotal moments in his economic rhetoric. Third, each speech had a real impact on voter perceptions. Examination of each text will include evaluations of its ideological, personal, and rhetorical constraints, and the rhetorical choices made by George Bush from the available means of persuasion. The chapter concludes with a synthesis of the research data collected and examined.

Politics is perception. As this chapter demonstrates, a rhetoric that ignores this axiom fails.

THE PRAGMATICS OF POLITICS

Political scientists have much to say about how and why political actors and voters behave the way they do. The language, inquiry, and measurement of political decision making is of great value to rhetorical analysis because it allows the rhetorician to better understand both the audience's and the speaker's motivations, decisions, and actions.

Economic Perception

There is a widely held notion that presidents who govern during times of economic prosperity are reelected. Much research supports this notion.[3] Yet this literature, as Marc Hetherington points out, assumes voters are able to aptly discern for themselves what the state of the economy is. He argues that "in terms of economic voting, voters' perceptions of economic indicators can be more important than the statistics themselves."[4] Thus, perception, not reality, often determines voter attitudes about the economy. This observation should undergird any discussion of presidential approval.

Issue Salience

Almost every study of presidential approval is based on how issues affect voters' attitudes and evaluations.[5] It makes sense that certain issues would weigh more heavily in a voter's evaluation of a president than others. Thus, the salience of an issue largely determines how much it will affect a voter's view of a decision-maker. Again, perception factors in heavily. Whether or not a constituent's perception of salience agrees with political realities, it still affects his or her evaluation. George Edwards III explains that most political science studies assume issue salience is a constant variable, when actually it is quite malleable. As voters' perceptions change, so do their determinations about which issues are important to them and which ones are not.[6] The rhetorical implications for this phenomenon are important. If what a voter considers to be salient can change, then so must the speaker's message change in order to meet the "needs" of his audience.[7] Hence, the central question arises: who or what causes an issue to become salient to the electorate at a given point in time?

Media Influence

The influence of the mass media on voter cognition is undeniable. The debate over media influence typically turns on the question of whether a liberal or conservative bias exists in news coverage. As Craig Allen Smith points out, most people "are still back at the 'bullet model's' all-powerful transmitter, presuming that messages mold people's minds."[8] Because consumers (voters) have myriad media from which to select, such a debate is often misguided. Political science studies, however, add greater depth to the discussion.

Political science studies suggest that the greatest impact the media have on voters' decisions is by *priming* and *framing*.[9] Priming is the process whereby the media stress key issues that "prime" people to base their political decisions on those issues. By priming the public, media distributors are, in essence, setting the agenda upon which voters are expected to make their evaluations. This is similar to Robert Denton and Gary Woodard's notion that mass communication establishes the political agenda and defines political realities.[10] If this is true, determining which issues are considered salient by voters means looking at which issues are being emphasized by the media.

Shanto Iyengar argues that the media can influence how voters assign credit or blame on a given topic. This is done through framing. Iyengar explains that there are two types of framing in which the news media can engage: episodic and thematic. *Episodic framing* encourages viewers to place blame on individuals outside the political process. *Thematic framing* encourages the viewer to blame institutions or elected officials for problems. This understanding of the assignment of blame has powerful implications, but it is necessary to show that media framing actually affects viewers' attitudes.[11]

John Zaller argues that voters do not really have attitudes. He holds that "attitudes" merely represent the sum of the positive or negative information an individual accumulates. Thus, a constituent's decision of how she stands on a given issue is influenced by the amount of negative or positive information she receives. The "tone" of news and information transmitted through mass media outlets thus becomes increasingly important in determining the positions voters take on issues. Hetherington and Edwards both conclude that mass media play a significant role in shaping voter perceptions. In his study of the 1992 campaign, Hetherington states that "media consumption and attention to the presidential campaign through the mass media negatively shaped voters' retrospective economic assessments."[12] Edwards, in his study on issue salience in 1992, similarly concludes that the more attention the mass media give to a salient issue, the greater the impact on presidential approval.[13] The strength of any body of scholarly research is revealed by its applicability to specific circumstances. Relating political perception, issue salience, and the media's impact on voter evaluations to the events surrounding President George Bush gives a clearer image of the political waters he had to navigate rhetorically.

Political Currents

On the surface, understanding President Bush's fate seems rather simple. In many ways it is tempting to dismiss his failure in a simple syllogism: All presidents governing when the economy is weak do not get reelected. George Bush was president when the economy was weak. Therefore, President Bush was not reelected. However, the syllogism is incomplete and misleading because it ignores the importance of issue salience and the power of perception. These two variables enhance our understanding of the reasons why the 1992 presidential race ended the way it did, and help to show how rhetoric could have played a crucial role in changing the election outcome.

By 1992 it was clear the economy was the issue most salient to voters (see Tables 1 and 2).[14]

It is evident that Americans believed the nation's economy worsened in both 1990 and 1992 in dramatic fashion (Table 1). In many ways they were correct. America's economy entered into a recession. According to the National Bureau of Economic Research, the recession began in July 1990 and ended in March 1991.[15] Americans' confidence in Bush's economic policies eroded, resulting in the highest percentage of Americans (44 percent) ever recorded (by the National Election Studies data) concluding that the federal government's policies were to blame for poor economic conditions (Table 2). However, something is rather peculiar about these findings. If 72 percent of Americans believed that in 1991 the nation's economy had gotten worse, why did Bush's approval rating stay high throughout the recession?

George Edwards III calls this phenomenon the "Bush paradox." He asks, "How could the president be so high in the polls if the public accorded the same weight to economic policy that it did to other important policies?"[16] Edwards uses a combination of Gallup, CBS News, and *New York Times* polling

Table 1. **Condition of Nation's Economy over the Last Year 1980–96**

Percent	1980	1982	1984	1986	1988	1990	1992	1994	1996
Gotten better	4	12	43	24	19	4	5	35	38
Stayed same	13	18	34	42	50	22	23	38	45
Gotten worse	83	69	24	35	31	74	72	28	17

Table 2. **Have Economic Policies of Federal Government Made Things Better/Worse 1984–96**

Percent	1984	1986	1988	1990	1992	1994	1996
Made better	36	25	20	**	4	18	23
No difference	41	52	57	**	52	67	60
Made worse	22	23	23	**	44	16	17

Source: National Election Studies.

data to reveal that between July 1990 and March 1991 (time of recession) the president's approval ratings never dropped below 56 percent and by March were at an amazing 87 percent.[17] Using time-series regression analysis, Edwards shows how the impact of issues changes. What is salient at one point in time will not necessarily remain so. He attributes the change in issue salience to the role played by the media. Hetherington argues that "more than telling people that the economy was an important issue in the campaign, the media actually influenced voters' assessments of it."[18] Thus, Thomas Patterson concludes that "the networks' portrayal of the economy got worse as the economy improved."[19] Indeed, well after the recession had ended in March 1991, media coverage remained focused on the economy. The sheer number of stories about the economy was an integral component of Zaller's two-sided information flow model, which resulted in a net negative impact on voter perceptions of Bush's handling of the economy. Hence, Edwards concludes, "More media attention to the economy and its greater salience to the public mean greater impact of the public's perceptions of the president's handling of the economy on his overall approval. . . . If foreign policy is especially salient and he [Bush] ostensibly handles foreign affairs well, his ratings will benefit. If economic policy is more salient, however, even high ratings on foreign policy will not prevent him falling in the polls if the economy sours."[20] Thus, the media's ability to engage in priming gives cues to voters about which issues should be salient to them. As they consume media messages, according to Zaller's model, the more negative messages viewers receive, the more likely they will be to adopt negative "attitudes." Hence, they were more apt to perceive the economy as anemic in November 1992, when in fact the economy had been out of recession for nineteen months. This conclusion is expressed in the words of C. Boyden Gray, counsel to President Bush, who said: "I believe that the economy is what mostly determines presidential elections . . . the economy was thought to be terrible in 1992, although it wasn't, but that perception is why Clinton won."[21]

WHY STUDY BUSH'S ECONOMIC RHETORIC?

If quantitative studies by political scientists have "figured it all out," why does Bush's economic rhetoric matter? After all, the dynamics of the election can be explained using complex quantitative models that seem to reveal how the disparate elements all fit together. Isn't political rhetoric mere icing on the cake of a presidency? Not necessarily. If rhetoric is the catalyst that produces the exogenous and endogenous phenomena that political scientists examine, then it is worthy of serious attention and analysis.

Perceptions matter greatly, and they have been shown to be the product of the tone and framing of repeated news coverage. A president commands more sustained and systematic media coverage than any other person. His every move is covered, and he possesses some ability to shape and dictate the images, words, and ideas Americans consume through mass media. If the president so desires, he can influence issue salience by orchestrating mass media messages through the vehicle of rhetoric, as Ronald Reagan repeatedly demonstrated.

Because tone is crucial, because perception, not reality, is vital, Bush's dark economic past might have heralded a bright political future, or so the political science literature seems to suggest. But what such research does not reveal is how Bush's rhetorical decisions throughout his presidency undermined and constrained his ability to craft strategic messages designed to garner support and mold voter perceptions. Reneging on his famous "Read my lips: no new taxes" pledge delivered a devastating blow to faith in the president's character, a blow from which he never truly recovered. With the tools of the modern Washington press corps at his disposal, Bush failed to use "the available means of persuasion" to benefit himself.[22] Bush's audience analysis failed to recognize that issue salience is malleable. By communicating messages not salient to voters, he made his rhetorical problems worse. Bush did not seize the myriad opportunities presidents enjoy to shape citizens' perceptions through the vehicle of rhetoric. Thus, an analysis of his rhetoric offers considerable insight into *why* perceptions of the economy were unfavorable for Bush.

PERSONAL PROFILE

Much of how a rhetor chooses to communicate is contingent upon his or her ideological makeup. Bush's ideological composition has been described as that of a Tory.[23] Tories by nature are slow moving and deliberative, and favor a hands-off approach to problem solving until a broad consensus has been formed. Tories view compromise and deal making as essential elements; they hold pragmatic decision making at a premium. The status quo is their solution of choice. But when it becomes evident that change is necessary, they prefer incremental solutions to large-scale ones. This explains why Bush struggled so much to master "the vision thing." Tories are not visionaries. Bush's rhetorical abilities did not help to compensate for his visionary deficit. Marlin Fitzwater said of Bush's rhetorical abilities, "He never felt he was good at it. He thought it was a weak part of his repertoire."[24]

Bush himself said, "I'm not good at expressing the concerns of a nation— I'm just not very good at it."[25] The view that Bush was simply an inept communicator is, however, misguided. Bush was, in many ways, an "episodic" communicator. He knew that for him to perform well, practice and time were essential. When Bush did practice, he was often effective. Roger Ailes coached Bush through the 1988 debates and was one of the few "handlers" to whom Bush ever really listened.[26] His performance was strong, and he proved himself an able debater. But, unfortunately for Bush, he viewed rhetoric as anathema to true leadership. Deputy chief of staff Andy Card believed that Bush's inattention to rhetoric possessed policy implications: "I feel that if the president had had more [rhetorical] style, more people might have listened to his good policies."[27] But a lack of rhetorical style was just a symptom of a larger problem.

Press Secretary Marlin Fitzwater felt that the president's relationship with rhetoric was much worse than merely an inattention to style; it was almost as though Bush would go out of his way to avoid any stylistic flourishes. Fitzwater says, "President Bush had a disdain for rhetoric."[28] This was evident in how Bush discussed his speeches. He believed style and substance were separate things. On January 15, 1989, President Bush sent Brent Scrowcroft a memo containing a revision for an upcoming speech. In the memo of suggested revisions, Bush never mentions his speechwriters by name. Instead he writes, "Get speechwriters to improve my language." He also writes, "To Brent: Please review this . . . and then get comments to Speechwriters. I am sending this to you only at this time because of 'substance.' . . . But it must get to writers soon." At the end of the memo he writes, "(speechwriters can *embel[l]ish* but I want to suggest . . .)."[29] Bush clearly sees a distinction between the serious business of leadership ("substance") and the role style plays in persuasion.

George Will said of Bush, "He discounts rhetoric because he discounts persuasion of the public."[30] To Bush, "words meant nothing," Fitzwater explains, but "emotions meant everything."[31] This strong dislike for rhetoric was only exacerbated by an equally strong distaste for campaigning. Bush's deputy chief of staff Andy Card explains: "President Bush clearly relished the role of governing and disdained the role of campaigning. As a result, he was much better at governance than he was at campaigning. As president, if he were to see a document that said, 'This is how you should say this,' I think that his knee-jerk reaction would say, 'Well, then, that is the way I *won't* say it!' He didn't want to be handled. He didn't want to be scripted in such a way that it violated his own intellect. I don't think he wanted to be known as 'The Great Communicator.'"[32] However, Bush was smart enough to understand that political expediency often dictated using rhetoric for functional ends. In many ways, his lack of respect for the power of rhetoric led him to make rhetorical choices that ultimately cost him his reelection.

In the 1988 presidential campaign George Bush defeated Michael Dukakis by capturing forty states with 53.9 percent of the popular vote. "Read my lips: no new taxes" offered the chance for Bush to assert, in a definitive way, his economic vision. Peggy Noonan explains the reason she came up with the line: "It's definite. It's not subject to misinterpretation. It means, I mean this."[33] He needed some sort of "vision," and the line provided it. However, the vision he pledged would soon become one of the most constraining elements of his economic policy and ultimately of his reelection efforts. Bert Rockman says that the slogan "was no doubt not an uncalculated line, but it was a line calculated to make his life more difficult if he got elected."[34] The level of "difficulty" the statement created was monumental, leading Bush to state after his presidency: "I wish I'd never said, Read my lips, no more taxes."[35]

Marlin Fitzwater vividly recalls the day the official breaking of the pledge occurred, an action that he calls "perhaps the biggest mistake of the administration."[36] He explains how he tried to stop the chief of staff, John Sununu, from releasing the cautiously worded statement that explained there would be "revenue increases." One of Bush's greatest rhetorical triumphs was to become his worst trial. On September 26, 1990, the pledge was officially broken, and so was Bush's *ethos,* as he himself now admits: "Raising taxes was a tremendous political mistake for me," Bush says, "because I shot a lot of credibility."[37]

The loss of credibility on the tax issue did not end with just the average voter. Perhaps more damaging was the loss of confidence within the Republican leadership and among members of Congress. The decision on September 26 was made without warning to many in the Bush administration and with no warning at all to the Republican members of Congress. Assistant secretary of the treasury for legislative affairs Bryce L. Harlow later said the president's advisers—Dick Darman, Nick Brady, and John Sununu—should have told the president to inform Republican members of Congress in advance so they would be prepared to answer questions about the decision. Again, Bush eschewed making a rhetorically strong case for the decision both to members of his party and to the American people. Harlow explained that Capitol Hill Republicans viewed the administration as untrustworthy and relayed their distrust to the Republican voters. Harlow says, "President Bush was never able to recover this trust even after the Gulf War. As a result, Bill Clinton was elected."[38]

Bush's Tory leadership style, his disdain for rhetoric, and his campaign pledge on taxes established rhetorical constraints that remained with him throughout his presidency. Each one affected his ability to communicate and to use the bully pulpit of the presidency to shape public perceptions about the economy.

ECONOMIC CLUB OF NEW YORK SPEECH, FEBRUARY 6, 1991

Americans had much on their minds by February 6, 1991. By this point the U.S. economy was in its seventh month of recession. Also, as Bush points out in his speech, "Three weeks ago tonight, at just about this time, we announced that the liberation of Kuwait had begun."[39] The body politic was tired, fearful, and insecure. The speech at the Economic Club of New York was intended to offer solace for Americans' economic fears, to provide reassurance for their international concerns, and to paint Bush as a leader with a sense of direction.

The speech's immediate audience was composed of business leaders who had paid $1,350 per table, for a total of $324,000.[40] In his introduction Bush thanked the members of the audience for standing to applaud. "I want to thank you not for standing up to greet me, for heaven sakes, but for standing up for all those fighting against aggression tonight in the Persian Gulf."[41] The introduction here serves two distinct purposes. First, it reminds the audience of his deferential nature. At a moment when most politicians would be claiming credit for military success, Bush appears humble. Second, the notion of "standing up for all those fighting" is a carefully crafted attempt to suggest that part of American support for the war effort means enduring the economic recession at home. Bush's opening keeps him on comfortable ground by highlighting his foreign policy strengths before moving into a discussion of the economic recession.

Presidents governing during economic downturns must chart a careful course. Bush needed to show Americans he was in touch with their fear of economic recession, while at the same time not drawing unnecessary attention to the issue. This was very difficult to do, both because of his earlier tax pledge and because, as a fiscally conservative Tory, Bush believed in the power of the unfettered market. This belief essentially required him to tell anxious Americans to sit tight and ride out the economic downturn. Such a stance hardly met the needs of the electorate for reassurance. Bush began his argument by noting that the last eight years had been the longest peacetime expansion in American history. Next, he built up the fundamentals in the economy and made the argument that the recession would be shortlived. "But make no mistake. The current recession does not signal any decline in the fundamental, long-term health or basic vitality of our economy. America is a can-do nation. . . . Our administration's economic policies are designed to strengthen the foundation for a solid recovery."[42] Bush invoked the American spirit of being a nation that overcomes adversity and suggested that the same would occur on the economic front. The body of the speech addressed the future prospects of recovery and what was necessary to achieve that goal.

Bush referenced three "pillars" from his state of the union address, which created the foundation for his prescription for economic stabilization: "encouraging economic growth, investing in the future, and giving power and opportunity to the individual."[43] He outlined how his actions supported the three pillars. In so doing, he briefly conceded that the national deficit "is high, unacceptably high."[44] But he then went on to suggest that the savings and loan scandal, the war itself, and the economic downturn all exacerbated the deficit. This portion of the speech received more media attention than any other, and it provides an interesting view into Bush's rhetorical instincts.

On February 7 the *Washington Post* headline read, "President Skips Over Difficulties in N.Y. Economic Pep Talk." The article went on to charge that the president "barely touched on the record federal deficit expected for the current fiscal year—$318 billion." During the revision process of the speech, after reviewing an early draft, Bush wrote a memo saying, "I think we need some mention about the deficit . . . large and horrible though it is maybe a sentence or 2 at 'A' on page 3."[45] Ultimately, Bush's political instincts made certain that at least a token statement was made about the deficit. Earlier drafts had omitted the topic. But the brief mention proved not to be enough, and the media made him pay for it.

In an attempt to allay fears, Bush explains to Americans that there is no need to worry because "thanks to the budgetary reforms that began last fall, the deficit will be virtually eliminated by 1995."[46] He reestablishes his ideology by stating "I really believe that the market must be allowed to work without unnecessary Federal intervention." On the one hand, he wants to convey that he, as the leader of the nation, is doing something to regain America's financial footing. On the other hand, he needs to be true to his firm belief in the power of the market to correct itself. As Bush concludes the speech, he tries to appeal to emotion, but fails. This failure foreshadows future charges about his lack of compassion for American economic suffering.

Bush sets himself up for charges of insensitivity to Americans' economic plight by stating that "by any historical standard, the current downturn is expected to be mild and brief." At the conclusion of the speech Bush accepted questions from the audience. One audience member asked, "The outlook right now is not as great as it should be for the economy. What's your prediction for the rest of your term—this and your next term?" Bush gave a lengthy response and said, "So, basically, I'm optimistic. I think we've had too much pessimism. I can understand why, and if I were an auto worker laid off I guess I'd have every reason in the world to have doubts. But I think the fundamentals are still there."[47] In those few sentences Bush exposed the reason he would later endure so much criticism. Interestingly, his answer seems to reflect the tensions between the president's advisers. Marlin Fitzwater recounts: "I can remember very vividly Darman, Boskin, and Brady sitting on one side of the president's desk telling him that we should be claiming that the economy is in recovery and that it was getting better. And on the other side of the desk were Teeter, Skinner, Fitzwater, and Demarest and others saying that the reality was that people were hurting."[48] This tug-of-war over the president's strategy seemed to surface in his answer to the questioner. He seems to attempt both to claim economic security and to recognize fears. In the process, he does neither well.

Bush appeared disconnected from the "rhetorical needs" of his broader audience. By choosing to address an emotional topic (job security) in an unemotional, logical way, Bush fueled the impression that he lacked empathy for or understanding of the struggles of ordinary citizens. Clayton Yeutter (RNC committee chairman, counselor to the president for domestic policy in 1992, and deputy chair of the Bush/Quayle presidential campaign) remarked: "When President Bush and others in the administration began speaking of a recovery, no one believed them. It didn't feel like a recovery for the large number of people who were unemployed or frightened about losing their jobs." Yeutter says that this led people to say, "The President is disengaged; he does not know what is happening around the country. We are in the midst of a deep recession and he doesn't know it."[49] The seeds of perception were being sown.

DETROIT ECONOMIC CLUB, SEPTEMBER 10, 1992

As the 1992 presidential election approached, political realities began to take form. The political climate Bush created was hardly conducive to winning reelection. Americans perceived the U.S. economy as weak, despite the end of the recession, and they believed the president lacked an economic plan. The Bush reelection team understood as early as March 16, 1992, that the absence of a written plan was harmful to the president. In a memorandum to the president, Fred Steeper, head pollster and key strategist for Bush, wrote: "Clinton and Tsongas are important. They both have 'economic plans.' The advantage of their plans is that they exist only on paper—voters can find hope in their plans. We are moving to a situation where it will be a choice of one of their 'plans' against our track record. If there is no recovery, this choice is not a good one for us."[50] The pressure for the president to join the field of candidates with tangible economic "plans" increased substantially over the next six months.

The Bush reelection team was well aware of the need to challenge the dominant perceptions in the electorate as they related to the economy. Thus, in a memorandum under a heading labeled "Recommendations," David Hansen, who worked alongside Fred Steeper on polls and focus group research, wrote, "We need to counter the perception that the President has mostly ignored the economy for three years."[51] But what form that refutation would take remained unclear until Bush unveiled the "Agenda for American Renewal."

On September 10, 1992, President Bush offered his solution. The "Agenda for Economic Renewal" became the administration's attempt to show Americans how Bush planned to handle the struggling economy. The Economic Club of Detroit became the site chosen to unveil his "Agenda for Economic Renewal" to the nation.

On September 4, 1992, Bush's reelection team met to develop a strategy to handle existing negative sentiments regarding the president's mishandling of the U.S. economy. Fred Steeper, one of Bush's pollsters, told the group that his research showed Bush needed "a dramatic economic program." Voters believed Bush had no economic plan, and many voters perceived President Bush as the reason for the sour economy. [52] They wanted answers.

Bob Zoellick and Jim Baker were the primary craftsmen of the "Agenda for American Renewal." They built upon Fitzwater's "Agenda Five" (5 percent cut in White House and congressional salaries, 5 percent tax rate cut across the board, 50 percent cut in White House and congressional staff, and 5 years to reach a balanced budget). This became the foundation for the booklet titled, "Agenda for American Renewal."[53] Baker's return to the Bush team was critical. Fitzwater explained how Baker's authoritative style helped produce the Bush economic plan: "When Baker came in, that's the first thing we did. He said, 'We've got to have a plan and a message. And I want it by Monday morning!' And he [Boskin] wrote that over the weekend, he brought it in, Baker rewrote it. We had a meeting where everybody reviewed it and looked at it, and Baker said, 'This is it. This is our message. This is what we stand for, this is what we're going to run on, this is what every speech is going to be about. The president's going to give it next week to introduce his economic plan and I want it to be the basis of every speech.'"[54] With the economic blueprint in hand, Mary Matalin, one of Bush's campaign strategists, knew that "selling" the plan would be the most crucial element for a successful turnabout of public opinion. The Bush/Quayle campaign purchased five minutes in prime time on ABC, NBC, and CBS in an effort to target as many likely voters as possible. The stage was set for a potential defining moment. James Carville said of the speech, "We were very scared of this one. This is where we went into what we called Def Con Five. We had our people ready to analyze and scrutinize and tear that speech apart. . . . We were convinced that this was really going to help Bush, and we were panicked."[55]

The rhetorical act was designed to address the exigence of an economy perceived as performing poorly and, in so doing, to gain electoral support. Bush sought to convince voters that he possessed a workable economic vision. Also, the speech needed to reveal a president who understood the concerns and fears of a country facing economic uncertainty. Finally, the speech was aimed at reminding voters that they could trust Bush with their future and that they should support him with their votes.

Shortly after the introduction the president quickly defers the credit for ending the Cold War with the line, "The American people have just completed the greatest mission in the lifetime of our country: the triumph of democratic capitalism over imperial communism."[56] He also appeals to the Reaganesque image of "Go West, young man" with the phrase, "That's the lesson I learned as a young man, packed up a Studebaker and moved to Texas after another war, at the start of another era. I saw jobs, prosperity, an entire future, built with the hands of ordinary men and women with extraordinary dreams."[57] This "common man" appeal is effective in reinforcing the idea that Bush is ultimately a man of goodwill, a hard worker, a pioneer. He predominantly uses the plain style to reinforce this message, yet the speech is peppered with some stylistic devices.

One of the major goals of the Economic Club of Detroit speech was to reestablish the notion that despite the perceived economic incongruities, Bush was an able, tested, and effective leader. In the speech, he tries to build his credibility by proclaiming: "My background has also prepared me for the task of bringing our foreign policies and our domestic policies together to turn our strength as a world power to our advantage as an economic power, to match the security we feel militarily with the economic security that we must build at home." Bush tries to link his leadership abroad to the potential for a successful domestic policy, particularly on economic grounds. However, the audience's prior distrust of Bush on economic issues could not be overcome with a single speech. Ultimately Bush needed to reinforce why he could be trusted now when he had reneged on an earlier promise. No such reason is offered in his Detroit speech. Hence, Bush's attempts at enhancing his *ethos* ultimately fail. The speaker's appeal to logic is similarly misguided.[58]

In rhetorical terms, as a result of not firmly establishing powerful *ethos,* the audience calls into question the speaker's reasoning or *logos.* Many initial reviews of the speech were quick to criticize President Bush's economic solutions on just these grounds. Steve Mulson, writing in the *Washington Post,* noted: "Bush said he wants lower taxes, but in 1990 he signed a budget agreement that included $137 billion of tax increases."[59] Rhetoric did not match reality. It actually worked against Bush because it served as a reminder that his conservative ideological rhetoric was not in step with his actions.

The speech operates within Bush's ideology of reducing the size and scope of government to increase prosperity, freedom, and ultimately virtue. These views serve as the premises for the speaker's arguments. Bush states them as follows: "I reject the shopworn logic that sees poverty as a simple lack of income, a kind of economic shortfall that can be replaced with a Government check. A conservative philosophy of empowerment must have at its foundation the creation of character through the ownership of property, through the dignity of work. That means . . . making individual discipline and self-reliance the goal of all of our programs."[60] The argumentative logic, if put in the form of a syllogism, might look something like this:

Major Premise: The development of character occurs "through the owner-ship of property and through the dignity of work." Anything that stifles the de-velopment of character must be rejected.

Minor Premise: Government involvement stifles the ownership of property and work.

Conclusion: Therefore, we must reject Government's attempts to injure the creation of character.

The argument lays the foundation upon which the speaker can offer poli-cies and actions for the audience to support, actions that are consistent with his logic.

Using statistics, President Bush justifies his proposal of an across-the-board tax cut, reducing the White House budget as well as federal employee salaries, implementing tort reform, and doubling the economy's size. As a result of Bush's inability to address his credibility deficit, however, audi-tors rightly call the speaker's logic into question and are left wondering, "Why should we trust the logic here when we watched you renege on an earlier pledge you made in the 1988 campaign? Isn't this just another empty campaign-season promise?" Many asked just that question. Ann Devroy of the *Washington Post* observed, "Bush has been widely criticized for going from one election year economic plan to another."[61] Margaret Warner said, "He has a big credibility and trust problem here with the economy."[62] Mark Shields put the dilemma another way: "The President last week said in one day the economy was anemic, sick, lousy, we've been through economic hell in this country, and I'm the only guy to get us out of the mess we're in. . . . That's a tough message to sell, that this is terrible, the last three years have been mis-erable, but I, who have been in control, can get us out of it."[63] The "sell" was a failure rhetorically because the speech failed to address why Bush was the only leader who could lead the country out of the economic doldrums. For this to work, the rhetor would be required to use emotional appeals in a very cautious and calculated manner.

Bush needed to accomplish two broad objectives in relation to emotional appeals to the audience. First, he needed to befriend his audience. Aristotle defines a friend as "one who shares pleasure in good things and distress in grievous things, not for some other reason but because of the friend."[64] The speech tries to accomplish this identification. "We feel the uneasiness in our own homes . . . we see the difficulties . . . we face great risks."[65] Bush ac-knowledges that the country is facing economic problems, in an effort to show he understands the plight of individual Americans. This was, of course, the lesson learned from his New York Economic Speech question-and-answer session about the fictional plight of the autoworker. The attempt to achieve identification with his audience became an integral part of repairing the breach that existed between voters and Bush.[66]

Bush knows he must offer relief from the existing fears within the electorate in order to achieve reelection. He accomplishes this in the speech by appearing confident and certain of his ability to lead the country out of the dismal economy. "I intend to fight for this agenda, to fight as hard as I can. . . . My agenda draws together our people and our Government to meet this challenge. We will create a $10-trillion economy, and we will renew America, and we will win the peace."[67] The *polysyndeton* and the martial metaphor serve as strong appeals to the listener that the president is in charge, competent, and invigorated. Bush invites the audience to recast in economic terms their image of him as a deft commander in chief of the military. According to Bush, he will henceforth be the defender of peace and security not only abroad, but at home as well. While this linkage of military success to potential future economic success is skillful, it is the president's use of pathos that stands out most strongly.

Yet Bush's failure to address the questions about his *ethos,* as well as his inability to translate his argument into a logical appeal that resonated with American's economic concerns, continued to hurt his ability to effectively communicate his message and achieve his rhetorical goals. J. Clarke Rountree notes that members of the immediate audience were highly skeptical of Bush's ability to enact the proposal, as well as of the significance of the "Agenda" itself.[68] Voters felt they had heard a similar sales pitch earlier. While Bush's appeals to emotions were largely successful in this speech, it is the synergistic effect of the three modes of appeal—*ethos, logos,* and *pathos*—that yield a positive rhetorical outcome.

The lack of follow-up on this effort to portray Bush's economic vision dramatically reduced its potential for long-term influence. Baker's attempt to instill a strict "message" discipline failed. Marlin Fitzwater explained that after the Detroit Economic Club speech, the reelection team had a problem carrying the message further. "Now as to the issue of follow-up, the problem there was that we were so late in the game in getting it out."[69] Thus, the speech's timing left it open to characterization as another example of an empty election-year promise.

THE 1992 PRESIDENTIAL DEBATES

The events leading up to the 1992 presidential debates were disastrous for the Bush/Quayle ticket. Debate negotiations between the Clinton/Gore camp and the Bush/Quayle team were fraught with disagreement over debate format, leaving Bush vulnerable to accusations that he was afraid to debate Clinton. This became the Clinton strategy, and it worked. The first debate was supposed to occur on September 17, 1992, in Lansing, Michigan, but was canceled due to the negotiation impasse. The Clinton team seized this opportunity by staging an event at the place where the debate was supposed to occur. Clinton proclaimed, "I showed up here to debate today. I guess I can't blame him. If I had the worst record of any president in fifty years I wouldn't want to defend that record either."[70] Bush, with his back against the negotiating wall, was now forced to accept a much less advantageous proposal.

There would be three presidential events, with different debate formats. The first debate would use a panel of reporters (Bush's preferred format); the second would use a talk-show format that would include audience participation (Clinton's preferred format); and the last debate would be split, with the first portion using a single moderator and the second a panel of reporters.[71] The multiple formats were far from Bush's initial desire to have all the debates follow the format of the 1988 election debates, which had featured panels of journalists. The multiple formats strongly favored Clinton, who as Bush himself admitted was a strong debater. "I'm not a professional debater. I'm not an Oxford man—and I think he's good at that. . . . I know I'm up against a formidable debater."[72]

Richmond, Virginia, October 15, 1992

Rhetorically analyzing the second presidential debate is important for three reasons. First, an examination of quantitative data produced by National Election Studies (NES) reveals that 25 percent of voters had not decided whom they would vote for until the last two weeks of the campaign or election day.[73] Polling data compiled by media organizations immediately after the Richmond debate show similarly that a third of all voters were either undecided or only weakly committed to their chosen candidate. Second, people were actually tuning in to the debates. The Richmond debate attracted 84 million viewers. The "audience" would soon be involved in deciding Bush's fate at the polls. A *USA Today*/CNN/Gallup poll at the time showed that 80 percent of voters were giving "a lot of thought" to the election, making the candidates' messages even more powerful in the perceptions of voters. Finally, the second debate is worthy of rhetorical analysis because Bush inadvertently confirmed Americans' view that he was out of touch with economic reality and lacked credibility with regard to solutions to the perceived economic crisis of the time.

The Bush campaign team did not look forward to the debates.[74] The consensus after the first debate in St. Louis on October 11 was that Bush finished last, with Clinton finishing second and Perot taking first place. The stage for the second debate was set for a do-or-die scenario. Bush needed to come out much stronger and with increased vigor. The format for the second debate was a talk-show format with Carole Simpson as the host. Governor Bill Clinton recommended the format for strategic reasons. The debate style was highly conducive to Clinton's delivery strengths—namely, increased movement, emotive expressiveness, and personal interaction with questioners. Also, by this time Clinton was very comfortable with the format because he had held similar "town hall" meetings throughout the country. Bush stood to lose much.

No moment in the debate was more injurious to Bush than the moment when a woman in the audience asked all three candidates a question on the personal impact of the economy on the candidates themselves: "Yes, how has the national debt personally affected each of your lives? And if it hasn't, how can you honestly find a cure for the economic problems of the common people if you have no experience in what's ailing them?"[75] The questions screamed for an answer laden with emotional appeals. Perot jumped on the question first, relating how his privileged life meant he had a duty to ensure prosperity and financial security for his grandchildren and the children of America. Bush went next.

The fumbled exchange would prove fatal to Bush's attempts to reinforce the impression created in his Detroit Economic Club speech regarding his concern, care, and empathy for those experiencing economic hardship. Ironically, the lethal bumbled response and interaction with the questioner and host were caused by a simple misunderstanding of terms. In any case, Bush's performance was an enormous rhetorical missed opportunity. With 84 million viewers tuned in, Bush had an extraordinary moment to challenge the media framing and "attitude" assimilation that had occurred up to this point about his handling of the economy. In the end, the perception left with viewers did more to validate than to challenge the dominant notion that Bush was indeed out of step with the concerns and fears of the electorate. The exchange went as follows:

President Bush: Well, I think the national debt affects everybody. Obviously, it has a lot do with interest rates—

Ms. Simpson: She's saying you personally.

Questioner: You, on a personal basis, how has it affected you?

Ms. Simpson: Has it affected you personally?

President Bush: Well, I'm sure it has. I love my grandchildren. I want to think that—

Questioner: How?

President Bush: I want to think that they're going to be able to afford an education. I think that that's an important part of being a parent. If the question—maybe I get it wrong. Are you suggesting that if somebody has means that the national debt doesn't affect them?

Questioner: What I'm saying—

President Bush: I'm not sure I get it. Help me with the question, and I'll try to answer it.

Questioner: Well, I've had friends that have been laid off in jobs—

President Bush: Yes.

Questioner: I know people who cannot afford to pay the mortgage on their homes, their car payment. I have personal problems with the national debt. But how has it affected you? And if you have no experience in it, how can you help us if you don't know what we're feeling?

Ms. Simpson: I think she means more the recession, the economic problems today the country faces rather than—[76]

The exchange was devastating. Bush was left standing there needing to have the host and the questioner/voter *explain* the question to him. He took the term *national debt* literally. Mary Matalin explained that when the exchange occurred, "everybody in our room was saying, 'What's the question? What is she talking about?' . . . To us, 'national debt' was an economic term of art. . . . Beyond the Beltway, normal people mentally translated 'national debt' to 'recession.' We didn't."[77] Bush and the questioner were literally speaking different languages. Bush's lexicon viewed economic terms through the rhetorical lenses of a policy wonk. As Matalin points out, the questioner was using the common idiomatic usage of the term. The confrontation left Bush appearing so far out of touch that he couldn't even understand the language of Americans. Even worse, in the midst of the communicative impasse, Bush managed to utter the devastating phrase, "I'm not sure I get it." This gave Clinton an opportunity that he was quick to seize:

Governor Clinton: Tell me how it's affected you again? You know people who have lost their jobs and lost their homes?

Questioner: Yes.

Governor Clinton: . . . I have seen what's happened in this last 4 years when, in my State, when people lose their jobs there's a good chance I'll know them by their names. When a factory closes, I know the people who ran it. . . . What I want you to understand is, the national debt is not the only cause of that. It is because America has not invested in its people. . . . It is because we are in the grip of a failed economic theory. And this decision you're about to make better be about what kind of economic theory you want . . . [78]

Clinton's response had everything Bush's lacked. He understood the question. He related to *pathos* in a way Bush failed to do. Also, Clinton challenged Bush's economic record and the voters to decide whether they wanted to continue down the path of perceived disparity.

James Carville found this piece of political drama to be a pivotal moment, too. As he later explained, "The woman said 'the national debt'; she meant 'the recession.' . . . If there's one thing I would fault Bush and his campaign on, it was that one question. . . . Clearly Bush's biggest problem was that people thought he was out of touch. . . . If I had been running the Bush campaign I would have said, 'That is the one question we want.' I would have *paid* to have that question asked."[79] The question possessed the potential to begin reshaping viewers' perceptions and attitudes by addressing the most salient issue of the campaign in a way that revealed a sympathetic (*pathos*), trustworthy (*ethos*), and well-reasoning (*logos*) leader. Governor Clinton effectively seized Bush's missed opportunity and exacerbated the existing negative perceptions of him. He even managed to remind viewers of Bush's *ethos*—destroying Bush's tax pledge through a cleverly crafted joke, "We all have ideas out here, and Mr. Bush has a record. I don't want you to read my lips, and I sure don't want you to read his. I do hope you will read our plans."[80]

The second debate razed the positive appeals to emotion built in the Detroit Economic Club speech and at the same time left the questions about Bush's logic and vision for economic recovery unanswered. Finally, by bringing up Bush's broken pledge from the 1988 campaign, Clinton smartly and subtly reminded voters that Bush was not to be trusted on economic matters.

CONCLUSION

Presidential rhetoric is critical because it holds the potential to mold voter perceptions. In an electronic age of increasing media outlets and competing providers of information, rhetoric's importance and impact on the decisions citizens make will continue to increase. While the findings of political scientists reveal much about *how* voters and political actors behave, less emphasis has been placed on *why* they act the way they do. Understanding the *why* question is crucial because it offers insight into what could strategically have been done differently to change political outcomes. Perhaps the reason rhetoric has been largely overlooked by political scientists is that rhetoric is largely a normative issue that is not easily quantifiable. This is, of course, an important distinction. Social scientists are concerned with the rigors of statistical accuracy and the definitive quality of numbers. But to assume that such analyses completely and fully explain the story of a president is misguided at best. Indeed, multiple variables, acting in concert, shape and reshape any political terrain. Politics cannot exist without communication. Because communication is the cohesive element that bonds human experiences, rhetoric matters. Likewise, the tools and instruments of the political scientist offer numerous benefits. Only by the synergistic effect of the two together can a complete and full account be crafted.

Political science research teaches that political perceptions, not political realities, are most important in determining attitudes. The degree to which an issue's salience can vary represents a challenge to rhetors to continuously adapt and reshape their messages to meet the demands and needs of their audience.

President Bush did not effectively use the resources that the office of president affords. Management and manipulation of the media is crucial to success in influencing voter attitudes. Bush was unwilling to use the rhetorical potential of the presidency, largely due to his disdain for rhetoric. Bush needed to take more chances than he was willing to risk. In March 1992, Fred Steeper sent a rather prophetic memorandum to Bob Teeter (campaign chairman and longtime pollster) and Charlie Black (senior consultant). The memo, entitled "Taking Risks," appears to have gone unheeded.

> I mentioned the other morning that I thought if we suddenly were in a 30 day campaign against Clinton, we would lose. . . . Step back a moment from the immediate choices and consider: We face a 20 month recession, a 78 percent "wrong track" number, and a Southern Conservative Democrat. In my mind, this is our worse [*sic*] political nightmare. . . . we obviously, and very significantly, do not have prosperity working for us this election year. . . . Nothing is inevitable. But, I would consider this axiom: The lower the probability we think there is for an economic recovery this year, the greater the political risks we should be willing to take. One sports analogy. Don't think of us as the team with the superior size, power, and speed. We are the underdogs (against the theories of presidential elections). To win, we need an imaginative, creative, take-them-by-surprise offense and defense. We need to do some things we would not normally do.[81]

Ultimately, Bush rejected this advice and did the things he normally would do. Thus, voters were influenced by the mass media's largely negative, unchallenged coverage of the national economy.

In 1992 the economic reality was that the U.S. economy *was* in a recovery. But the perception at large was antithetical to that reality. Voters therefore adopted the view that Bush was to blame for the state of the economy. Carville's slogan "It's the economy, stupid!" rang true with the mass perception that Bush was unaware of the state of the economy at home and more concerned with foreign policy ventures. Thus, the fictional autoworker Bush spoke of in his question-and-answer session at the New York Economic Club was, by the end of the campaign, far more representative of public opinion than he calculated. The strength of the fiscal "fundamentals" were not central to voters' overall evaluation of Bush's success on economic policy. Instead, voters saw an economic landscape riddled with fear, lack of confidence, and uncertainty.

What seemed impossible had happened. A president who enjoyed unprecedented approval ratings had been defeated by a relatively unknown Arkansas governor. Fitzwater calls this conundrum "the great unanswered question of 1992." He explains: "Between January of '92 and Jim Baker, there was no leadership, and why did the president not recognize it? That's the whole issue. Why do you allow it to stand? I think he allowed it to stand because he just didn't believe Bill Clinton could be elected. . . . And I think it was just over-confidence. . . . How could anybody believe that a draft-dodging philanderer could ever be elected in American political history? . . . But it happened."[82] Perhaps President George Bush himself has most eloquently explained the role economic perception played in his defeat in 1992: "I'm convinced that the American people didn't know my heartbeat and I can't blame anybody but myself for that. . . . My failure was not being a good enough communicator at the end of my presidency to convince people that the economy had recovered."[83] Bush now recognizes both his inability to use rhetoric to advantage, and also the power and import of rhetoric in the development of voters' beliefs and attitudes. In the end, President Bush paid the price of misperception.

NOTES

1. Lloyd F. Bitzer, "The Rhetorical Situation," *Philosophy and Rhetoric* 1 (1968): 1–14.
2. David Demarest, telephone interview with author, April 14, 2000.
3. Morris P. Fiorina, *Retrospective Voting in American National Elections* (New Haven: Yale

University Press, 1981); V. O. Key, *The Responsible Electorate* (Cambridge, Mass.: Harvard University Press, 1966); Gerald Kramer, "Short Term Fluctuation in U.S. Voting Behavior 1896–1964," *American Political Science Review* 65 (1971): 131–43.

4. Marc J. Hetherington, "The Media's Role in Forming Voters' National Economic Evaluations in 1992," *American Journal of Political Science* 40 (1996): 372–95.

5. George C. Edwards, William Mitchell, and Reed Welch, "Explaining Presidential Approval: The Significance of Issue Salience," *American Journal of Political Science* 39 (1995): 108–34.

6. Ibid., 119.

7. Craig Allen Smith, *Political Communication* (New York: Harcourt Brace Jovanovich, 1990).

8. Ibid.

9. Shanto Iyengar, *Is Anyone Responsible?* (Chicago: University of Chicago Press, 1991); Shanto Iyengar and Donald R. Kinder, *News That Matters* (Chicago: University of Chicago Press, 1981).

10. Robert E. Denton Jr. and Gary C. Woodward, *Political Communication in America* (New York: Praeger, 1985).

11. Iyengar, *Is Anyone Responsible?*

12. Hetherington, "Media's Role," 372.

13. Edwards, Mitchell, and Welch, "Explaining Presidential Approval," 119.

14. The exact questions used for Table 1 were: "How about [1996: "Now thinking about"] the economy [1990, 1994 and later: "in the country as a whole"]? Would you say that over the past year the nation's economy has gotten better, stayed [all years except 1984: "about") the same, or gotten worse?" The exact questions used for Table 2 were: [1988, 1992 and later: "Over the past year"] Would you say that the economic policies of the federal government have made the nation's economy better, worse, or haven't they made much difference either way? (IF BETTER/WORSE:) Would you say the economy is much better/worse or somewhat better/worse?"

15. Robert D. Hershey Jr., "This Just In: Recession Ended 21 Months Ago," *New York Times,* December 23, 1992, C1, 15.

16. Edwards, Mitchell, and Welch, "Explaining Presidential Approval," 110.

17. Ibid., 123.

18. Hetherington, "Media's Role," 390.

19. Thomas Patterson, *Out of Order* (New York: Alfred A. Knopf, 1993).

20. Edwards, Mitchell, and Welch, "Explaining Presidential Approval," 121.

21. C. Boyden Gray, "The President as a Leader," in *The Bush Presidency: Ten Intimate Perspectives of George Bush,* ed. Kenneth W. Thompson (Lanham, Md.: University Press of America, 1997), 3–22.

22. Aristotle, *On Rhetoric,* trans. George A. Kennedy (New York: Oxford University Press, 1991). Noted presidential scholar Fred I. Greenstein supports this notion and places particular emphasis on Bush's inability to manage perceptions rhetorically. He says that "in leaning over backward to avoid Reaganesque oratory, he [Bush] deprived his presidency of the teaching function that enabled presidents such as Roosevelt, Kennedy, and Reagan to frame public perceptions." Fred I. Greenstein, *The Presidential Difference: Leadership Style from FDR to Clinton* (New York: Free Press, 2000), 169.

23. Bert A. Rockman, "The Leadership Style of George Bush," in *The Bush Presidency: First Appraisals,* ed. Colin Campbell, S.J., and Bert A. Rockman (Chatham, N.J.: Chatham House Publishers, 1991), 1–35; Joel D. Aberbach, "The President and the Executive Branch," in *Bush Presidency: First Appraisals,* ed. Campbell and Rockman, 223–47; Herbert S. Parmet, *George Bush: The Life of a Lone Star Yankee* (New York: Lisa Drew/Scribner's, 1997).

24. Marlin Fitzwater, telephone interview with author, December 10, 1998. Similarly, deputy chief of staff Jim Cicconi believed that Bush was insecure about his own rhetorical skills. Cicconi said, "I don't think he had a great deal of confidence in his own ability to deliver a really good speech. All of us saw him do it, but I'm not sure that he believed in himself, as we did, as a person who was a very good public speaker when he wanted to be." Jim Cicconi, telephone interview with author, June 28, 2000.

25. R. W. Apple Jr., "Capital," *New York Times,* September 6, 1989, 15.

26. Deputy chief of staff Jim Cicconi played a major role in the drafting and editing of speeches for Bush. In a personal interview, Cicconi laughingly explained to me the important role that Roger Ailes played in getting the president to rehearse his speeches. "Roger had a particular way of making him do it. Roger is the type of guy who would go, 'Damn it! You have to practice the speech! You have to deliver it right or you will screw up badly and lose the election if you don't!' . . . He [Ailes] had an ability to focus people on what he wanted them to focus on [laughter]. The great thing about Roger was (a) he was right; (b) he had a tremendous amount of experience with that subject; and (c) he didn't give a damn and would say what he thought." Jim Cicconi, telephone interview with author, June 28, 2000. Rhetorical scholar and former Bush speechwriter and speech consultant Craig R. Smith notes that during his tenure working with Bush, he noticed a disdain for practice as well. However, Smith says that this behavior was less about insecurity and more about desire and masculinity. According to Smith, "Bush never took it [speech rehearsal] seriously and thought rehearsal was unmanly." Craig R. Smith, e-mail interview with author, April 13, 2000. Also see Craig R. Smith, "George Herbert Walker Bush," in *U.S. Presidents as Orators: A Bio-Critical Sourcebook,* ed. Halford Ryan (Westport, Conn.: Greenwood Press, 1995).

27. Andrew H. Card Jr., telephone interview with author, April 20, 2000.

28. Marlin Fitzwater, *Call the Briefing!* (New York: Random House, 1995).

29. President George W. Bush, Memo, "Memo to Brent Scrowcroft from Camp David," January 15, 1989, George Bush Presidential Library, Box 10 [OA 6789].

30. George Will, "It's Not Modesty, It's Arrogance," *Washington Post,* October 12, 1990, A21. Former Bush White House aide James P. Pinkerton essentially agrees with Will's conclusions, noting: "He lacked respect for words and the ideas behind them." James P. Pinkerton, *What Comes Next: The End of Big Government and the New Paradigm Ahead* (New York: Hyperion, 1995), 161.

31. Fitzwater, quoted in Parmet, *George Bush,* 115.

32. Andrew H. Card Jr., telephone interview with author, April 20, 2000.

33. Peggy Noonan, *What I Saw at the Revolution* (New York: Random House, 1990).

34. Rockman, "Leadership Style," 9, 13, 30; Paul Quirk, "Divided Government and Cooperative Presidential Leadership," in *Bush Presidency: First Appraisals,* ed. Campbell and Rockman, 69–91; Barbara Sinclair, "Bush and the 101st Congress," in *Bush Presidency: First Appraisals,* ed. Campbell and Rockman, 155–84; Anthony King and Giles Alston, "Good Government and Politics of High Exposure," in *Bush Presidency: First Appraisals,* ed. Campbell and Rockman, 249–85.

35. George W. Bush, interview by David Frost, *George Bush: A President's Story,* History Channel, November 28, 1998. Rhetorical scholar Amos Kiewe's chapter on Bush's "Read my lips" line argues that Bush's decision to renege on his tax pledge created a political crisis that could potentially have been rectified had the president used his rhetoric in a more forthright fashion to educate Americans about the economic situation. Amos Kiewe, "From a Rhetorical Trap to Capitulation and Obviation: The Crisis Rhetoric of George Bush's Read My Lips: No New Taxes," in *The Modern Presidency and Crisis Rhetoric,* ed. Amos Kiewe (Westport, Conn.: Praeger, 1994), 179–202.

36. Fitzwater, *Call the Briefing!* 214.

37. Bush, interview by David Frost, *George Bush: A President's Story,* History Channel, November 28, 1998.

38. The Gulf War's success and Bush's correspondingly high approval ratings may actually have done more harm than good. According to David Demarest, the president's impressive poll numbers convinced the two strongest voices in the White House, Darman and Sununu, that no work on a domestic agenda would be necessary. Demarest told me in an interview, "It wasn't until after the Gulf War that some of us were saying, 'You gotta have a domestic agenda.' That was Andy Card, that was Gregg Petersmeyer, me. And Dick Darman and John Sununu said, 'You guys are out of your fuckin' mind!' . . . They said, 'No way! He's won this. We've got this election in the bag.'" David Demarest, telephone interview with author, April 14, 2000. Bryce L. Harlow, "The Budget Process," in *Bush Presidency: Ten Intimate Perspectives,* ed. Thompson.

39. George W. Bush, "Remarks and Question and Answer Session at the Economic Club of New York," February 6, 1991. Online document available at: <http://www.csdl.tamu.edu/bushlib/papers/1991/91020607.html>.

40. Frank J. Murray, "Bush Vows Resumption of 'Robust Economy,'" *Washington Times* February 7, 1991.

41. Bush, "Economic Club of New York."

42. Ibid.

43. Ibid.

44. Ibid.

45. George W. Bush, "Personal Memo to Speechwriters," February 1, 1991, Bush Library, Box 10 [OA 6789].

46. Bush, "Economic Club of New York."

47. Ibid.

48. Marlin Fitzwater, telephone interview with author, December 10, 1998.

49. Clayton Yeutter, "Accomplishments and Setbacks," in *Bush Presidency: Ten Intimate Perspectives,* ed. Thompson, 45–67.

50. Fred Steeper, Memo, "Research Findings and Strategy: Current Status and Recommendations," March 16, 1992 [Fitzwater Files] Box 25, Bush Presidential Library.

51. David Hansen, Memo, "Notes on Birmingham, AL Focus Groups," January 13, 1992, Box 22, Bush Presidential Library.

52. Fitzwater, *Call the Briefing!* 356. The role that economic perception and *ethos* began to play became dire as election day approached. The exact prescription from Steeper regarding the seriousness of Bush's lack of credibility on the economy can be found in the memo that Steeper circulated the day before the September 4 meeting. Under the heading, "Summary of Bush Expansion Voters and Conclusions: Attitudes, Perceptions, and Characteristics," Steeper writes, "The President needs a major improvement in his credibility on the economy with the target voters." Peter Goldman, Thomas M. DeFrank, Mark Miller, Andrew Murr, and Tom Mathews, *The Quest for the Presidency 1992* (College Station: Texas A&M University Press, 1994), 716.

53. Fitzwater, *Call the Briefing!* 356.

54. Marlin Fitzwater, interview with author, College Station, Texas, September 27, 1999.

55. Mary Matalin and James Carville, *All's Fair* (New York: Random House, 1994), 332.

56. George W. Bush, "Remarks and Question and Answer Session at the Detroit Economic Club," September 10, 1992. Online document available at: <http://www.csdl.tamu.edu/bushlib/papers/1992/92091000.html>.

57. Ibid.

58. Ibid.

59. Steven Mulson, "Bush's Economic Message Clearer Than Administration's Actions," *Washington Post,* September 11, 1992, A11.

60. Bush, "Detroit Economic Club."

61. Ann Devroy, "President Outlines Second-Term 'Agenda for American Renewal,'" *Washington Post,* September 11, 1992, A10.

62. Transcript from *Capitol Gang,* televised broadcast, September 12, 1992, CNN Transcript #36–1.

63. Ibid.

64. Aristotle, *On Rhetoric,* 134.

65. Bush, "Detroit Economic Club."

66. Kenneth Burke, *A Rhetoric of Motives* (Berkeley: University of California Press, 1969).

67. Bush, "Detroit Economic Club." The reason that I claim Bush *knew* he needed to offer a positive and solace-laden speech is twofold. First, Steeper's September 4 summary memo, written before the speech, states, "The President's appearances and advertising need to do a particularly good job [of] portraying him as optimistic and confident." See Goldman, DeFrank, Miller, Murr, and Mathews, *Quest for the Presidency 1992,* 716. Second, we know that Bush actually viewed these numbers before the memo was drafted for the other members of the campaign team because of his diary entry that day, which read in part: "I went for a run on the White House grounds, analyzing the Teeter poll results which were most discouraging." George Bush, *All the Best, George Bush: My Life in Letters and Other Writings* (New York: Lisa Drew Book/Scribner's, 1999), 566.

68. J. Clarke Rountree III, "The President as God, the Recession as Evil: *Actus, Status,* and the President's Rhetorical Bind in the 1992 Election," *Quarterly Journal of Speech* 81 (1995): 325–52.

69. Fitzwater, interview.

70. Clinton, quoted in Gwen Ifill, "The 1992 Campaign: The Democrats; Where Debate Was to Be, Clinton Shows Up for Rally," *New York Times,* September 23, 1992, A21, 1.

71. "Details of Campaign Debates Are Settled in Hours of Talks," *New York Times,* October 4, 1992, A15.

72. Bush, "Detroit Economic Club." Certainly, statements like these were part of the normal "expectations game" that campaigns play before a presidential debate. Nevertheless, the statement contains much truth.

73. "Time of Presidential Election Vote Decision 1952–1996," National Election Studies (Ann Arbor: University of Michigan, Center for Political Studies, 1997).

74. Fitzwater, *Call the Briefing!* 357.

75. George H. W. Bush, "Presidential Debate in Richmond, Virginia," October 15, 1992. Available online at: <http://bushlibrary.tamu.edu/research/papers/1992/9210500.html>.

76. Ibid.

77. Matalin and Carville, *All's Fair,* 415.

78. Bush, "Presidential Debate in Richmond." For more on the 1992 debates see Robert V. Friedenberg, "The 1992 Presidential Debates," in *The 1992 Presidential Campaign: A Communication Perspective,* ed. Robert E. Denton Jr. (Westport, Connecticut: Praeger, 1994): 89–110.

79. Matalin and Carville, *All's Fair,* 415.

80. Bush, "Presidential Debate in Richmond."

81. Fred Steeper, "Taking Risks, March 11, 1992" [Fitzwater Files], Box 25, Bush Presidential Library.

82. Marlin Fitzwater, interview with author, College Station, Texas, September 27, 1999.

83. Bush, interview by David Frost, *George Bush: A President's Story,* History Channel, November 28, 1998.

Afterword

Evaluating the Rhetorical Presidency of George H. W. Bush

MARTIN J. MEDHURST

Insofar as presidents try to communicate their ideas to an audience, they are rhetorical presidents. Some clearly succeed in this endeavor better than others, but all are rhetorical, whether successful or not. The last quarter of the twentieth century was remarkable for featuring two of the best and two of the worst rhetorical presidents in American history. Unfortunately, George Bush was one of the worst. Even more unfortunate is the recognition that it need not have been so. Bush had the tools to be a perfectly acceptable, perhaps even good, public communicator. He simply refused to use those tools, or to allow others to develop them on his behalf.

I assert this with a high degree of confidence, because I once had the pleasure of sharing a platform with George Bush after his presidency. In December 1996, former president Bush delivered the annual fall lecture for the Program in Presidential Rhetoric at Texas A&M University. His audience that night was composed of 750 people, primarily undergraduates enrolled in communication courses. While the setting did not bode well, George Bush rose to the occasion magnificently, speaking for over an hour and holding his audience in rapt attention from beginning to end. As a speaker, he was funny, using a self-deprecating humor, as well as informative, insightful, slightly profane, clear, and persuasive. He successfully identified with those students and made one of the better speeches of his entire career. It was so successful that he adapted it for various audiences over the course of the next several months.[1] Clearly, the problem was not that George Bush could not give a public speech. The problem was that neither he nor his lieutenants adopted a rhetorical stance toward governing.

The chapters in this book underscore the point. From start to finish, George Bush's problems were primarily rhetorical in nature. From the outset, he failed to realize that the presidency is an inherently dramatic office, an office that is charged with the care and maintenance of the American Dream. In refusing to articulate his version of that dream, refusing to share with the American people his vision of a better tomorrow, he effectively severed the most powerful part of any president's rhetorical arsenal. Successful presidents are those who become so identified in the public mind with their dreams or visions that the person and the dream become forever fused in historical memory—FDR, Kennedy, Reagan, to name only a few. By surrendering this power to define and shape a vision, Bush squandered an opportune moment—what in rhetorical theory is called *kairos*—and instead allowed others to substitute their visions for his and, simultaneously, to criticize him for lacking one.

Rhetorically speaking, Bush started from a one-down position. He exacerbated that position by certain choices he made during the opening days of his administration: refusing to allow any Reaganite to hold the same position in the Bush administration, allowing Sununu and Darman to dictate communications policy, downgrading (at least in terms of experience) the speechwriting office, and refusing to accept the kind of help that his press secretaries, communications officers, and speechwriters repeatedly tried to offer.[2] Craig R. Smith got it exactly right when he noted that George Bush's worst enemy was none other than George Bush. Without a rhetorical sensitivity at the top, there was no expectation of one further down the line.

Bush was most effective rhetorically during the Gulf War conflict. That comes as no surprise, as that was the only period during which communications and policy were closely coordinated. As Demarest recalled, "one of the reasons that the Gulf situation was so successful was because we were all on the same page. And that, to me, was the most rewarding time. . . . it was the most fun for me, too, because I felt empowered to really drive a set of messages and I had all the tools to do it. Whereas, on the domestic side, it was all over the lot, and we did not have the unanimity of purpose around 'what is the theme we're trying to get across?'"[3] During the Gulf War period Bush successfully merged his role as agent with the various agencies of communication. The two worked in tandem to achieve a single goal. But that was the only period during which policy and communications about that policy to various audiences worked smoothly.

For most of his presidency, Bush was repeatedly thwarted in his attempts to persuade either the public or the Congress to adopt his ideas. Some of these problems were, of course, structural. Bush did face a majority opposition Congress all four years of his tenure. There was a serious problem with the budget deficit. Yet other presidents have faced similar problems in the past and emerged with more of their agenda intact. And they did so by being better at persuasion, both public and private. The Bush administration was characterized by a series of rhetorical faux pas that involved such basic matters as timing, follow-through, coordination, focus, liaison with constituencies, scheduling, and the like. Sometimes these problems were the result of a real chasm between Bush's governing principles and the desires of various audiences. More often they were the result of antirhetorical decisions made internally that had devastating external consequences.

This brings us, once again, to Bush's insistence that rhetoric was a part of campaigning, not a part of governance; it was viewed as politics or show biz or image making, not substance. But, of course, rhetoric is both. And by far the most important part is the substantive: the effort to discover new ideas, to shape them in ways that advance one's agenda while simultaneously appealing to one or more audiences, to engage in the give and take of internal debate and discussion, to reach decisions in light of those discussions as well as of the impact of those ideas on particular audiences, to consider the language that one uses and the actions that one undertakes in light of audience concerns and expectations. Most of all, one learns to adapt rhetorically to different situations, audiences, and exigencies. As these chapters reveal, Bush often lacked the rhetorical antennae to pick up on these kinds of signals. Missing the substantive, he instinctively rejected the stylistic or imagistic parts of rhetoric as well.

Curt Smith, who wrote more speeches for Bush over the course of his presidency than any other person, summed up the situation:

> We should have pushed him more. It's difficult to push the president. I was always trying, in the memoranda that I would write, to show the country the Bush that we knew. We didn't do it. We didn't understand. We had too few people that understood that politics is poetry, not prose; politics is art, not science; it's not programmatic, it's not specific. . . . But establishment Republicans have a very difficult time in understanding the emotions and values and intuitive viscera that move the average voter. The two Republicans that have won landslide elections in our time—Richard Nixon and Ronald Reagan—understood that to the marrow of their core, which is why they could reach and convert tens of millions of Democrats. But the corporate banker, the Fortune 500 Republican doesn't understand that—and would feel uncomfortable with it even if he did. We had too few people who understood that in the Bush White House, which is why, perhaps, if we'd had more of those people they would have gently persuaded the president that this is not simply in your best interests, but the American people want to know about you as a human being. . . . Bush, of course, is a hero. Bush was an exemplary human being. Had people known that, he would have been reelected—there's no question in my mind.[4]

While it is anything but clear that Bush would have won reelection even if his assistants had been more persistent, Smith touches on a central problem of the

Bush presidency: who the real George Bush was and whom he was believed to be by the electorate. Rhetoric, for good or ill, operates in the realm of perceptions: not the reality of George Bush, but his perceived identity. After the 1990 budget deal, many people perceived Bush as a man who did not keep his word. In Aristotelian language, Bush had a problem with his ethos—the perception of his character. Of all the modes of proof, ethos is the most powerful. It is also the most volatile, because it goes directly to the issue of credibility. Once audiences seriously begin to question a person's ethos—sincerity, veracity, good will, and moral character all rolled into one—the damage is done, at least in the short term. And election cycles are short-term events.

The Bush presidency ended after four short years. George Bush, who refused to learn the lessons of what rhetoric could do *for* him, instead learned the much harder lessons of what rhetoric did *to* him. Failure to think and act rhetorically not only results in failure to communicate one's ideas. It can also result in the attribution of all kinds of negative inferences, based not only on what one says and how one says it, but also on what is left unsaid and what audience needs are left unmet. In that sense, rhetoric can be a rather unforgiving art form—one of the many lessons learned during the rhetorical education of George Herbert Walker Bush.

NOTES

1. Even in rhetorical triumph, Bush could not bring himself to appropriate the full resources of rhetoric, including the media. He refused to grant permission for C-SPAN to cover his speech.

2. One exception to this rule was Marlin Fitzwater who did occupy the same position in the Bush White House as he had held in the Reagan White House, press secretary to the president of the United States. But even this exception is, perhaps, not so exceptional when one realizes that Fitzwater worked for Bush as vice president before he was elevated to Reagan's team. So, in a sense, Fitzwater was a Bush acolyte before he was a Reaganite. Bush also retained two cabinet members from the Reagan administration: Nicholas Brady at Treasury and Richard Thornburgh as attorney general.

3. David Demarest, interview with author, tape recording, College Station, Texas, 29 March 2001.

4. Curt Smith, interview with author, tape recording, College Station, Texas, 27 January 2000.

CONTRIBUTORS

Martín Carcasson is assistant professor of speech communication at Colorado State University, Fort Collins. His work has appeared in *Quarterly Journal of Speech, Presidential Studies Quarterly,* and *Rhetoric & Public Affairs,* among other outlets.

Wynton C. Hall is an instructor at Bainbridge College, Bainbridge, Georgia. His work has appeared in *Presidential Studies Quarterly* and *Western Journal of Communication,* among other outlets. His most recent work (with Dick Wirthlin) is *The Greatest Communicator: What Ronald Reagan Taught Me about Politics, Leadership, and Life.*

Rachel Martin Harlow is an instructor at Texas Tech University, Lubbock. Her work has appeared in *Rhetoric & Public Affairs.*

William Forrest Harlow is an assistant professor of communication studies at Texas Tech University. His work has appeared in *American Behavioral Scientist.*

Amy Tilton Jones is an instructor of communication at Del Mar College, Corpus Christi, Texas.

Roy Joseph is assistant professor of communication arts and sciences at Duquesne University in Pittsburgh. His work has appeared in the *Journal of Applied Communication Research.*

Catherine L. Langford is an assistant professor at Texas Tech University, Lubbock.

Holly G. McIntush is a student at New York University School of Law. Her work has appeared in *Rhetoric & Public Affairs.*

Martin J. Medhurst is distinguished professor of rhetoric and communication at Baylor University, Waco, Texas. His work has appeared in *Quarterly Journal of Speech, Communication Monographs, Presidential Studies Quarterly, Armed Forces & Society,* and many other outlets. He is the founder and current editor of *Rhetoric & Public Affairs.*

INDEX